How to Build a Corporation's Identity and Project Its Image

How to Build a Corporation's Identity and Project Its Image

Thomas Garbett

Lexington Books

D.C. Heath and Company/Lexington, Massachusetts/Toronto

Quote on pages 171–172 is reprinted with permission from TV Guide®
Magazine. Copyright © 1982 by Triangle Publications, Inc. Radnor,
Pennsylvania.

Library of Congress Cataloging-in-Publication Data

Garbett, Thomas F.
   How to build a corporation's identity and project its image.

   Includes index.
   1. Corporate image.   I. Title.
HD95.2.G37   1988   659.2   86-45370
ISBN 0-669-13312-4 (alk. paper)

Published simultaneously in Canada
Printed in the United States of America
International Standard Book Number: 0-669-13312-4
Library of Congress Catalog Card Number 86-45370

The paper used in this publication meets the minimum requirements of
American National Standard for Information Sciences—Permanence of Paper
for Printed Library Materials, ANSI Z39.48-1984. ∞™

   89 90 91 92   8 7 6 5 4 3 2

To my wife and partner, Carolyn

Contents

Figures and Tables

Preface

Today's corporate communication executives have one of the most demanding jobs in American industry. Faced with a suspicious and frequently antagonistic press, as well as activist groups for every conceivable issue, they must try to project an image of their corporation that is at once stable and yet exciting, aggressive yet public spirited, somewhat diversified but focused in key areas, generous to its employees but lean and mean as an investment.

All too frequently this image-building job is complicated by management's lack of a clear understanding of what the company's real identity should be. In other cases, the identity of the company shifts as new businesses are acquired and others divested, each move sending out a shimmering picture of the company which may change even before the old one is established.

This book is an effort to help those faced with the responsibility of building their company's identity and projecting that image in today's hectic business environment. This book does not offer any new business theory or buzz words, it just tries to help executives deal with the ones that already exist. I am not a professor or a business writer but rather a practitioner in the field of communications.

The advice and counsel offered here covers many of the common problems faced by communicators in their day-to-day operations: the routine work of *public relations, research, corporate advertising, investor relations,* as well as not so routine problems, such as *mergers, changing the company's name, selecting new agencies,* or *dealing with a news disaster.* I have tried to offer the same kind of counsel I provide my clients when I am invited in to examine their programs.

This hands-on advice is based upon a long career that has been divided roughly into thirds. The first third involved the advertising, sales promotion, and often product publicity for clients of four different ad agencies. Two of these were house agencies, which viewed their activities as part of the parent company's operation. The range of products even surprises me as I look back at what was a relatively stable career for the advertising industry. Thom McAn Shoes of the Melville Shoe, Company, Kinney Shoes, Rootes Motors, Dan River Mills, Pro Toothbrushes, Listerine, and a long line of pharmaceutical products from Warner-Lambert were an eclectic beginning. Lavoris, Vicks Vaporub, and a seemingly endless line of cold medications for Morse International, the house agency for Richardson Merrill Inc., added to the list. The old Doyle Dane Bernbach agency provided an opportunity to work on the Volkswagen account in its exciting early years, which included the introduction of the Microbus and the Karman Ghi. That account was followed by those of American Airlines and Pfizer Products, such as Pacquin Hand Creme and Barbasol.

Then came General Telephone and Electronics and the second part of my career. This stage largely involved corporate advertising for GTE and the advertising run by their seventeen telephone companies throughout the United States. Each company's public relations department has its own campaign, which often was corporate in nature. The Allied Chemical Company became an account, and rapidly became the Allied Corporation, and then Allied-Signal, as it acquired Bendix and other high-tech companies that changed Allied's entire business focus.

The old marketing disciplines from the first third of my career died hard in the world of corporate communications. In an attempt to bring order to what first appeared to me to be the confused and undisciplined world of corporate advertising, I wrote *Corporate Advertising, the What, the Why and the How,* which was published by McGraw-Hill in 1981. That led me into my third and final (I hope) career, that of consulting.

When you have written a fairly successful book, especially when it is the only book on the subject, you are credited with the rank of expert in the field. Other companies began to share their problems with me and to discuss ways of dealing with their communications needs. At first this was through the offices of DDB and its clients, through potential new clients, and then through private consulting. DDB (now DDB Needham Worldwide) became a client, along with more than a score of other corporations and ad agencies. Studies and special analyses of a variety of communication problems led to a yet broader view of business communication. Working with the Association of National Advertisers on their annual research into corporate advertising practices, as well as engaging in other speaking and writing assignments, extended my contacts to even more companies. It all just sort of grew.

The result has been an unusual opportunity to gain an insight into current communication problems in major U.S. corporations. What I have seen convinces me that the problems have never been more acute. Unfortunately, many companies today are not aware of how serious their identity problems are or of the price they are paying for their indistinct and inaccurate images.

Today's business landscape is littered with a confusion of corporate images that often do not begin to serve the marketing interests of their companies. Indistinct and inaccurate perceptions are more prevalent than ever. Preoccupied with multiple survival problems, businesses focus more on internal than external matters.

Many companies seem also to disregard the need for a distinct identity even among publics vital to their very existence. We see, for instance, national corporations advertising in the same business journal using a confusion of nonnames such as ones like ABC, ACF, ACL, ADR, AEG, AGA, AIG, AMF, ANR, ARA, or the longer ones like AGIP, AMAX, AMCA, ARCO, ASEA, AVCA—and we are still in the A's.

Some of this image clutter has been brought about by new companies' springing up in new or expanding industries. These companies have not as yet had time to establish new names and reputations, but the confusion is just as prevalent among established concerns. Nor is the image problem confined to alphabet soup. Well-known names from the past, such as Pullman, Singer, GE, and Colt (to name just a few), are attached to businesses that have roamed far afield from their beginnings.

Much of this confusion can be attributed to the pressures applied to business in the past decade. In the first half of the 1980s American businesses were forced to reexamine virtually every aspect of their operations in response to an unprecedented assortment of problems.

Competition from overseas extended deep into traditional American industry strongholds. It was no longer confined to a few vulnerable categories such as automobile manufacturing and electronics; it went back to the beginning of the production stream to the basic materials, steels, machine tools, and heavy production equipment. Accustomed to the high inflation rate of the 1970s with its pat solution of a price hike each year to stay ahead of rising costs, many companies had to rethink completely their product lines and production efficiency when inflation was gradually brought under control.

At the same time, many industries, such as the airlines, telecommunications, banking, and trucking, were preoccupied with adjusting to an increasingly deregulated environment. Deregulation brought with it many new start-up companies unhampered by heavy entrenched labor and facility costs. Competitive price cutting commanded the full attention of the larger, older companies, forcing them to restructure and readjust constantly, to the new competitive rules. Some of these businesses thought their problems could be met with diversification. Increasingly through the mid-1980s American industry reshuffled its production and business portfolios through acquisitions, write-offs, and divestitures to reposition itself into business segments, where strategic planning led. Business portfolio management became a time-consuming game for management committees across the country. The strategic planning was calculated not only to improve these companies' competitive positions, but also, they hoped, to make them more attractive to the financial community. According to W.T. Grimm & Co., a Chicago mergers and acquisitions firm, 1985 saw more than 3,000 merger, acquisition, and divestiture deals. This was up from 1,089 in 1980, a 50 percent increase in just five years. The total value of these soared from $44.3 billion to $179.6 billion in 1985.

Unfortunately for many companies that had hoped to make themselves more attractive on Wall Street, the financial community is not consistent in its likes and dislikes. The chemical industry, for instance, had been out of favor for a decade on Wall Street, not only because of its stagnant growth, but also because of its environmental risks. Chemical companies reacted to this by diversifying into oil, consumer products, or pharmaceuticals. Today almost all of them can be classed as "diversified chemical companies." For many, their strategic planning left them little better off after the oil glut hit the petroleum industry. So too excitement about the financial potential of the health care industry cooled in the wake of government and social health care cost containment efforts. Even the seemingly endless magic of high-tech industries began to fail for those who had branched out into this promising area. Some of the acquisitions worked, more probably did not. All of the acquisitions left the companies far different from the way they were perceived by their publics.

Attacks by unfriendly raiders resulted in the dislocation of many more corporations. In their efforts to become less attractive takeover targets, these firms often sold valued segments to reduce the spread between the value of their assets and their equity. The cash from the sale of these assets was frequently used to buy back the company's own stock, thereby increasing its value and making the raider's job that much more difficult. Just the enormous time needed by top executives to plan and execute "shark repellent" programs, as many antiraider techniques are called, took management's attention from more normal marketing concerns. All this has left many companies quite different in a very short space of time. Singer is now 80 percent an aerospace company. U.S. Steel (now called USX), for instance, is now about two-thirds an oil company. G.E. is heavily into financial businesses. International Harvester, now called Navistar, is out of the harvester and agricultural implement field. American Can Company is into financial and retail services and is known as Primerica. On it goes.

The strategic planning of the early eighties did leave companies far more efficient, productive, and better able to compete. Many have moved into industries with brighter futures. It has also, however, left many companies with images that no longer reflect their current realities. A massive re-education job is needed to rebuild correct industry associations with American companies.

Along with these changes and shifts in product lines has come a change in the cultures or personalities of the businesses involved in the acquisitions and divestitures. The integration of often very different corporate life-styles can have a major effect in unsettling the images a corporation sends out about itself. Employee and community loyalties have been shaken as people have felt the aftermath of mergers: plant closings and the elimination of redundant jobs. Their insecurity, skepticism, anger, or the common postmerger depression spreads not only through their internal contacts, but out into their dealings with the many publics important to the corporation.

The customers of these companies have had to adjust too. Sometimes they have had to adjust repeatedly, as they have seen their familiar resource change hands and in the process become an entirely new company. In some cases their resource has been passed along again to yet another new parent. The customers have had to learn to accept new airlines, new telephone companies, new banks, and new high-tech suppliers at an astonishing rate. Never have so many businesses changed so dramatically in such a short period, and never has the public been forced to rethink so many of its accustomed buying habits.

Interestingly, all this is happening at a time when American business and industry appear to be rediscovering strategic marketing. Having restructured themselves into those businesses with which management feels secure, they need now to go back to the fundamentals of marketing. Their houses are now far more in order; now they must readdress the marketplace. Fundamental to this process will be rebuilding their images and reputations.

In 1985 Coopers & Lybrand and Yankelovich, Skelly & White, consultants and research firms, conducted their third business planning study among executives in more than 140 corporations. This study predicted a revival of strategic marketing. The study further noted that greater attention will be placed on so-called niche marketing, the segmentation of discreet market needs for specific products.

The new trends will also lead to more collaborative arrangements among corporations to market each others' products and/or manufacture for each other. Both of these trends will place greater reliance on a strong corporate reputation. The Coopers & Lybrand and Yankelovich, Skelly & White research states that

> the issue of how best to utilize their "corporate reputations" will become more important . . . American corporations are "out to win," and they in turn want to deal with winners in collaborative ventures and in supplier relationships. Similarly, as companies move into niche markets with more limited communications budgets (compared to huge national rollouts), a compelling CORPORATE REPUTATION may be the key to initial product/service considerations and trial.

They go on:

A major concern of the surveyed larger "marketing oriented" corporations that enjoy strong name or brand reputations is how to best utilize these reputations more effectively. Some of the key questions being asked are:

- Exactly what messages do particular well-known names convey to the marketplace?
- How "elastic" are these names with regard to the breadth of products and services that could be convincingly marketed under their umbrella?
- What liabilities are attached to the extension of names to new product and service areas?
- Is there a risk of overusing names and thereby reducing their long-term value?

Corporations that are interested in capitalizing on their reputations must become increasingly sensitive to how they manage their relationships with both their customers and their suppliers. In effect, they must establish highly efficient conduits for supplying their customers with the most suitable products and services at consistent levels of quality and price. Organized and systematic management of corporate reputations—substantially beyond traditional efforts with the financial community—is becoming the focus of management attention under the new marketing agenda.

If the Coopers & Lybrand/Yankelovich, Skelly and White study is correct, the pressure for an enhanced corporate reputation is increasing, at a time, ironically, when American business reputations have never been in greater disarray.

You, who must rebuild these shattered company images today or establish whole new ones, will require skill and imagination. The ideas, advice, and counsel on the following pages are for you. I hope you will find them a useful guide.

Acknowledgments

I'd like to thank the hundreds of clients who knowingly or not provided a great education in communications and human nature.

A special thank you to my secretary, Michele M. Dupey.

1
Company Image—Control It or It Controls You

Companies work within an environment that is, in good part, pre-established by their own reputation or lack of it. An unknown company does not start with a clean slate. Everyone with whom it must deal starts with a negative collection of doubts about the company. These can be seen to diminish as the familiarity with the company increases.

A company's image is governed by these six factors: the reality of the company itself, the newsworthiness of the company and its activities, the diversity of the company, the company's communication effort, time, and memory decay. Working together, the positive and negative messages sent out by a company will, over time, build a body of public awareness, familiarity, and attitudes. This is to a degree controllable.

Studies have shown those characteristics that are of the greatest importance in establishing positive feelings toward the company. Work done by *Time* magazine and the *Wall Street Journal* provides surprisingly consistent evidence of the importance of the company's being well managed and offering high-quality products or services. Other characteristics are shown to be of either more or less concern to investors than to customers.

A convincing argument for the value of a strong company reputation came from a young salesman for a small Connecticut industrial wholesaler. He was enthusiastically describing his day on the road with the factory representative from 3M.

I found out today it is a lot easier being a salesman for 3M than for a little jobber no one has heard of.

We were visiting some of our customers and he was showing me how they sell their products. What a difference. First, the receptionist seemed to know us, some of them even smiled. There was no explaining who we were, what the company does or why we were there. No one asked what we were selling. And that was just the receptionists. The plant managers acted as though they knew all about 3M and were just waiting to hear what it was that we had that was new. It was as though the customers were proud that a big company like 3M would send a man around to see them, and you know something else? It made me start off with a whole different frame of mind when I began to talk to the customer. When you don't have to waste time justifying your existence, or explaining why you are there, it gives you a certain amount of self-assurance. And, I discovered I came across warmer and friendlier. It made me feel good and enthusiastic to be "somebody" for a change.

Communication helped establish that 3M reputation. It set the stage for that important first impression. Compare it with the first impression the neophyte salesman made on customers who had never heard of his company. It is sometimes mistakenly assumed that the company no one has heard of at least starts off with a clean slate. This is not true. In fact, the unknown company starts off dragging with it the baggage of "just another company I know nothing about; they could be dishonest, they could have shoddy products, they could just be like all the rest, why not stick to the companies I know." Even a company with a reputation that is only vaguely familiar has an advantage over the company that is totally unknown. Why? Because of an interesting human characteristic: a willingness to credit positive attributes to those things with which we are most familiar. Conversely, people are more likely to attribute negative characteristics to the unknown. In this case it might be said that familiarity breeds content—contentment with the acceptability of a company as a resource. That is not to say that even greater familiarity with a company, its products, and the good things it does is not an added advantage. It is. The more positive things known about a company the better, but this does suggest that even modest effort at broadening a company's level of awareness pays off.

That a good reputation for a company can make selling a lot easier is pretty obvious. In fact, a company's reputation affects its whole operation in hundreds of subtle ways management rarely considers. The ease of access for a salesperson is only one of the more obvious advantages. The self-assurance it gives the salesperson in dealing with the customer is another. In fact, this self-assurance will be enjoyed by employees of all sorts. People take greater pride in working for a company when they do not have to explain who the company is and what it does. The company's prestige is transferred to them in their social dealings, in their community, at their clubs, and at their banks. Employees respond to this status in positive ways that can improve morale and productivity.

Reputation also has an effect on commercial banks' views of a company. Investors find it more comfortable holding stock in companies with a better reputation. The business press is more likely to run news releases from the better-known companies, and reporters from all media will seek out the most respected companies to speak for the industry when it comes to commenting on industry or public issues. Even government bodies, which should be expected to treat companies of all sizes and reputations equally, are all too human and will treat companies with the respect they think they deserve.

Therefore to a large extent companies work within an environment that is pre-established by their reputation or lack of it. It is a silent advantage or a handicap that accompanies them and modifies everything they do.

Six Factors Controlling the Company Image

All corporations have an identity and project an image of some sort, whether they are aware of it or not. It may be good, bad, or just blah, but it is always with them. In some respects, it is like the weather—you tend to notice it more when it is extremely good or extremely bad. Both can change with only partial predictability because they are both affected by a multitude of forces that are only imperfectly understood. Fortunately, a company's image is far more subject to control and modification than the weather. Its dynamics appear to be governed by six factors:

1. *The reality of the company itself.* The company's size, structure, the industry it is in, the products it makes or the services it provides are all the raw material that contributes to making up the image. The number of employees and the degree to which they interact with society shape the fundamental nature of the company. Clearly, an industrial company is inherently different from a chain of stores. The sheer magnitude of a company and the scope of its activities directly affects the degree of its familiarity. So does its inherent importance to society. The company producing trivial novelties cannot compare with the company producing sophisticated aircraft, electronics, or services such as health care.

2. *The newsworthiness of the company and its activities.* What the company does may be interesting, and it may affect people's lives importantly and in positive ways through products and services, or it may be making important contributions to society that are newsworthy. In a negative way, poor products, product recalls, financial failure, or social and environmental transgressions may be just as newsworthy. Adverse news will in fact raise the awareness level of a company, although at the same time it will build poor associations and attitudes toward it. Most companies are not especially newsworthy one way or another. In truth, companies have to work at making the commonplace interesting to publicize itself successfully. Searching through companies' products and activities for things that promise high interest should be an ongoing project of a communications department.

3. *Diversity of the company.* The more varied and diverse the activities of the company, the more diverse will be the messages sent out by the corporation. A true conglomerate may be sending out such diverse signals as to have little cohesiveness. Conversely, the more monolithic a company is, the more related the messages it sends out will be. The effect of this fact of life is that a conglomerate will find it more difficult to establish a reputation than will a single product-line company.

4. *Communications effort.* There is no question that companies that work at communication, those that spend money building the

company's image, become better known and usually have more positive reputations.

5. *Time*. None of this happens overnight. A building process is involved in establishing any reputation. Even the most startling new product or major new ad campaign usually will cause only a peak in the level of familiarity with the company for a comparatively short period of time. If the peak is strong enough, the level of familiarity may settle back to a new plateau, at a level higher than before. Good corporations wear well with time; their images, which have been built over the years, will be far more lasting.

6. *Memory decay*. You pour forth the image of a company into a very leaky bucket. It is a constant communications effort to just stay where you are. It takes even more effort to build a company's image. Memory decay, or the public's tendency to forget, is more rapid than people imagine. "Top of mind" awareness about a company goes first and in a surprisingly short time. This is particularly true if the company has not had ample time to build and reinforce its image over the years. This is caused to some degree by a change in the audience, as some people retire and a new generation comes on the scene, as customers change jobs and new people come in to take their place. This process, however, also simply results from the familiar's crowding out by new and more demanding information and interests.

How these six factors interrelate to create a corporate image can be seen in the following rough formula (see figure 1–1). Although this formula may not be subject to quantification, it illustrates the approximate effect each factor has in contributing to the company's image.

In practice the multiple impressions made by a company will vary greatly from very positive to the negative. Many of the impressions will be merely neutral reinforcements of the name. These impressions will be falling on an audience that changes with time. The people in the various publics will gradually change. People die, retire, change jobs and new people enter the audience in a constant flow that makes up the fluid nature of the company's important target groups. Most of all, these publics forget and the impressions made on them, if left unreinforced will gradually fade.

$$\begin{array}{c} \text{Reality} \\ \text{of the} \\ \text{Company} \end{array} + \begin{array}{c} \text{Newsworthiness} \\ \text{of Company} \\ \text{Activities} \end{array} \div \begin{array}{c} \text{Diversity} \\ \text{(Lack of} \\ \text{Cohesiveness)} \end{array} \times \begin{array}{c} \text{Communication} \\ \text{Effort} \end{array} \times \text{Time} - \begin{array}{c} \text{Memory} \\ \text{Decay} \end{array} = \begin{array}{c} \text{Company} \\ \text{Image} \end{array}$$

Figure 1–1. *The Corporate Image Equation*

In real life, news is not only mixed good and bad, but it also open to interpretation by each public hearing the news. These different publics will interpert news more strongly one way than another. A consumer advocacy group, for instance, might view the closing of an environmentally troublesome plant far more positively than would employees in that community. The financial implications of the closing, which could be either negative or positive, would be viewed by the investing public in terms of the effect the closing will have on the bottom line. The complexity of the messages, their interpretation, compounded by the number of mixed messages sent out by employees who interact with various publics, compounded by time make this far too complex a model to lend itself to practical quantification in any real life situation. However, understanding the general interaction of good and bad news against a changing population is essential to understanding the continuing need for communication effort to build and maintain a company's reputation.

Although the company image portrayed must reflect reality, it is entirely possible as well as desirable to select and promote those characteristics that harmonize with the strategic plans of the company. The characteristics should also be those deemed desirable by the publics important to the company. The mid-1980s have seen an effort by many companies to assume the posture and attributes that seem to them to be most popular and "in" at the moment. Much like the political scene, which uses opinion surveys and polls as a basis for determining popular causes, business has turned increasingly to research to learn the characteristics most admired by the general public, customers, the trade, and particularly the financial community. Just as politicians may use the research results to find out where everyone is going and then rush to the head of the line to take a leadership position, so companies turn to the research to become what is popular, even if that is not always precisely what the company is. The studies can direct companies to make changes in the style and structure of industry posture which will mold the company toward its perceived ideal.

Most of these studies involve offering the respondent a preselected list of characteristics that he or she is asked to rank in importance. Since a preselected list of attributes is based on the research company's or its clients' common sense and experience with previous similiar research, several characteristics turn up in most surveys of this sort. Typically the surveys will examine the relative importance of company characteristics by determining whether the company:

1. Is well managed
2. Is a responsible corporate citizen
3. Provides quality products
4. Is committed to customer satisfaction
5. Is innovative
6. Is committed to research and development
7. Is advanced technologically
8. Supports cultural activities in the communities
9. Has shown consistent growth in profitability
10. Is well positioned in promising industries
11. Is well established
12. Is good company to do business with
13. Is reliable
14. Offers good investment potential
15. Would be a good company to work for
16. Is concerned with ecology
17. Is a large multinational company
18. Is diversified
19. Has a good reputation generally
20. Is financially sound
21. Is well focused
22. Offers good, long-term investment value
23. Gives evidence of the wise use of corporate assets

Although these studies find great similarity, some notable shifts have occurred over time reflecting business and social changes. Once diversified companies were in; now companies with well-focused, more compatible areas of business seem most popular. There are also variations according to the publics being surveyed. As one might expect, the consuming public is more concerned with product quality, customer satisfaction, and good corporate citizenship; these are elements more likely to touch their lives. The investing community, by contrast, almost invariably ranks management quality and long-term growth investment possibilities in position one or two. Interestingly, innovativeness is judged by both groups as quite important but probably for very different reasons. Consumers are more interested in finding new and interesting products, while the investing community evaluates innovativeness highly as a competitive advantage for future growth.

Research on the Subject

Many research companies, including Yankelovich Clancy Shulman, Roper, ORC, Harvey, AHF, and Erdos & Morgan, have conducted surveys of this type. In general, they agree in their conclusions; however, such survey work is usually done for individual corporations and constitutes a body of proprietary information unavailable for publication. But examples of the results of two such surveys are available for publication and are presented here.

One was conducted among readers of the *Wall Street Journal* by the *Wall Street Journal* Marketing Services Department; and the other, among the somewhat more general, though still upscale, readers of *Time* magazine. The latter survey was conducted in 1985 by National Family Opinion Research among a national sample of 1,000 *Time* readers; the survey was conducted by mail. The 760 who responded provided a reliable base. The questionnaire asked the readers to rate the importance of eleven traits of U.S. corporations, ranking them on a four-point scale from extremely important to extremely unimportant. The results can be seen in table 1–1.

David H. Thomas, corporate advertising manager of *Time*, notes that the overwhelming importance of commitment to customer satisfaction would seem to suggest the changing attitudes of today's better-educated consumers. This finding fits admirably with another, that of a move in importance from quantity to quality, from price alone to value. Although males and females largely agreed on the importance of these various traits (see table 1–2), women were more concerned with customer satisfaction than were males. This is very similar to findings of other surveys relating to

Table 1–1
Importance of Various Traits for U.S. Corporations Today
(in percentages)

Company Traits	Extremely/ Very Important	Important/ Somewhat Important	Unimportant/ Somewhat Unimportant	Extremely/ Very Unimportant
Committed to customer satisfaction	91	9	—	—
Innovative/take advantage of trends	71	27	2	—
Responsible corporate citizen	70	27	2	1
Good company to work for	68	27	4	1
Concerned with ecological issues	68	30	2	1
Good investment qualities	63	32	4	1
Communicate company's goals to society	57	34	7	2
Broad based and diversified in business	28	48	20	4
Multinational in scope	20	42	30	8
Major corporation	20	56	20	4
National-only in scope	14	42	36	8

Source: National Family Opinion Research Study among *Time* readers

product quality. Note too that innovativeness was of somewhat less concern to females.

In 1984 the *Wall Street Journal* Marketing Services Department, under the direction of vice president of marketing, Bernard T. Flanagan, began a semiannual survey among *Wall Street Journal* readers, referred to as the corporate report card. They employed Erdos & Morgan, an independent research firm. The first wave of interviews was fielded in January 1984. A total of 700 companies were selected, 500 industrials, 50 diversified financial, 50 diversified service, 50 transportation, and 50 utilities. All were from the Fortune 1983 rankings. To this, they added 7 new telecommunications companies formed by the breakup of AT&T. Since only parent companies, whose stock is available on public exchanges,

Table 1–2

Importance of Various Traits Ranked by Sex Extremely/Very Important

Company Traits	Total	Sex	
		Males	Females
Committed to customer satisfaction	1	1	1
Innovative	2	2	5
Responsible corporate citizen	3	3	3
Good company to work for	4	4	2
Concerned with ecological issues	5	6	4
Good investment qualities	6	5	6
Communicate company's goals to society	7	7	7
Broad based and diversified	8	8	8
Multinational in scope	9	9	10
Major corporation	10	10	9
National-only in scope	11	11	11

Source: National Family Opinion Research Study among *Time* readers

were to be measured in this study, a total of 78 companies were eliminated. Also eliminated was Dow Jones, the *Wall Street Journal's* parent company, although it is listed on the exchange.

The *Wall Street Journal* continues to revise and refine the study, but the first quarter 1985 report is typical in that 629 companies in 30 industries were evaluated. Three versions of the questionnaire were distributed randomly among them: each questionnaire version was mailed to a sample of 1,500 *Wall Street Journal* subscribers for a total mailing of 4,500. To reduce the effect of the listed sequence of companies within an industry, a reverse-order version was mailed to half of each sample.

In that study, a total of 3,040 questionnaires—67.9 percent of the net total mailout—were received by Erdos & Morgan. Response rates for all of these *Wall Street Journal* studies have been consistently better than 66.67 percent. In a random sampling of this size, 95 percent of the studies will show no more than a 6 percent variation in either direction, as compared with interviewing all of the universe—in this case, general subscribers.

The principle results of this study provide a continuing report card on the familiarity of the *Wall Street Journal* audience with major, publicly held corporations; but in addition to familiarity, the study also evaluates three other qualities: (1) whether the company is considered well managed, (2) whether it has a good reputation generally, and (3) whether it is considered a good investment. The report results are held in strict confidence between the *Journal* and each company measured. Information on the performance of an individual company is available only to that company through a *Wall Street Journal* advertising sales representative. The report shown to each company contains only that company's own data as a rank and percentage above a high average and low achievement level in each category. The peer companies included in the study are listed, but figures for the other companies are not disclosed.

In addition to ranking the companies, the study probes other information useful to corporations. In the early studies, respondents were asked to rank, in importance, the company attributes they considered in making an investment. The results, shown in table 1–3, ranked high to low, are of interest.

Despite their investment orientation, the *Wall Street Journal* audience continues to rank "high-quality products and services" high among considerations. It is also clear that among investors of greatest concern is how well managed a company is. This is universal in such studies among the entire investing community.

Table 1–3
Ranking of Company Attributed by Respondents

Company Attributes	C.R.C. No.1	C.R.C. No.2	C.R.C. No.3
Is considered well managed	79.9%	79.5%	79.3%
Offers high-quality products or services	62.6%	63.8%	63.7%
Has a good reputation	53.4%	53.3%	55.3%
Has a high earnings growth rate	48.4%	46.4%	46.1%
Has a record of stable or increasing dividends	45.7%	47.7%	47.9%
Has a high rate of return on equity	42.1%	41.3%	40.4%
Belongs to a high-growth industry	39.5%	37.2%	34.0%
Has sufficient levels of investment in R & D	26.5%	23.6%	24.4%
Was recommended by a broker	15.9%	14.4%	14.7%
Was recommended by an investment service	10.9%	9.6%	9.6%
No answer	4.2%	3.9%	5.3%

Source: *Wall Street Journal* Corporate Report Card

Just one example is a study by the *Financial Analysts Journal*, which found that portfolio managers and security analysts rated "quality of management" the most critical factor in evaluating the long-term potential of a company.

The importance of this factor led the *Wall Street Journal* to focus on the issue of what makes investors believe a company is well managed. By including this question in a number of their "Corporate Report Card" surveys, researchers found that *Wall Street Journal* subscribers considered the criteria appearing in table 1–4 important.

Not surprisingly, the performance of the company as an investment determines most strongly whether it is considered well managed. This view is understandable, although it presents a chicken-and-egg type of dilemma.

Over a long period of time better-managed companies will perform better than poorly managed companies. Yet undeniably some companies that are poorly managed do well for a period of time as they ride industry or market trends. Conversely, even extremely well managed companies can run into periods of poor performance.

Table 1–4
Important Critera in Investors' Evaluations

Company Traits	Percentage of Investors Who Consider This Important
A record of above-average earnings growth	77
Return on assets consistently above average	60
Consistently high return on shareholder equity	60
A history of successful new product or service introductions	56
Management that clearly communicates its plans for growth and profitability	46
Earnings derived from diverse sources	33
Invested heavily in research and development	30
Management that is quick to divest money-losing operations	29
A record of successful acquisitions	21
Top executives who are familiar to me	13

Source: *Wall Street Journal* Corporate Report Card

How to Present a Positive Image

How then can you convey this element of being well managed when the record says otherwise? What other traits are considered, particularly by analysts and institutional investors who follow companies closely, as characteristics of a well-managed company? How do these professional investors judge what constitutes good management? There is little uniformity in how these investors make their judgments, but certain criteria appear to arise with some frequency among analysts evaluating a company:

- Comparison of past communication by the company about its plans, projections, and forecasts, with current results. A conservative management that does not overpromise can be believed in the future. Credibility and honesty go hand in hand and count for a lot of good management signals.

- A willingness to communicate directly with analysts in meetings or on a one-to-one basis as a sign of confidence.

- Good financial control procedures, showing evidence of planning and consistent budget procedures.

- Evidence that management has found its business on a long-range strategic plan that is being followed.

- An obvious preoccupation with marketing by top management is a plus.

- A clear appreciation of innovation as evidenced by an R & D program geared to maintain an industry advantage is essential in many industries.

- A realistic structure for control of both domestic and foreign activities is preferred to a loosely run collection of companies.

- The look and sound of success in its communication program involving the company's identity system, signage-advertising, internal publications, and press releases make the management sound and look as if it is in control.

- Management industry experience is valued more highly than it was. Fading is the once popular notion that a good manager can manage any business.

- Depth of management is important—autocratic rule is suspect. A balance in ages is preferred with heir-apparent backups for an orderly succession.

- Stability in management is important. Frequent changes in senior people—high turnover—is a sign of poor management. Long tenure is usually viewed as a strength.

- Stockholdings by executives, particularly regular buys in the market by top officials, are viewed as evidence of confidence. Conversely, sells could flag trouble.

This then is some of the raw material from which images are shaped—but just how are forces within the company channeled to develop the desired reputation?

2
Will the Real Corporation Please Stand Up

A prerequisite to a cohesive corporate communications program is an agreed-to corporate mission. This is a statement describing the basic character of the company. It usually contains a company description, company objectives, and operating principles. The more specific these can be, the better.

The business philosophies expressed in these statements, while covering a relatively limited list of issues, can result in highly distinctive company character descriptions. The emphasis placed on the issues of quality, growth, employee relations, profits, customers, competitive attitudes, responsibility to stockholders, dealers, and public involvement will show a company's priorities.

Ethics statements are becoming more common, either as part of the mission statement or as a separate element. These standards of conduct guidelines, sometimes only moral puffery in the past, are becoming increasingly more effective by spelling out, in detail, the ethical behavior expected of employees.

A third basic tool is the company "fact book," which can be prepared in numerous ways and in modular form to make it a useful tool internally as well as with investors and customers.

Before the strategy, before communication planning, even before communication objectives can be set, there must exist an understanding of what the company is and what it is striving to become. Set down and agreed to by management, this is the corporate mission. Whatever your corporate communication program is asked to achieve, it will flounder and be unproductive if you do not start with a very clear understanding of the essential character of your corporation. You must know what the company is, what it stands for, and where it is going. It is the corporate admonition tantamount to "Know thyself" and "To thine own self be true." All your communication efforts must be compatible with this basic "vision of the company."

The Corporate Mission Statement

The corporate mission is somewhat analogous to the product positioning statement used in product marketing. Its importance lies in developing communication that is consistent over time and among the many voices emanating from the corporate body. Setting down such a statement in writing is not an academic exercise.

Ad agencies, public relations firms, marketing, communication, and identity consultants all agree that establishing the mission is an essential first step. Each service, in its own way, will attempt to aid a company in developing such a mission statement. They may advise and give guidance in its development, but the very top management of the corporation must make the final determination of what the company is and what its vision for the future should be. Communication advisers also agree that most poor corporate communication programs result from starting with a poorly defined corporate mission.

The mission statement itself is usually composed of a number of parts: company description, company objectives, and operating principles. Variations in its form are virtually endless. Generally, the statement starts with a description of the business. These examples will serve to illustrate how succinct these descriptions can be:

> Hewlett Packard Company is a major designer and manufacturer of electronic products and systems for measurement and computation. HP's basic business purpose is to provide the capabilities and services needed to help customers worldwide improve their personal and business effectiveness.

Ford Motor Company is a worldwide leader in automotive and automotive-related products and services as well as in newer industries such as aerospace, communications, and financial services.

Digital Equipment Corporation is the world's leading manufacturer of networked computer systems and associated peripheral equipment, and is the leader in systems integration with its networks, communications and software products. The Company's products are used worldwide in a variety of applications and programs, including scientific research, computation, communications, education, data analysis, industrial control, time sharing, commercial data processing, graphic arts, word processing, personal computing, health care, instrumentation, engineering and simulation.

Du Pont is a diversified chemical, energy and specialty products company with a strong tradition of discovery.

The Upjohn Company is a worldwide research-based manufacturer and marketer of pharmaceuticals, health services, chemicals, seeds and agricultural specialties.

These short company descriptions are usually only a sentence or two and may be thought of as describing the company in its most basic sense and in the fewest words. The descriptions will be enlarged upon to include other basic facts about the company, such as its size, where it operates, number of employees, years in the business, and other points of pride. For example:

Upjohn continues . . . with corporate headquarters in Kalamazoo, Michigan. The company completed its 99th year of continuous operation in 1985; it currently has research, manufacturing, and sales distribution facilities in more than 200 locations worldwide. Business segments within the company are Human Health Care and Agricultural.

United Technologies is a broad-based designer and manufacturer of high-technology products, with global headquarters in Hartford, Connecticut, U.S.A. The corporation employs over 193,000 people, operates about 300 plants, and maintains sales and service offices in 57 countries around the world. Sales are balanced among the aerospace and defense, building and automotive businesses, with electronics important throughout. The corporation's best-known products include Pratt & Whitney aircraft engines, Sikorsky helicopters, Norden defense systems, Carrier air conditioners, Otis elevators, Hamilton Standard controls, Essex wire and cable and automotive components and systems.

For most companies, the descriptive part of the mission statement will be relatively simple. Even as complex a giant as Allied-Signal succeeded in reducing its diversity to this one sentence:

Allied-Signal Inc. is an advanced technology company whose businesses are focused in three segments: aerospace, automotive and engineered materials.

The next section of mission statement will require the most time, careful consideration, and management attention. This is the heart of the statement concerning the operating principles of the company, its future visions, and its philosophies. Deciding on these guidelines may take months. Refining them and updating them is frequently an ongoing process. It is here that the individuality of the company is most evident. The personality and the values of the company will be revealed not only by what is said, but also through the tone of the statement. Contrast, if you will, the mission statements of United Technologies and General Motors. Both have been carefully worded and each is excellent, but they reflect entirely different company "societal orientations."

United Technologies issued a written statement in 1976 listing six elements that make up its corporate credo. Following a description of the company are six points,

Profit. To do good, we must first do well . . . We believe our ability to make a profit in the ethical manner is the single most important measure of our contribution to society. From profit we make the investments that guarantee the future of our corporation and provide job security for our employees. Our business requires people, money, tools, materials, and time. When we manage these resources efficiently and effectively, our customers buy our quality products and services at a price greater than our costs to produce and distribute them. This difference is our profit, the value we add to our resources. Without profit, no company can exist for long. To serve our customers well, to offer people rewarding employment, to provide a fair return to our shareholders, to finance growth, and to make contributions to society depends upon our skill in generating an adequate profit. Obviously, making a profit means achieving good gross margins and that means lowest possible cost consistent with highest quality. It would be relatively easy to improve our profits on a short term basis. We would reduce the levels of our investment in research, customer service, plant, equipment, and maintenance. These are shortsighted actions and we will not take them. Our management is charged with determining and maintaining the proper balance between short term profit performance and the necessary investment in our future growth and strength. United Technologies is in business for the long term.

This superb explanation of the need for profit, virtually an apology for the capitalist system, is followed by somewhat shorter but equally well done discussions on the importance of *satisfied customers, satisfied employees, satisifed shareholders, growth,* and *good citizenship.*

Note the difference in emphasis in the mission statement of General Motors, which starts thus:

The fundamental purpose of General Motors is to provide products and services of such quality that our customers will receive superior value, our employees and business partners will share in our success, and our stockholders will receive a sustained, superior return on their investment.

This short statement is followed by General Motors' eleven guiding principles, which deal with commitments to *product excellence, meeting customer needs, employees, dealers, quality leadership, seeking new business opportunities, offering a full range of products, maintaining strong manufacturing and technology units, operating with clearly articulated, centralized policies and decen-*

tralized operational responsibilities, and *participating as a responsible citizen.*

Both these statements serve to express each company's philosophies equally well, yet they are worlds apart. Some of the difference in the two approaches may be attributed to General Motors' consumer product orientation. Part of the difference may also be explained by the different audiences for such statements outside the respective companies. But the major part of the difference must certainly be attributed to the mindset of the managements and how each views the corporation it is guiding.

Important Elements of the Mission Statement

The business philosophies expressed in mission statements are a balance and mixture of the company's views. Generally they cover a relatively limited list of issues. The importance of "quality" and "excellence" to companies makes this an almost universal subject in mission statements. Here are a few more examples:

Quality

> *Xerox* is a quality company. Quality is the basic business principle for Xerox. Quality means providing our external and internal customers with innovative products and services that fully satisfy their requirements. Quality improvement is the job of every Xerox employee. . . . [Emphasize] Leadership Through Quality.

> (*Procter & Gamble*) We will provide products of superior quality and value that best fill the needs of the world's consumers.

> (*Fireman's Fund*) We believe success requires . . . [a] relentless commitment to excellence—to being the best—in our expertise, efficiency and service quality.

> (*Ford*) Quality comes first—To achieve customer satisfaction, the quality of our products and services must be our number one priority.

In addition to profits and product quality, other topics are frequently included in positioning statements:

Growth

(*Hewlett Packard*) [As an] objective to let our growth be limited only by our profits and our ability to develop and produce innovative products that satisfy real customer needs.

Whirlpool, in its chosen line of business, will grow with new opportunities and be a leader in an ever-changing global market.

Employee Relations

(*Proctor & Gamble*) We will employ, throughout the company, the best people we can find without regard to race or gender or any other differences unrelated to performance. We will promote on the same basis. *We recognize the vital importance of continuing employment because of its ultimate tie with the strength and success of our business. *We will build our organization from within. Those persons with ability and performance records will be given the opportunity to move ahead in the company. *We will pay our employees fairly, with careful attention to the compensation of each individual. Our benefit programs will be designed to provide our employees with adequate protection in time of need. *We will encourage and reward individual innovation, personal initiative and leadership, and willingness to manage risk. *We will encourage teamwork across disciplines, divisions and geography to get the most effective integration of the ideas and efforts of our people. *We will maximize the development of individuals through training and coaching on what they are doing well and how they can do better. We will evaluate Procter & Gamble managers on their record in developing their subordinates.* We will maintain and build our corporate tradition, which is rooted in the principles of personal integrity; doing what's right for the long-term; respect for the individual; and being the best in what we do.

(*United Technologies*) Satisfied employees. Our people are our strength . . . We work hard to meet employee needs and to provide job security. We want our men and women to take pride in their work, knowing their efforts contribute to the success of United Technologies and our mutual benefit. We expect the very best from our employees and respect, appreciate, and reward their efforts.

(*Ford*) Our people are the source of our strength. They provide our corporate intelligence and determine our reputation and vitality. Involvement in teamwork are our core human values.

Customer Focus

(*Dun & Bradstreet*) Customer focus is not a destination, it is a journey.

(*Ford*) Customers are the focus of everything we do—Our work must be done with our customers in mind, providing better products and services than our competition.

(*United Technologies*) Our customers are valued business associates who have a right to expect and to receive the best from us. This means the ultimate in craftsmanship, the finest service promptly rendered, and the greatest possible value for their money. We strive for excellence in everything we do.

Competitive Attitude

(*Du Pont*) To be more successful than our competitors, we must never be satisfied with the status quo.

(*Westinghouse*) Globally competitive—a leader or significant participant in its selected markets.

(*Fireman's Fund*) We value and reward competitive spirit: a commitment to doing things better than others, to being aggressive, to winning.

Responsibility to Stockholders

(*United Technologies*) Satisfied shareowners. A fair return for our shareowners ... We believe the owners of United Technologies are entitled to a fair and continuing return on their investment. Management is gratified by the trust and confidence placed by shareowners over the years. Our responsibility is to continue to conduct business in a profitable way to keep United Technologies an attractive investment. Further we believe we have a responsibility to conduct the affairs of the corporation in such a way as to make our shareowners proud of their corporation—its people, products, services, and actions.

(*Fireman's Fund*) We are in business to provide an attractive return on owners' capital, targeted to average 15 percent over time.

(*Xerox*) Implement realistic plans for revenue and profit growth to assure progress toward achievement of our long term ROA goal of 15%.... Continue to improve profitability in key geographic markets.... Continue progress towards competitive benchmark levels in quality, cost and asset use.

Dealer and Trade Relations

(*Ford*) Dealers and suppliers are our partners—The Company must maintain mutually beneficial relationships with dealers, suppliers, and our other business associates.

Marketing Objectives

Aetna will compete in selected domestic markets and gradually expand in international areas. We will establish and build competitive advantages in those markets where we operate and will be a leader in providing value to our customers by producing quality products and services efficiently and effectively. We will undertake new business opportunities only when they add value to our core businesses.

Public Issue Involvement

Aetna will play a significant role in the development of positions on regulatory, legislative and environmental issues that are important to the achievement of the objectives. The company will recognize its responsibility as a corporate citizen by becoming involved in those social issues and concerns where it can make a positive contribution and by providing opportunities from employee voluntarism.

Ethics

(*Fireman's Fund*) We value and reward honesty and integrity, to ourselves, to our customers, in the way we work and in the open way we communicate.

(*Warner-Lambert*) We are committed to being good corporate citizens, actively initiating and supporting efforts concerned with the health of society, particularly the vitality of the worldwide communities in which we operate. Above all, our dealings with our constituencies will be conducted with the utmost integrity, adhering to the highest standards of ethical and just conduct.

(*Aetna*) The company will maintain the highest ethical standards in conducting its business and will discharge moral as well as legal responsibilities.

Other Values

Individual companies also espouse a wide variety of positive values, which are shared by the company and its employees. These positive values include such things as honesty, integrity, clear thinking, hard work, teamwork, sensitivity, courage, vision, creativity, and innovation. Many companies also express their positive attitudes toward research and development if they are in technology areas, and science and laboratory development of new drugs if they are in the medical field.

It is also appropriate to include in these statements discussion of the internal structure employed by the company to realize its visions. Discussions concerning centralized versus decentralized management are not infrequent. Many companies update these statements with current specific goals regarding financial objectives, acquisition, and divestiture aims, all of this reflecting the kinds of information of interest to employees and investors.

Standards of Conduct Guidelines

Many corporate missions include statements on ethical conduct, but increasingly many companies also issue separate ethics guidelines to their employees. In some cases these are incorporated into employee standards and policies handbooks and become a part of regular employee indoctrination. In other cases, companies provide separate pamphlets on the subject of ethical behavior. These often spell out, in great detail, what is expected of the employee, using examples, questions, and answers. Companies that sell to or work with the government or defense contractors are particularly careful to go on record as to what they expect from employees in dealing with these customers. They will even spell out dollar value differences between acceptable and unacceptable business gifts.

Standards of conduct booklets help set the ethical tone of the company and serve not only to educate employees, but also to give evidence to the rest of society of the high moral standards set by the company. Some of the pamphlets carry an almost threatening tone to employees and are obviously no-nonsense rules of company policy on honesty. Other pamphlets appear to be written more for their effect on nonemployees and tend to be more general essays on ethics. Of the two, the former is more convincing to both employees and nonemployees. It is an area where tough, firm language is not only acceptable but most believable.

Generally, the subject matters covered in such pamphlets include the following:

1. Proper marketing practices

2. Offering of business courtesies

3. Accepting business courtesies

4. Conflict of interest

5. Use of company time, materials, equipment, and proprietary information, including software

6. Policies on political contributions

7. Policies on antitrust

8. Policies on equal employment opportunity

9. Policies on sexual harassment

10. Policies on environmental conservation, special policies pertaining to government employees

11. Policies on confidentiality of information likely to affect company stock price

12. Policies on travel and entertainment

An interesting variation in the use of a standards of conduct statement is employed by Warner-Lambert. The company combines the standards of conduct statement with its mission statement to produce "A Creed." These are guidelines appropriate to a pharmaceutical manufacturer. Although the ethical conduct portion is probably not sufficiently detailed for a government contractor, it is more than adequate to make clear the ethical expectations of the company to employees from very diverse backgrounds around the world.

Warner-Lambert Creed:
Our mission is to achieve leadership in advancing the health and well-being of people throughout the world. We believe this mission can best be accomplished by recognizing and meeting our fundamental responsibilities to our customers, employees, shareholders, suppliers and society.

To Our Customers: WE ARE COMMITTED to providing high-quality health care and consumer products of real value that meet customer needs. We are committed to continued investment in the discovery of safe and effective products to enhance people's lives.

To Our Employees: WE ARE COMMITTED to attracting and retaining capable people, providing them with challenging work in an open and participatory environment, marked by equal opportunity for personal growth. Performance will be evaluated on the basis of fair and objective standards. Creativity and innovation will be encouraged. Employees will be treated with dignity and respect. They will be actively encouraged to make suggestions for improving the effectiveness of the enterprise and the quality of work life.

To Our Shareholders: WE ARE COMMITTED to providing a fair and attractive economic return to our shareholders, and we are prepared to take prudent risks to achieve sustainable long-term corporate growth.

To Our Suppliers: WE ARE COMMITTED to dealing with our suppliers and all our business partners in a fair and equitable manner, recognizing our mutual interests.

To Society: WE ARE COMMITTED to being good corporate citizens, actively initiating and supporting efforts concerned with the health of society, particularly the vitality of the worldwide communities in which we operate.

ABOVE ALL, our dealings with these constituencies will be conducted with the utmost integrity, adhering to the highest standards of ethical and just conduct.

Communicating the Company Philosophy

The business description, the mission statement, and standards of conduct constitute the profile of a company and its values. These are expected to be shared and followed by the company employees. This will require communication. Merely printing and distributing a document will not be enough, but it's a start. Reworked and reexpressed in speeches, in articles in the company newsletter, and in staff memos, the fundamentals of the mission will need reiteration and elaboration on a continuing basis. The simpler the theme, the sharper its focus, the more effect the mission statement will have in determining the culture of the corporation. Repeated in various forms by the chief executive officer, it should become the company's theme song. As Charlie Moritz, chairman of Dun & Bradstreet, has said, "The process of being a CEO is one of finding a million and one ways to deliver the same message over and over again." In his case, it is a message that stresses "customer focus." Whatever your company focus it will require continued communication.

The philosophy that the company will live by should be understood not only by employees, but by other stakeholders as well: shareholders and the investment analysts that follow the company, the trade, suppliers, and customers. Each should be reached with appropriate versions of the message. Obviously, the annual report is a natural vehicle, but so too are other company mailings, press releases, and even package stuffers. Some companies reduce the message to a single laminated card that can be carried in a wallet. Some issue it as a large display, and it appears on company bulletin boards. Almost all provide pamphlets to accompany their regular communication. Consideration should be given to making the advent of a new mission statement the basis for a new fact book.

Whether it is a modest brochure for a small company or an elaborately bound book for a major corporation, the fact book is one of the first tools needed for good communication. For the smaller company it can serve multiple purposes, acquainting suppliers and customers, new employees and the financial community with the fundamental facts about the company. Larger corporations may wish to have a separate book for the investing community. This may include a bound-in copy of the latest Annual Report. The fact books are usually divided into the companies' major business units, providing all pertinent facts and figures. A good fact book should include at least an outline of the company structure and the principals in charge of the various divisions and departments.

Although a single fact book can serve multiple purposes, it is wise to take the principal need and develop the book for that specific purpose, adapting later as necessary for other uses. For a publicly held company, the fact book is usually compiled with the investment community in mind. As a result, it may be heavier in investment information than a customer-oriented document would be. Conversely, it will generally be lighter in product data. It is possible through spiral binding to develop great flexibility if a single format is used. Appropriate sections can be added or subtracted to the book for the different publics. In this way, even strictly in-house types of employee information may be effectively combined with other material to form excellent employee fact books on, say, compensation.

The fact book should project the desired appearance and personality of the company. It should express the same tone of voice as other company communication. You may wish to consider the following types of material in at least some versions of the fact book. However, there is no special merit in length, and certainly providing information that is not pertinent to a particular group is a mistake. A balance must be maintained between enough and too much. Here are some possible fact book subjects:

- An outline of the company's major business segments.

- A mission statement explaining why the company is in business and its position as it relates to employees, customers, the community, investors, society, nationally and/or internationally.

- An ethics statement.

- A company history, or perhaps historical highlights leading to the formation of the company.

- A summation of the company's corporate strategy.

- A statement about the company's current marketing and financial positions within its industries and society.

- A statement concerning any important environmental or other public issues.

- A presentation of the organization and management of the company. Frequently, these are accompanied with pictures of the principals and brief biographies/résumés. These may be combined with simplified organization charts, financial data, financial achievements.

- Information on the statistical standing of the company, such as ranking, size, profitability, market share, and so forth.

- Pertinent research findings that help position the company as to reputation or achievements.

- Major accomplishments of the company, such as number of patents, new products.

- General statistics, including number of personnel or plants. This data may be associated individually with the various business units.

- Branch offices and locations.

- Useful addresses and telephone numbers.

- Competitive position of major business units vis-à-vis the principal competitors. Market data, such as product share, industry penetration, and sales trends could be included.

- Product lists, possibly matrixed with their markets.

- Information on recent acquisitions and divestitures, new plant openings and closings.

- Latest R & D developments, with their future implications.

- In the financial section, include information on the financial management structure, consolidated balance sheet, summary of income, financial data by segment, and the board of directors; include also a statement on capitalization and a discussion on current financial concerns and achievements.

A fact book that accurately reflects the mission and style of the company is a solid accomplishment, one that puts you well ahead of many companies today. Now you must address the planning, staffing, and coordination necessary to project this identity.

3
The Players

Communication was once something companies just "did." Today it requires organization and understanding by all concerned as to who says what to whom and under what circumstances. This organization and structure will depend in part on the size of the industry the company is in and on the goals the organization sets for itself. A consumer products company, employing heavy consumer advertising, probably finds that most of its communication needs should be under the guidance of marketing. A highly regulated utility may find that its communication function is handled best under a public affairs officer. A defense contractor may find that communications led by military experts is the logical approach. A highly decentralized, multi-divisional company will find that most of its corporate communications are with the investment community, and that a financial/investor relations (IR) officer may be a logical choice for directing communications.

A communication audit is a logical first step. This may mean a graphics audit, a media audit, a communications content audit, or all three. How to conduct such audits and do so successfully will be examined in this chapter.

A generation ago communication wasn't considered a separate function. It was just something everyone did in the course of doing their regular jobs. If you were employed in the financial function of a company you were expected to communicate with stockholders, analysts, portfolio managers, and the financial press. Those in the legal department normally communicated with regulators and government agencies. Marketing employees were expected to communicate through advertising, packaging, and sales material, and perhaps through product press releases. The manufacturing function handled the communications with each plant community, and so on. With each division handling its own communications, the public relations department was limited largely to dealing with the press, communicating through press releases and personal contact, but it was to some extent isolated from the communication of others in the company.

Very little effort was made to coordinate these diverse communications to send out a cohesive picture of the company. A cohesive corporate image was more or less a question of how strong a personality the CEO had. If the company was lucky he or she set a leadership style that other employees could follow and reflect in their own communication.

A number of trends combined to make it essential that companies bring some discipline to this casual approach to communications, to make communication a function rather than simply a happenstance.

One of these trends was the growing diversity of companies, which became not only multiproduct but multibusiness. As companies became more complex, the resulting diversity in communication led, in some cases, to babble. An equally important trend has been the rise in consumerism and in government demand for more information about products, their manufacture, and environmental impact. Today's management routinely communicates information it previously would never have considered revealing. This is equally true in the financial side of business. A whole new function called investor relations has sprung up in response to the Securities and Exchange Commission (SEC) requirement for the disclosure of information that might affect the price of the company, either positively or negatively. Saying nothing is no longer the safest route. In fact, it is often illegal.

These changes made communication a necessary function, not simply a corporate option. The initial response to this need to provide control and direction to communication was usually to broaden the responsibility of the public relations director. Frequently, this new responsibility was not accompanied by increased authority or even by the opportunity to be a participant in the inner circle of management. The result was that policies were often established and company activities conducted with little or no thought given to their communication implications. Simply making the public relations director a vice president of corporate communications in title is insufficient. It must be accompanied with the muscle, the brains, and the structure to make the communication effective.

Robert Townsend, the president of Avis Corporation during its halcyon days, passed on this relevant (but irreverent) advice to business on how to deal with public relations on page 178 in his 1984 book *Further Up the Organization:*

> "P.R. Department, Abolition of" Yes, fire this whole department. Two: If you have an outside P.R. firm, fire them. . . . So we eliminated the P.R. staff and we called in the top ten or so people in the company and the telephone operators and told them they were the P.R. department. The telephone operators were given the home phone of the ten people and asked to find one of them if any of the working press called them with questions.

Townsend explains that these ten people were given the framework within which they could be themselves, and, according to him, the system worked very well.

For a company with a single product or service, a clearly defined direction, and a shared philosophy throughout the organization, this would be a most effective method of handling public relations. The press appreciates nothing more than talking to an executive in charge. The philosophy works particularly well if a single-minded purpose has been established throughout the company, as it was in the Avis case. The "We Try Harder" advertising theme worked its magic through all employee levels, down to desk clerks and parking attendants, virtually forcing an enthusiastic demonstration of the company's dedication. This, of course, is the best form of communication a company can have.

It is a rare company today that is so simplified in structure that its ten top executives can speak with a single voice. If they can, Townsend's approach is still a good one. With growth diversification, however, most corporations structure their communication into a function called "corporate communication." What was once a function performed by the CEO, either wittingly or unwittingly, needs in most cases to be largely delegated to a professional communicator with sufficient training, authority, and support to be effective.

How best to organize and structure the communication function will depend on the goals the company sets for itself. There is no single best way. It also depends on the company's size, diversity, and the industry it is in. Each company's communication needs must be tailored to these goals. It is hardly an overstatement to say that no two companies are alike. This can be readily seen by citing some extreme examples:

1. A consumer products company employing heavy consumer advertising for products sharing the company's own name may think that its communication needs are virtually all met successfully under the guidance of the marketing discipline. Communications with the financial community are considered totally separate and are confined to the financial officer's regular activity.

2. A highly regulated utility may find that communication functions best in the hands of a public affairs officer, who responds to regulators and local consumer groups. Marketing considerations may be less important in this less competitive area.

3. A defense contractor may find that communication led by military experts works fine if it is tempered with public relations sensitive to the increasing demand for congressional control.

4. A highly decentralized, multidivisional company operating more as a holding company may find that its principal corporate communications function is financial and is run by a financial/IR officer, which leaves consumer or trade communications to the individual subsidiaries.

These four brief cases begin to suggest the variety of forms corporate communication may take. In practice, it is a balance among a variety of communication needs which will differ from one company to the next. In some, marketing will be dominant; in others, public relations or financial relations considerations will determine the types of expertise required by the staff. Size and budget for the function will also be determined by understanding the goals set for communication. This will become more apparent when the goals are examined in terms of the appropriate audiences that will need to be reached and the ways in which these contacts will be made. The most logical way to gain a picture of a company's communication needs is to start with a communications audit of those communications which already exist.

The Communication Audit

There are three principal types of communication audit: (1) graphics audit, (2) communication content audit, and (3) media audit.

The media audit will be the most useful in determining the staffing and structural requirements for your communication program. Because all three audits are highly related and each informative in its own way, there is efficiency in conducting all of them at the same time. Agencies and communication consultants will frequently suggest conducting such audits and may be helpful at this stage. However, there is some validity to the charge that a consultant is someone who, when asked the time, borrows your watch in order to tell you. In fact, the most useful information for making companies run better comes from within the company itself. The consultant's ability lies in understanding what to do with that information. It's a little like knowing what to do with all the numbers on the watch in relation to the big hand and the little hand.

Whether you elect to seek help or not, most of the work will still be internal. You should start by assembling all the examples of communication you can identify, and this requires the authority to request and receive samples of every form of communication sent out or used by all departments, divisions, and subsidiaries of the company.

Graphics Audit

This is the simplest audit and consists only of the collection of names and logos as they appear throughout the company on letterheads, business cards, public relations releases, and advertisements, as well as snapshots of signs in and around plant sites. It will include the logo as it appears on novelty items, house organs, brochures, as it is used alone and in combination with other companies and partners, such as jobbers or joint ventures. This is a useful exercise for companies of any size and any degree of diversity. It almost invariably results in a dramatic demonstration of how discordant the company's "look" is. It is a very good sales tool for a consultant to use in persuading management that a new identity system is required or that policing of the old one has been neglected. Most identity consulting firms insist on this as a first step. This type of audit also reveals the various forms that communications take that will require special logo handling.

The first examination of a collection of such material can be intimidating. Order will emerge from the initial chaos if you first examine each division and its own subsystem of identity and try to understand how it was conceived and is supposed to work. Examine it for its principal strengths and weaknesses and for what appear to be fundamental requirements, like lining up a brand name to a subsidiary name or connecting the subsidiary name to the parent company name. Such an examination will provide valuable clues on the real needs of the subsidiary that will have to be dealt with in any new linkage system. It will be helpful to have an understanding of the relative importance of the different forms of communication by each subsidiary. Obviously, having someone take you through the material who is knowledgeable about it will be a big help.

Next, concentrate on the more important forms of identity used. Regroup the material to get a picture of the diversity of look that exists across the various businesses. That is, examine all the business cards, examine all the plant signs, all the executive letterheads. Fundamentally, you form a grid by company and by the type of communication. A large cork wall or a table area you can tie up for a few days is a big help.

Content Audit

The graphics audit will have given you a good start in the direction of the content audit. You will also need to assemble whole samples of the more important company communications. These consist of ads, press releases, house organs, form letters, and prepared speeches by company principals. A communication audit can also examine how the press refers to the company. Studying press clippings and broadcast extracts is valuable and revealing but is a different exercise and should not be mixed or confused with the content audit. However, it is interesting to contrast what you say in your press releases and what is actually picked up.

In assembling communication material, include a few negative form letters, such as job applicant turndowns and second notices on delinquent accounts. Just as the graphics audit required a certain sense of visual style and taste, the content audit will require a sense of language. Allowing for the obvious differences in style required by a letter concerning a delinquent bill and an advertisement, try to "listen to the language" and hear whether the communication could be coming from the same company. If not, you have identified a problem.

Notice particularly whether communications to the same audience are compatible. Does the annual report have the same tone of voice as the press releases to the financial community? Does the trade advertising sound as though it could be coming from the same company that is talking to wholesalers and jobbers in the deal sheets? Cross-check, as well. Would a customer, who owns stock in the company, be jarred by the difference in attitude in advertising communication and the annual report, or would their differences simply be those naturally expected by content and subject matter change?

Your quest here is for a fundamental compatibility that communications are at least coming from the same company. More than that cannot really be expected. In fact, in multibusiness companies it may be entirely appropriate for some subsidiaries and products to have their own individual character that is shaped for their particular marketplace. The tone used by producers of soft drinks or children's toys will probably not be appropriate in communication from a sister pharmaceutical division, for instance. Common sense must be applied liberally in a content audit.

Media Audit

The media audit should reveal your staffing and structural requirements. It consists of assembling a list of your principal avenues of communication. The term *media,* in this case, should be thought of as a communication opportunity, whatever the format. It will include such things as annual and quarterly reports, as well as the annual stockholders meeting. Regular mailings to analysts and portfolio managers and meetings with analysts should be included on the list, as should any regular participation in business associations, councils, or roundtables of executives of the firm. Each of these is a communication event in its own right, requiring some preparation and requiring staffing and skills to ensure that it is a positive event. The various classes of press that are regularly contacted and trade and customer mailing lists that are frequently used should be included. At the same time, internal media should also be considered. The company newspaper, regular staff memos, even internal closed-circuit television if it is employed at plant sites, should be included. Taken together, the internal and external communications media audit will provide an idea of the existing communication workload, which in turn will give some idea of the staffing requirements and skills needed.

The paid media, or advertising, portion of the audit should be considered somewhat separately, not only from a workload standpoint—since it will be, in all likelihood, written and produced by outside agencies under company direction—but also from the standpoint of achieving media efficiencies. This is really a separate project but one worth conducting. A multibusiness, decentralized company may discover that major economies can be achieved just by taking advantage of improved contract rates offered by the media through combining divisional schedules. Such media coordination and contract control may be assigned to a single ad agency for implementation; this does not take away any of the divisions' advertising prerogatives. Depending on the degree of overlap in the target audiences of the different advertising campaigns, long-term savings achieved by such an audit more than repay the time and effort.

An appraisal must be made of the existing communication workload revealed by the audit and of that that will be required by the new corporate communication program. Don't base your structure only on past needs, but interpret the new needs brought about by new communication objectives.

Where the Communications Activities Belong

The next step is to examine the communications activities to find out where they belong, whether centralized within corporate communications, as an activity of another department, or as a function of a subsidiary or division. It is generally simplest to start by identifying the activities that clearly must be handled by corporate headquarters first, leaving the activities that might properly belong with separate divisions to be dealt with later.

The activities should be thought through twice. First, where does the conceptual or planning stage belong, and then, an implementation stage? A central group within corporate communications could be charged with the responsibility not only of implementing the material requirements of the financial, human relations, and other headquarters departments, but also of functioning as the writing, art, and production resource that will fill many divisional needs. It is possible that a company is so dominated by a division's marketing communication needs that the creative and production resource should be a part of marketing and should be used as required by headquarters. The variations that can be satisfactorily employed are almost as diverse as the companies themselves. Allowances must be made to maintain headquarters's role in the communication process. Corporations must have the ability to add not only to the strategic input but at the conceptual stage as well. Equally important, some monitoring system of the final output is required for policing purposes, but also, more importantly, to provide feedback for improvement and modification of future conceptual planning.

Although the strategy decisions for some communication will

obviously be made at divisional level, for a corporation to isolate itself completely from the communication activities of the division assures a highly fragmented company image. Even the most decentralized holding company requires at least some input/output communication feed with its operating companies. Though this may not be appreciated by the companies, it is essential to the proper running of even a holding company's financial interests. Today's portfolio managers and analysts are far too sophisticated to appraise a corporation's value only in terms of the communication output from headquarters. They read the division's activities and how the business components are faring in the marketplace to get at the fundamental marketing strength of the parent company. A company with activities in several industries will find the analysts interpreting the individual divisions not just through their market share but also their other achievements within each industry. In fact, a subtle but convincing way to reach analysts is through the vertical press of the major industries the company is in. What a pharmaceutical company says in medical journals is every bit as revealing to a good analyst as what he or she is told by the company's headquarters in the business press. *Aviation Week,* for example, can be at least as revealing to an analyst as one of the financial publications if the company he or she is following is in the aerospace industry.

Each communication activity will have to be examined in this way to determine where its planning function belongs and where its executional needs can best be met. An examination of this sort requires an understanding of the organization's structure—that of headquarters and of the division. Your organization's chart is a must. You will have to question the entire existing structure. Which existing services can be employed? Which activities can be combined? Will a central staff constitute the most economical approach? Where should it be located? Furthermore, you will need to consider available personnel in relation to the actual needs. Is the talent available? Where are they located? Will geographical consolidation be necessary?

When the structure appears to make sense, its logic should be tested by envisioning a control system to make the structure work. If anything, the system of control is even more important than the structure itself. The system should allow those with the greatest expertise to act upon the principal functions at an early stage, and it should ensure access by those charged with communication responsibility to secure all necessary information from the various parts and levels of the company. Communication is obviously possible only when there is something to communicate. This must come from within the company and all its parts and pieces. The system must allow for this in such a way that the most interesting news and stories, the tidbits that make up good company messages, are made available to those charged with preparing the communication.

It is also essential that the sources providing this information be given the opportunity of review to be sure that what they have provided has been accurately handled. This process is in addition to the review that will have to be built into the system to assure that legal and trademark questions are cleared in all communication.

Two Difficult Decisions

In practice, most of this process of evaluating the structural and system needs is simpler than it sounds. Most of the activities fit logically into a scheme appropriate for your individual company, its size, industry, and communication goals. Experience suggests that the most difficult decisions will arise in two areas: (1) centralization versus allowing a division free rein to communicate, and (2) the corporation's image needs versus product marketing requirements. The reason for centralization is principally control, to assure that a single voice comes from the company. The messages must reflect management position and the interests of the *whole* company, not just those of a division. Centralized communication close to the CEO level can assure that messages take into account longer-range company needs, financial and stockholder interests of the company, as well as the political, regulatory, and government interests of the company. Centralization affords economies in staffing as well.

Despite these powerful reasons for centralization, marketing requirements must come first. As business seems to be relearning after its spate of reshuffling its business portfolios, the essence of business is still sales, and that takes marketing. Without sales, the paper shuffle for Wall Street ultimately collapses. Communications must be geared to meet marketing needs. If this requires communication autonomy for a division, so be it. But some controls are still necessary. If it is thought, for example, that centralization removes the production of product press releases too far from marketing, the decision should be to leave it with marketing and/or the division.

The problem is more complex when it involves evaluating the centralization of advertising needs, particularly in a relatively monolithic company whose product and identity are closely allied. In a multibusiness company, allowing each separate business unit and/or product and brand its own separate marketing advertising approach may be valid, but the danger of this decentralization is that the advertising may take a form that detracts from the parent company's image. In a competitive industry that has reached a stage of maturity in which price, promotional or other short-range sales advantage types advertising or sales promotion predominates, it will be found that the quality image of the company will suffer in the long term. Such advertising detracts from a company's reputation. Corporate advertising, under the control of the corporate communication group, differs in its objective, which is to build the corporate image, not tear it down. Its aid to immediate sales is secondary.

Sales advertising, on the other hand, can often be seen actually hurting a company's product. In fact, the pressure for immediate sales may result in advertising that can even hurt the long-range prospects for the product itself. Distress sale advertising is the simplest example of such communication. Here again, a balance is needed. Very likely, a separate corporate communications program is required to offset the effect of such detrimental advertising.

Studies by the Association of National Advertisers among its members and by the Conference Board both show that corporate advertising is performed within the public relations hierarchy in most instances. This is based on the thinking that as important as marketing is, as dominant as sales and profits are to the life of a corporation, marketing does not represent the full scope of considerations involved in developing and executing corporate advertising programs. Recent ANA findings suggest that advertising is becoming more marketing oriented. Good! This new trend has been particularly noticeable among companies that market to the business community, where high overlap of audience exists between the marketing needs and the government and investment needs of the corporation. But once again, marketing should not be the only consideration under these circumstances. A balance must be maintained to be sure all company interests are met.

In summary, make an examination of the existing communication activities throughout the company. This will establish a current base line. Compare the new communication program to the current activities. This should reveal any new needs to handle these new programs. The activities are then apportioned to the logical departments and divisions or the activities may be centralized.

Finally a control system is developed to assure good executive input/output, to provide specialized internal informational channels for gathering company news and to set up clearance channels. You should incorporate a feedback mechanism. This process may include a research stage that will facilitate learning from practical experience gained in conducting the program.

4

Picking an Agency

To get the most from either an ad or a public relations agency, know yourself and your needs. The relationship should be a close one—this implies compatibility. Compatibility depends on the agency's own business objectives, executive personalities, and the agency's ability to meet your specific needs. This requires an understanding of what you expect from an agency. A suggested method for examining your needs and comparing them to agency capabilities is described, along with a questionnaire for learning what each agency can offer.

The agency selection process is explained step by step, and the fundamental differences between public relations and ad agencies in terms of structures, costs, and staffing are also described.

A public relations agency and—if your program calls for paid media—an advertising agency are essential partners for any serious communications effort. Think of them as extentions of your staffing requirements. Usually offering broad capabilities, they can employ specialists whom you would otherwise find impractical to retain on your staff on a full-time basis.

The relationship between a company and its agencies should be a close one. If you think of the agencies simply as vendors or suppliers, it is a sure indication that you are not getting all you should from the relationship. This would be true even if the assignment were limited to product advertising or product publicity. But when it comes to corporate relations and corporate advertising, complete trust in the agency is necessary so that it may be given in-depth knowledge of the company's activities.

It is difficult to discuss the requirement of an agency relationship without calling up the analogy of marriage. Certainly the selection process resembles nothing more than the courtship period. The nervous smiles from the agency, the profuse exchange of amenities can leave a prospective client with a feeling he or she may be handed a bouquet of flowers at any moment. The first few weeks parallel the honeymoon, both sides looking forward with anticipation to what they can accomplish together, finding out as much as they can about each other, and generally making light of any minor shortcomings or transgressions. Just how well the marriage progresses will, in part, depend on how well suited you were for each other in the first place and on how much you both have worked to make the relationship a good one. It does take work, but more about that later. Eventually, there may come a time when a separation seems in order, particularly if the minor differences haven't been dealt with as they have arisen and an accumulation of problems have begun to sour. Some breakups include trips to the lawyers and can rival the acrimony of a real divorce.

If your company already employs an agency, don't jump to make a change. Whether it is a public relations or an advertising agency or an agency you are currently using for product promotion and product advertising, examine the relationship thoroughly. Changes are disruptive, and there may be far more potential in the relationship than you realize. More and more companies are making it a practice to go through periodic, usually yearly, reappraisals of their agency relationships. This can be as simple as a serious luncheon discussion with the principals of the agency, or it can be a very elaborate review conducted by an outside consultant who specializes in this kind of "marriage counseling" work. Many agencies are, therefore, accustomed to making periodic account stewardship reports.

There is a tendency to drop agencies, particularly advertising agencies, more often than is necessary. Usually agency people, if they are smart, are all too willing to change their ways. If they are dumb, that is a terminal condition and you don't want them anyway. In the case of larger agencies, changes can be simply a matter of assigning new teams that can effectively offer a client a fresh start with fresh faces. What may simply be poor working habits and a failure to communicate, combined with a failure to address the problem over a period of time, can make a change appear more desirable than it really is. The apparent advantages of the change must be weighed against the pain and inconvenience of finding and re-educating a whole new group. Executive time involved in the search and selection process is considerable. A change in agency may interrupt an ongoing program and cause delays and loss of momentum. Three to six months may be required to find a new agency and another three to six months to get it up to speed. Finally, you run the risk of selecting an agency that is fundamentally no better than the one you had.

For these reasons, therefore, a complete re-evaluation of your present agency capability is a worthwhile venture. The examination has to get to the root of what has caused problems in the relationship. The findings will be of value to you whether you decide to stay with the agency or make a change. Various studies in this area conclude that many agency/client problems lie not just with the agency but with the client too. Changing an agency when the problem lies fundamentally on the client side can lead to a succession of unhappy relationships, which is not uncommon in the communications business.

Advertising Agencies versus Public Relations Agencies

Before getting into fundamentals for evaluating agency/client relationships, it is worth taking a few moments to examine some of the differences between advertising and public relations. On the surface, both types of agency appear to have a lot of similarities. In fact, many agencies offer the combined services. In the case of the smaller agencies, the account executives, writers, and others may have broad enough experience to offer a full range of required capabilities. This can be a convenience to a client who is cutting down on the size and number of meetings, since it makes coordination of programs easier and more a responsibility of the agency than of the client. Much of this advantage is also held by slightly larger agencies, those that have a separate but still internal public relations department. The account people (service representatives) can use the specialized skills found in the PR departments and coordinate these activities for the client. Medium-sized and larger agencies, when owned by the same company, usually operate their advertising and public relations services separately. This largely eliminates the advantage of one-stop shopping. Although these agencies still like to feature their "total communications capabilities," as a practical matter the client is usually left with the coordination problem.

The disciplines of public relations and advertising are dissimilar enough that with increased size the process tends to grow apart and to create distinct groups. The economies of running the two kinds of agencies are very different as well. The salary scales, for instance, are usually lower on the PR side than the advertising side. Public relations is a more people-intensive business, and profit grows more slowly as billings go up because more people must be added to the staff. Conversely, advertising profits grow more quickly with larger budgets. Once the initial ad production is completed, running in more publications or more expensive media simply increases the customary 15 percent commission to the agency without substantially adding to its overhead. This simple fact of life usually leads to dominance by the advertising function within a combined services agency. This results in internal strains that are best addressed by completely separating the two units.

If yours is a large corporation, therefore, you will probably be working with two separate agency groups even if they do appear to be owned by one corporation. These may but need not be the same agencies that handle the product publicity and product advertising that would be controlled through your marketing hierarchy. If yours is a relatively simple corporation working in one industry, with a single, well-focused product or service line, you probably will find a single advertising and single public relations firm the most efficient route. If, however, you are the communications director for a large corporation that is diversified, you may wish to employ separate agencies, one for product work and one for corporate. The latter should be skilled in public affairs, community affairs, investor relations, Washington relations, and other areas not normally associated with product publicity.

In the case of the advertising agency, a number of differences exist between corporate and product advertising which should be recognized as requiring somewhat separate advertising skills. Corporate advertising makes up less than 3 percent of all advertising; consequently, experience in it is relatively rare. In general, agencies are staffed with people accustomed to product advertising. The emphasis is on business and marketing experience for those who engage in the contact work. In fact, in recent years M.B.A.'s have been sought out by ad agencies for that position.

Advertising copywriters come from a much wider range of backgrounds than do public relations writers, who come principally from journalism. Today's advertising agency emphasizes writing for television. This demands a high level of idea generation but makes relatively modest demands on English language skills. It is not unusual to find advertising writers who can write little else than television. When this background is compared with the journalism background so typical of those employed by corporations in their corporate communications and public relations departments, it is easy to see how different the two worlds are and where many conflicts can arise in relationships.

Consider for a minute the relationship between a press release and an ad. A press release is written for two audiences, the editor and the target public. It is also written so it can be cut and still maintain its essence in the first paragraph or two. Advertising writers, on the other hand, write for a single audience and develop the copy in such a way that it should be read as a single short piece, carrying the reader on to the end. They know it will not be cut. Frequently they use the last sentence as the wrap-up for the copy, tying it back to the headline. Public relations people tend to think of their writing as news stories that may or may not have a photograph or two. Ads, by contrast, are thought of as a unit in which the art and copy are closely related. The advertising art director plays a major role in the ad's creation. The illustration may in fact be the major communication element. It is not unusual for the art director to originate the basic concept, the term generally given for the headline and the visual treatment presented as a whole.

Advertising copywriters are usually not overly concerned with grammar. They wish to speak in the vernacular of their customer target audience. Short phrases and incomplete sentences can effectively communicate ideas quickly and painlessly. That's not the kind of writing that most editors would appreciate in the press release. Nor is it necessarily the kind of advertising writing that is appropriate for corporate ads. Corporate advertising usually represents the voice of management, and not all managements are willing to present themselves using poor grammar. It is one thing when it is used to discuss your product. It can be an entirely different matter when it represents your company. Attitudes on this subject vary with the company along with the style and tone of the ad. The audience for the advertising makes a difference as well. Ads addressed to educators and the press may require a second look at the syntax.

The marketing background of many advertising people also makes them extremely goal oriented. They are usually much more willing to make waves with their communications to reach an objective. In fact, sound marketing usually considers it perfectly acceptable to run ads that may upset portions of the population, providing the ad generates meaningful and profitable sales. Compare this with the public relations person with a journalism background who is concerned about getting good ink, not just any ink or even any news content at all. Such a PR director may see a corporate ad that makes waves as a disaster. This is to be expected since the first people to write and complain are usually stockholders, major customers, subsidiary executives, and employees and their wives. These are important publics to any corporation.

Even as simple a question as how frequently to run an advertisement shows the fundamental difference in philosophy between journalism and marketing backgrounds. Years of substantial advertising readership research document that an ad can run three, four, or five times and lose none of its impact and readership. Most PR people in charge of corporate advertising are reluctant to repeat ads because of their concern for freshness and newsworthiness; they will be reluctant to repeat ad subject matter once it has been dealt with in a single advertisement. This difference in background and point of view sets the stage for a lot of problems between ad agency and corporate clients if these differences are not understood.

Fundamentals for Evaluating Your Agency Relationship

Before you can evaluate your agency, you must first evaluate your own company needs. You cannot determine how well suited your present agency is for meeting your needs until they are first clearly defined in your own mind. Your needs will probably be directly related to your company's size and complexity, as well as to the scope of the communications problem. Most of all, your needs will vary with your personal or company operating philosophy on whether to handle most work in-house or to rely heavily on outside resources.

Determining which way to go depends on a number of considerations. First, of course, is deciding whether each function is sufficiently time consuming to warrant hiring a full-time employee, which means determining how stable the need for the function will be. Is it a long-term or a short-term assignment? Is it year-round or seasonal? Would the activity be dropped with the first budget cut, or is it likely to be required in any economic development? If it is not a full-time function, would it fit well enough with other functions to warrant employing someone with more generalized skills? Usually the more specialized the skill required, the better off you are going outside for it. Does the function require extensive knowledge of the company and of its products and their manufacture? Although agencies will be expected to learn a great deal about your operation, they do not need the kind of in-depth industry and company knowledge an employee will attain. Many functions, such as developing customer case histories or employee activity information, depend on extensive contact with many people within the corporation. The success of such a function depends on the ability of the person to develop a network of internal information sources and to coordinate clearances among various divisions around the company. Usually such a function is better handled by someone on staff. Security is of growing importance and is easier to maintain with in-house staff. Defense contractors and others who operate with a high security requirement must take into account a generally higher turnover and looser security system than they might like.

One consideration frequently overlooked in the hiring process is how well the job function skills fit corporate career paths. To hire someone with highly specialized skills such as advertising copywriting or research may only be a practical solution on a short-term basis. Unless the employee's job fits well into a thought-out career path offering growth and personal development, the job will be a dead end. Dead-end jobs will lose you the best people until eventually someone with lesser ambitions and lesser career opportunity is assigned. You may then have effectively filled the niche with a lifetime hack. This can be a particularly difficult problem when people with distinct, specialty skills that demand a high level of creativity are being hired. Copywriters and art directors, for instance, can grow stale in an environment that requires them to deal with the same raw material for stories and advertisements. Agencies, by their nature, provide an opportunity for these people to treat a variety of different subject matters, and this helps to keep them fresh. Furthermore, an environment filled with other writers and art directors promotes a competitive spirit that helps to stimulate them and maintain a level of challenge that may be absent in a corporate environment.

When defining your communication needs, commit them to writing and be as specific as possible. Use this opportunity to rethink the services you really require, not just the ones you are getting from your current agency relationship. A starter list follows, but it is by no means complete. Needs will vary according to the special requirements of each company.

1. Complete communication strategy development and planning

2. Issues management

3. Marketing guidance

4. Investor relations guidance

5. Investor relations projects

6. Industry or constituency monitoring of emerging problems and issues

7. Government relations support, at federal, state, or local community levels

8. Washington assistance—legislative or Pentagon

9. Press relations contact work

10. Annual report, quarterly report writing and supervision

11. Executive speech writing

12. Byline articles

13. Opinion pieces

14. Promotional writing for general press

15. Business and financial writing for business and financial press

16. Technical writing—the technical press

17. Employee communications, house organs, writing and supervision

18. Annual meeting, planning and execution

19. Case history or industrial application writing

20. Advertising preparation and production

21. Production and executional services

In addition to the amount of work probably required in each one of these functions, consider the degree of skill required. Are you able to afford the level of expertise you would like for someone on your own staff? Can you get by with a generalist by combining enough functions? Will such an employee have enough expertise to do the job, or must you go outside?

Other questions that should be asked involve geography. Is assistance required in cities outside of your home office? Would a Washington office (for a public relations firm assisting in issue management) be important to you? Would a New York office (for an agency assisting you in investor relations) be important? Would offices internationally aid in coordinating your global communication needs? How about branch offices for major plant cities?

Finally, examine your needs in terms of your own individual style and work habits. Do you pride yourself on running a lean department? Or do you (at least secretly) recognize that a larger communications staff will enhance your own career, even at the risk of your being accused of empire building? Do you view yourself as the laid-back strategist and planner who makes the decisions and then delegates? Or are you either through personal inclination or departmental budgetary constraints a do-it-yourselfer who will even pitch in and stuff envelopes on occasion? The more realistic you can be about yourself, the more you accept your individual work habits, the more likely it is that you will find contentment in the working relationship you have with your agencies and your staff. Almost endless structures can work and be efficient; given good people—they are the key.

Don't Rush to Sever Your Present Agency Affiliations

When you are convinced that you have a good understanding of your own needs and where outside agency resources will be called

Table 4–1
Factors to Consider When Assigning Functions

Internal *Likely to be best handled* *within the company*	*External* *Likely to be best handled* *by an independent* *agency or consultant*
Heavy workload	Light workload
Long-term project	Short-term project
Year round	Seasonal
Combines well with other functions	Highly specialized
Deep company/industry knowledge required	Average company/industry knowledge required
Heavy internal contact and coordination needed	Little or no internal contact and coordination needed
High level of security required	Average level of security required
Fits well into company career path	Isolated function unlikely to provide adequate personal growth
Routine level of creativity required	High demand for originality and creativity

for, you are ready to start a search. Start by reacquainting yourself with your current public relations and ad agency affiliations. Don't assume you know everything about them. Particularly if the association has been a long one, you may be surprised at how your agencies have changed in recent years. The restructuring, merging, and purging of business has been going on as much in the agency field as in any.

Start by meeting with the agency's managements in a relatively informal way. There is no need in most cases to scare them to death. Explain that you are re-evaluating all of the functions within your department and would like to get from them an idea of all their current capabilities, how they have changed over the years, what new departments and new branch offices they may have, what new clients and kinds of projects they are currently involved with. Draw them out on how they like best to work with other clients. Do they seem happiest when they are developing a complete communication strategy, or do they seem more at home executing the plans of others? How does this fit your needs? Ask about their new accounts and any business they have lost. What are their future expansion plans? Are they profitable? And, specifically, is your account profitable? Do they seem content with the relationship? Do they seem to smell of success or failure?

Without necessarily revealing your own concern for a continued relationship, you may be surprised at how, in even a short discussion such as this, you can resolve questions about your next course of action. You may, for instance, discover there is more to the agency than you are aware of, more services than you are currently using but which fit nicely into your own plans. It may also be clear that you and your agency have grown apart, or that the kind of company they want to be is different from the kind you'll need for your own future growth. In all likelihood, however, it won't be that simple a decision. You will still have questions that cannot be resolved in one meeting. If so, rethink what you will need to find out in the privacy of your own office. Decide whether there are sufficient advantages to staying with your current agency, if its representatives were alerted to their areas of shortfall and agreed to make changes in the working relationship. If not, begin an agency search. If you are still not sure, include your old agency as a contender for the business.

At this stage, if you have a large corporation or a complex account, or if you are generally unfamiliar with the capabilities of alternate candidate agencies, you may wish to consider engaging an outside consultant. Consultants not only help you identify corporate agencies, but they can also help you evaluate your current one. Dealing mostly in well-established but troubled relationships, many consultants have developed sorting through such problems to a fine art. The role a consultant can play in resolving these problems is an interesting one. Consultants supply an objective evaluation of the agency and the way the company works. This can be quite different from the subjective appraisal you may have made. Usually their evaluations go beyond finding out what is wrong with the agency. They examine the relationship from both sides, also soliciting candid criticism from the agency to learn about the difficulties it has working with you, the client. In effect, consultants provide a report card on both sides. Furthermore, they can relate your agency's performance to that of other agencies. Typically, they also compare the long-term agency objectives to those of the client to see whether their growth patterns are likely to be compatible.

Some years ago, the Association of National Advertisers analyzed how agencies rated specific problems that confronted them in their client/agency relationships. They then asked the same question of clients. The results from the ANA paper shown here suggest a number of frequent troubled areas.

The first question asked was, What's wrong at the client?

The rank order of how each party responded to this question is as follows. According to the client:

1. Too many levels of approval
2. Unnecessary meetings
3. Don't give agency enough time
4. Unwilling to commit resources
5. Inability to plan ahead
6. Not willing to experiment, take risks

According to the agency:

1. Client doesn't give enough lead time
2. Client unfamiliar with costs

3. Unable to plan ahead
4. Client unwilling to commit resources
5. Too many levels of approval
6. Unwilling to experiment, take risks
7. Unable to stick to schedule
8. Not enough senior management involvement

The second question was, What's wrong at the agency? According to the client:

1. Agency turnover too high
2. Unable to stick to schedule
3. Agency needs too much lead time
4. Not enough senior management involvement
5. Failure to ask the right questions
6. Unwilling to listen to client viewpoint
7. Failure to show initiative

According to the agency:

1. Agency unable to stick to schedule
2. Agency unable to plan ahead
3. Failure to ask the right questions

While this study is now some years old it still reflects the difference in point of view between client and agency. It also shows a common frustration in the inability to plan ahead with sufficient time to deliver work on schedule. Some of this is due to a failure to get the right information from the right people in the first place.

The Agency Selection Process

If you decide to use a consultant, you will be guided through the agency selection process. A consultant can also give you some early anonymity as you assemble dossiers on candidate agencies, and you may appreciate this chance to avoid being inundated by unsolicited offers from volunteering agencies—the speed with which agencies find out there is a "client on the loose" can be frightening. If you decide to do it yourself, however, you will find that the project is really not so difficult. You must be prepared, however, to devote ample time to it. Some clients have told me they wouldn't go through another agency search and change for anything, claiming it takes too much time. At least two, however, admitted that "they kind of enjoyed it" and "it was a heady experience."

Identifying the Candidates

The list you compiled of your communication needs will be the basis for a new list, your "criteria for agency selection." In summary the agency must be able to provide the services you require and meet your geographic needs. Should the agency have branch offices? Where? Will it be helpful if the agency has offices internationally? If you anticipate a high frequency of contact, then the convenience of an agency in your own hometown is a valid consideration. If you are in a major city, it is reasonable to expect to find a suitable agency nearby, although, as was suggested earlier, the number of agencies with corporate experience is substantially smaller than those with product and marketing know-how. If you are in a small town, consider airline schedules. Weigh the possibilities of a New York agency no matter where you are located. The selection is wide, and if your job function includes investor relations, you can combine agency meetings with those journeys to Wall Street.

Now is a good time to decide what size agency is right for you. If you have a small company with a small budget, you will have little choice but to use a small or, at most, a medium-sized agency. The larger agencies, particularly ad agencies, have a hard time making a profit on smaller accounts. Don't feel badly about this— the bigger the agency, the greater the likelihood that you will be assigned people from the lower end of the staff. Though it might be nice to enjoy the assurance and prestige of working with a major name agency, you are probably better off with the services of an agency to whom you represent a meaningful portion of their billings. Regardless of agency size, you will probably still enjoy approximately the same number of work hours. This is determined more by workload than by agency size. Even though large agencies appear to have a cast of thousands available to work on your account, in fact their staffs consist of highly specialized people devoting only a portion of their time to a larger number of accounts. On the other side of the equation, higher-priced talent is usually available in the larger agencies, which pay higher salaries. Conversely, you will probably work more closely with agency management when you associate with a smaller agency. In the end it's the team that is assigned to your account that really matters.

You will also want to consider how important it is for your new agency to have a management familiar with your particular industry. If you have an industrial business, you may find that an agency accustomed to working with consumer product clients is lacking in understanding of trade practices and industrial standards, and even in media knowledge. In general, however, agencies, particularly their management, are quick studies in learning the fundamentals of a new business. Working in many different industries, they are subject to cross-pollination of different ideas and practices, which can be beneficial. The practice of avoiding competitive conflicts, particularly when dealing with advertising agencies, can make it difficult to insist upon finding an agency with direct experience in your particular field. On the other hand, it is really up to you, as the client, to decide whether two similar accounts at the same agency represent a competitive conflict. There may be justification for concern about maintaining confidentiality in highly competitive product and service advertising categories. However, corporate clients are usually unique in their problems and objectives, so that any transfer of knowledge or ideas shouldn't be detrimental, nor should it in most cases provide a competitive advantage. Lawyers, research companies, accountants, and marketing consultant firms benefit their clients and themselves by being able to service related and competitive clients. Corporate public relations firms and advertising agencies should be considered to have this kind of relationship too.

In addition to these criteria that you have set for your agency selection, there are fundamental things you will need to know about any agency you consider. Its financial stability is one important consideration. Does it pay its bills on time (if it is an ad agency)? Or could the agency give you, indirectly, problems by not paying charges on time that it has incurred on your behalf? Might it miss discounts? Does it have a credit rating that enables it to work freely and comfortably with all media and suppliers?

It is also worth determining the win/loss record on the agency's list of clients. Does the agency appear to be growing? Or is it losing accounts? All agencies lose accounts from time to time, but look into the reasons behind lost business to see whether the agency has fundamental weaknesses that could affect your dealings with them.

Finally, but most importantly, what is the creative record and reputation of the agency with existing clients? An agency is certainly judged by the clients it keeps and by the work it does for them. In fact, on this basis you will identify your initial list of agencies from which to choose. Whether you are tackling the agency selection process alone or with a consultant, at some stage you will need to list those companies whose reputations you most admire. List too the corporate advertising you most respect, if that is an intended part of your program. Examining *O'Dwyer's Directory of Public Relations Firms* (published by J. R. O'Dwyer Company, Inc., 271 Madison Avenue, New York, NY 10016), will help you track down the agencies that have been helping these clients with their public relations activities. This publication also indexes the firms by skills in fourteen areas of specialization. You will also find it helpful to acquaint yourself with the *Standard Directory of Advertising Agencies,* published by the National Register Publishing Company (a Macmillan, Inc., company, located at 3004 Glenview Road, Wilmette, IL 60091). Another helpful source is the annual issue of *Advertising Age* that is devoted to a review of ad agencies.

In addition to obtaining this published information, other services such as the Advertising Register Service in New York, can for a fee provide a list of ad agencies it considers appropriate to your needs. This service usually can provide anywhere from ten to thirty agency candidates, along with extensive dossiers on each company. These agency backgrounds have been provided to the agency register in advance by ad agencies, which pay to be included in the service. To a certain extent, therefore, this service may miss a portion of likely candidates. A consultant should be expected to provide additional candidates from his or her own experience.

Contacting The Agencies

When this process of identifying candidates has been completed, the next stage is to contact each likely agency by letter (send a questionnaire to get specific relevant information so you can further compare the candidates) and determine whether it is interested in soliciting your account. To aid the agencies in deciding how appropriate you would be as a client, you must provide them with the details of your needs as you understand them and with your communication objectives. You also should provide them with your approximate budget and tell them whether you expect this to be an ongoing level of expenditure and activity or whether this is a limited-term project. Without this information, they can't know whether you would be a practical client to service.

At this stage, a consultant can act as an intermediary to keep your identity quiet, although the general nature of your business, its size, and communication objectives must still be made clear. Your consultant should have checked, at least in a preliminary way, possible agency conflicts to avoid wasted effort on both sides before any contacts are made.

Allow the agencies reasonable time to respond, but give them a deadline to meet. At this stage, start a folder for each agency and note even their performances in answering your letter. Do they follow up with a phone call to check on details in the questionnaire? Do they attempt to provide you with ample additional information? Who is doing the contacting? Is it a principal? Does this person seem knowledgeable? Look for clues on how intelligently the agencies handle even the details and note them in the folder. Depending on how many agencies you have invited to compete, you will be glad to have a specific note later when you come to sort out the responses. A suggested questionnaire outline appears in appendix 4–A, at the end of this chapter. This questionnaire is not nearly as long and elaborate as those that many agencies receive. In fact, some popular agencies have problems in responding to many of these questionnaires, which ask elaborate and often meaningless questions, only adding to the problem of interpretation later on. The Association of National Advertisers and Public Relations Society of America (PRSA) have both made efforts to reduce this confusion somewhat by suggesting standard forms that enable agencies to give off-the-shelf answers. So far, these efforts have not been very successful, and agencies continue to get questionnaires that ask more or less the same questions but require that the details be calculated and put into a different form for each inquiry. There is, however, some justification for a somewhat specialized form in the case of corporate clients, whose needs, as was stated earlier, are special.

Before long, you will be receiving packages that represent the effort and imagination of each agency, as each puts its best foot forward to demonstrate its capabilities. Selection is largely an elimination process. After carefully studying the material each agency sends, you should be able to reduce the number of candidates to three or four, at the most. Contact these by phone to arrange a meeting in each agency's offices. Make it clear that you are interested in meeting the people who would actually work on your account, not just a new business team. Tell them you would like to hear what they have to say about their agency and their philosophy of doing business. They may ask you, at this time, for additional information about the company. You should provide them a kit, if you have not already done so, which includes your annual report, a recent speech or two by the CEO, any pertinent research you have, and plans for the company that you care to share with them. Do not expect, or solicit from them, a presentation of a proposed public relations plan or advertising creative work for your account. Such speculative work at this stage would be based on such a minimum of input that should they happen to guess right about a creative approach, it would be as much through luck as through sound evaluation and judgment.

Make it as nearly a work session as possible, and see how the individuals within the agency relate to one another. Do they appear to be a team and seem to enjoy the exchange of ideas, or are the Indians all sitting back and waiting for the chief to speak? Remember, you will probably be working more with those Indians than with the chief, so they had better be smart and have ideas of their own.

The meeting should include a period toward the end, after the agency has said its piece, in which you state the aims and objectives of your program. Or tell them of a problem, and solicit spontaneous (or nearly so) ideas and watch them react. This is the key to finding out how they work together and how comfortable you are working with them.

The Final Selection

When you have made your selection, it is courteous to call the losers as well as the winner. Sure, you can do it with a letter and maybe that seems easier, but you will probably get a phone call after they receive the turndown letter anyway. Those agencies you did not see but who filled out returned questionnaires should be told of your final agency decision. They can be handled by letter, but even here phone calls are preferred.

Finally, a word about contracts. Each agency will have submitted a sample of its typical contract form with the questionnaire. The agency will draft the final form after discussions with you. Naturally your lawyers will have to go over it. It is not unusual for this process to take a long period of time during which you simply work on a handshake and the understanding that if you both are not happy working with one another, the arrangement will be terminated after thirty days. Look at it this way: if the level of trust and cooperation is not good enough in the honeymoon period, no contract is going to improve it. In any event, file away the names of the also-rans.

Before an agency prepares any creative work, meetings with you and your management must be held in order to give the agency essential background. Generally it is sufficient to judge an agency on the work it has done for other clients, particularly if they are in a similar business. If you do elect to ask for a creative presentation at a final stage in the selection process, it is only fair to expect to pay the agency for its time and out-of-pocket expenses. Set a budget in advance for the work. Such an exercise should *not* be looked at or used as a fishing expedition to get new ideas. Creative work done by an agency ethically belongs to that agency and its client working together.

Ideas should not be lifted and given to another agency to implement. The new agency will, if it is any good, resent it. Paying for speculative work is especially needed when it comes to corporate advertising. The size of the advertising budget is generally small. The big dog-and-pony-show presentations you may have heard about may have some economic justification when a $30 million package goods account is in question, but hardly when the budget may be no more than a million dollars.

You may, however, wish to entertain the possibility of selecting a real assignment isolated from the rest of your program—such as a CEO speech, a pamphlet on an issue of concern to your company, or an ad on a particular issue—and assigning it to one or more agencies as a trial assignment. Pay the agency for it and see how it handles the work. If you choose this course, make sure everyone understands the ground rules and that it is not to be interpreted as a final decision to work with that agency.

Meeting at each agency's offices will give you a chance not only to meet your team, but also to see the agency's housekeeping and to listen to those things that the agency considers important about itself. Where do its people put the emphasis on how they work? Expect to hear them tell you some things that are not necessarily germane to your problem but about which they are proud. Bear with it—all of this will indicate where their mind-set lies. But if they are too far off target, beware. Meetings should last no more than two hours. Don't attempt more than one in the morning and one in the afternoon. Better yet, if you have the time do only one a day. Make notes right after each meeting. Rank each agency on your criteria, using a one to ten scale. This can be particularly helpful if you are touring the agencies in company with other executives from your company. Each of you should form opinions on your own before discussing final decisions. Try to make this final decision back in your own office, and do not be stampeded into an enthusiastic, premature selection until all the meetings are over. Look especially for good chemistry during these sessions.

Appendix 4–A
Agency Profile Questionnaire

1. Agency name, address, telephone number, and person to contact for follow-up.

2. Describe agency's ownership: Independent or a subsidiary? Stock or partnership? Affiliated agencies and year founded?

3. How many people do you employ full-time?

4. How do you normally charge for your services?

5. Approximate percentage of media billing in each category: spot TV, network TV, magazines, newspapers, radio, and outdoor.

6. Annual billings for your office in last three years.

7. Current account list and year acquired.

8. Pattern of account size.

9. List accounts gained and lost in the last two years.

10. What experience can you bring to bear on [state company's business category, such as "industrial account"] corporate advertising?

11. What experience have you in preparing and placing advertising overseas? (If pertinent.)

12. Please include, if available:*

    1. Credit references or other evidence of financial stability
    2. Annual report
    3. Your standard letter of agreement

Feel free to include any other material related to the agency's structure, staffing, operating policies, and advertising philosophy.

Speed and content are more important than neatness and form. Please make every effort to return by [date].

Thank you.

---

*Please provide two sets of material.

5
Tracking the Corporate Image

If your communication program is substantial enough to produce results, you will need some form of research to determine whether it's working. Recognition or awareness and attitudinal studies can be conducted before a program is started to establish a benchmark. Though the research requires professional handling, it is nevertheless advisable to have a good understanding of what you are trying to find out before asking for bids.

The qualities most frequently examined in such studies are listed, along with findings from a survey on the subject. Public opinion studies are examined as a source for news stories, as is their role in dealing with issue management.

Employee polling is examined as a means of uncovering trouble spots and as a method of opening up a dialogue between management and employees.

Qualitative depth interviews may be used to uncover underlying motivation for attitudes among the company's executives, customers, and other vital groups.

The popular focus group technique is examined for its advantages and disadvantages and is compared with one-on-one interviewing as a means of checking creative work and conceptual ideas.

Companies seem to do either too much or too little research in connection with their corporate communications program. Some study their problems to death instead of starting programs to do something about them. Other companies employ little or no research. They seem to think they already know the answers, although this notion may be based on nothing more than folklore among the executives who have repeated it often enough to each other to accept it as reality. The view management can get of its own company unaided is almost necessarily wrong. Friends, relatives, customers, and the immediate staff will all provide a variety of distortions reflecting their own interests when talking to the executive of a company. Between these two extremes of too much or none at all, research should play a role in communication plans.

Generally speaking, the larger the expenditure for a communication program, particularly if corporate advertising is employed, the more research should be employed to improve its effectiveness. In practice, this is exactly what happens. Studies by the Association of National Advertisers among members employing corporate advertising have shown that the larger the company, the more likely it is to use research. According to a 1986 ANA study, slightly less than three-quarters (71 percent) of responding companies used some form of market research to develop their corporate ad program. The 1987 study indicated a figure closer to 90 percent.

Virtually all forms of market research, opinion polls, and research techniques that were developed originally for advertising and marketing have some application and may be used with success in connection with different aspects of a corporate communication plan. Research should be considered any time there is a legitimate doubt in the communication process. This doesn't mean it should necessarily be used, but the option should be examined. The more fundamental the question, the more cost-effective the research can be. Programs that start in the right direction, from a solid base of facts, stand a much better chance of success.

In a perfect world, research would be used only to find out what you don't know. It is a shame to waste money proving what you already know. If you can follow that rule, you will cut out most extraneous research projects. Unfortunately, in the real world it is sometimes necessary to employ research to provide the evidence to do what may appear obvious to a professional communicator. If it requires a survey, however, to prove that your company is greatly misunderstood, so be it. In fact, that is exactly the kind of research that should usually be done before a new communication plan is put into effect. It is essential to start with a reliable understanding of the picture key audiences hold of the company. The 1987 study among the Association of National Advertisers showed that 90 percent of the members who used any research in connection with their communication program used a form of awareness and attitude study. Most did so on a more or less regular basis to determine changes in the extent and quality of their reputations. When corporate advertising is involved, such a study is absolutely essential. A benchmark study, followed by periodic (probably yearly) follow-up studies to track the results, is the only way to assure the continuation of the program. It is axiomatic among corporate advertisers that those programs without research to substantiate their effectiveness will be discontinued after a year or two or with the first change of management.

The information a benchmark study provides concerning opinions already held by key audiences about the company is invaluable in guiding the creative work as well. If you are to start on a journey you must know where you are to begin, or you will simply wander. From the starting point, you can measure progress along the way.

Although awareness and attitude studies among important publics constitute perhaps the key piece of research in communication work, virtually all of the market research tools that have been developed can, with minor adaptions, be useful from time to time. Here are some of the more frequently used research techniques used by corporate communication groups.

Recognition Studies

Recognition studies are also called awareness and attitude studies or familiarity studies. These are quantitative surveys to establish the degree of recognition among and the attitudes held by the group surveyed. They may be used as a one-time study to establish information about the reputation of the company at any point; or they may be repeated after a specific news event or ad campaign; or they may be conducted before, during, and after a communication program.

Don't wait too long after a campaign or event to test the results. Memory decay will start to be noticeable in only a couple of months. Studying the retention rate of the communication program can be done by repeating the survey after a substantial time lapse. The larger corporations generally employ a continuing series of recognition studies that provide ongoing tracking of the corporate image. Obvious care must be taken to duplicate the survey method, sampling techniques, and questioning in order to assure a reliable, readable trend.

At the risk of stating the obvious, you must start such studies by determining what you are trying to find out—the objective. Is it simply the recognition of the company name, or is it the ability to associate the name correctly with the industry the company is in? Is association with products an important factor? Do the major questions concern attitude toward the company, the quality of its products, environmental issues, social issues, or some other problem of specific relevance to your communication problem?

A useful device at this stage is to ask yourself to what use you plan to put the answers to such a survey. Will they be meaningful by themselves? Would a recognition level of, say, 30 percent be good? Would 30 percent be bad? Would a 50 percent association with quality products be considered acceptable as a level of achievement? Clearly your own set of statistics gained on a one-time basis will be of limited use. The same study repeated periodically will provide the trend data that will point the direction the company image is headed. But comparative data can make even the first study more useful!

Unless the survey questioning becomes so long and involved with your own company's interests, it is advisable to include study questions concerning your major competition. These "control" companies may be three or four other companies, or the entire industry list, if your principal concern is one industry, or leaders from several business areas in which your company operates.

It is probably better to limit the list to companies that you could select as the industry's yardsticks. This selection criteria varies. You may choose some because you admire their activity, they dominate the industry, they are highly successful financially, or they are faced with many of your own social or environmental problems. On whatever basis the choice is made, if these companies are kept as a constant in subsequent surveys, they will serve to show whether changes in attitudes toward your company are specific to you or whether they are shared by your industry. This can be particularly helpful in understanding downturns in attitudes, such as those experienced by the chemical and oil industries in former years. It may turn out that although you went down, you did well compared to competitors that went down farther.

Dozens of different research techniques may be employed to gain a good understanding of your company's awareness levels and reputation. Dealing with this broad array is not a job for amateurs. Whether you use a ranking scale of the qualities in question or draw a personality picture of the corporation based upon word association, or use open-ended questions or multiple choice—these are questions best left to the professionals.

Research companies will provide you with a written proposal and estimate in response to your request. You may wish to see your data displayed in relation to those of other companies in an interesting format called "perceptual mapping." In this approach, a quadrant or grid of qualities is laid out like a map, and your position is pinpointed along with that of the other companies.

You will need then to provide the research company with what you are trying to find out and the audiences of greatest concern. Even the very fundamental question of whether the survey may be handled through direct mail or whether telephone or personal interviews should be conducted should be left to the experts. Your own homegrown mail questionnaire can provide you with some of the most expensive research in the world, in that results can be so far wrong that they will send you off in the wrong direction.

Good recognition studies are expensive, and the larger, better-known companies are not cheap. They rightfully insist on sampling target audiences with great precision, ensuring absolute comparability if the study is repeated. Companies such as Opinion Research Corporation, Yankelovich, Clancy & Shulman, Inc., AHF Marketing Research, Erdos and Morgan, Inc. and others have a wealth of experience upon which to draw when helping you interpret the results. Some companies can even provide established norms to which you can compare certain findings. Generally, a survey such as this should include in the price a presentation to you and management as well as a finished document with the research company's interpretation of the results. Although the researchers will not give you the proprietary results of other studies, they can help you relate your company's findings to the range of results others have had.

It is useful to determine from the research company what experience it has had in surveying your particular target audience. For instance, if your concern is the financial community, an experienced research company will employ very different techniques in surveying individual investors and stockholders than it would brokers or portfolio managers or stock analysts. A number of companies specialize in reaching the more difficult target audiences and will offer shared costs or omnibus studies that invite a number of companies to participate. In these, the different companies share joint general information findings in addition to specific, company-related confidential questions. At this writing, some change is expected in the specialized shared costs studies offered by the major companies. However, in the past Yankelovich Clancy Shulman has offered periodic studies of brokers, portfolio managers, and individual investors. Opinion Research Corporation has offered studies of segments of the financial community, as well as of business executives, thought leaders, the press, and special groups in Washington. A few phone calls will uncover the current availabilities from these companies and from Roper, Gallup, Louis Harris, and others.

By and large, only the largest corporations or those with consumer products spend enough money to consider reaching the entire U.S. population with their corporate communication program. Most companies today focus on specific segments. These are selected based upon their communication objectives. One such popular segmentation is household salary level. The ANA 1987 study showed that households with annual incomes over fifty thousand dollars were the most frequent target of corporate advertising. Researching segments of the population by income level can present a problem in tracking over a period of years if inflation occurs. This problem can be solved, however, by expressing the target audience as a percent of the population as a whole. You might therefore sample, say, the top 10 percent or those with incomes equal to or above the median income level of the population.

Customer surveys present a pitfall so common as to warrant mention. The seeming ease of securing a customer list from the sales department makes it tempting to survey this group exclusively. But if you match up the customers with the noncustomers in the same category, you'll learn a lot more. You may also learn a great deal about your sales department's record keeping. Make sure it's not a stacked list of customers primed to be cooperative and procompany. This is particularly the case in the industrial area, where long-time friends are the rule. It is also an area in which relatively small studies among customer and potential customers can be especially valuable. This type of research is usually more successful when lists by Standard Industry Classifications (SIC) codes for the desired industry category are provided by the research company and it is allowed to distinguish the customers from the noncustomers for itself. Although this may be more expensive and time consuming, it eliminates the bias and provides a statistically stable base that can be used in follow-up studies. In these cases, however, it is essential to provide the research company not only with the industry SIC category, but also with the title or job description of the relevant position of the customers and potential customers—simply to say "buyer" is not enough. It may be design engineer or any one of literally dozens of titles, depending on the industry.

Another approach, somewhat simpler, is to use the services of certain industrial researchers, such as those provided by the McGraw-Hill Research Group or by Harvey Research in Buffalo, New York. Accustomed to working with publication audiences within individual industries, such as aeronautics, automotive, plastics, and so forth, these researchers are skilled at finding the right job category and reaching these people with a high degree of success. The results, when arrived at through these independent channels, can often be extremely helpful for communication purposes and even surprisingly useful to the sales manager (if handled tactfully).

Professional groups and associations may also be helpful in securing industrial lists. Trade publications may have lists to reach retailers, jobbers, and wholesalers in a variety of categories. They may also be valuable sources for secondary research or they may do periodic studies in which you can participate. Some will even aid with the use of their research facility to conduct your own custom study.

In studies of this sort, a selection will have to be made of which attributes are of major concern to your company. Attributes are, in a sense, the components that make up the total reputation. Which of these attributes should be emphasized in your company communications and which should be researched and tracked is important to consider.

Some variation in the importance of an attribute will exist, depending on the company. Purity of product is obviously more meaningful to a food or pharmaceutical company than, say, a lawn chemical company. Certain attributes, on the other hand, are important to all or most companies. Such things as "maker of quality products" and "has a good management" rise to the top in most such studies. The different research companies have their own lists of frequently surveyed attributes and will be helpful in their selection. It is important to recognize that company attributes achieve levels of importance that are different for different target audiences, as was pointed out earlier. Thus if you are talking to a consumer you will find that the quality of the product or service is more important than the caliber of management. Conversely, if you are surveying portfolio managers, you will discover that high-caliber management is usually of more concern than the quality of the products.

The study *Winning,* by the Brouillard Communications agency of New York, selected fifteen attributes for further study from preliminary qualitative interview work. These can be seen in table 5–1.

Respondents from four different categories were asked to rate these attributes on a six-point scale in evaluating what constituted "a winning company." Each group cited seven attributes as more critical. Five attributes were common across the four audiences. The other critical criteria varied somewhat in their evaluation by different publics. They did so in ways interestingly predictable. The results appear in table 5–2.

Table 5–1
Total List of Attributes Rated by Respondents

Quality products	Quality service
Concern for employees	Flexibility
Staying power	Honesty and ethics
Good communications	Good value
Clearly defined goals	Good corporate citizenship
Market leadership	High-caliber management
Financial performance	New products
	Size

Source: *Winning*, a study by Brouillard Communications

Opinion Studies

Somewhat akin to attribute studies, opinion studies usually deal with social subjects. They are popular with the press, and many companies have taken to conducting surveys on various public issues important to the company, making these results available with appropriate press releases. The findings of even a modest study, if the subject is of public interest, can receive a surprising amount of coverage. When the study is carefully related to the interests and activities of the company, it can serve to present the company as knowledgeable and expert in a particular sphere of interest. This technique has been used imaginatively by a number of companies, including the makers of Old Grand Dad bourbon, who made surveys of grandparents that found grandparents to be more vital than the stereotyped view of the old would lead people to believe.

Opinion polls on more controversial subjects will require care in setting up in order to establish their credibility. The need for this credibility exists in almost direct proportion to the degree of controversy involved. The use of universities and independent third parties to conduct the research may be worth considering to lend credibility in such situations.

Opinion polls have become so popular that at least one research company, Opinion Research Corporation, helps companies in searching out promising issues with which those companies may work in a communication program. This almost seems a reversal of the more natural order of things, in which a company being faced

Table 5–2
Top-rated Attributes by Audience

Affluent Consumers	Corporate Executives	Research Directors	Portfolio Managers
Quality service	Honesty and ethics	High-caliber management	High-caliber management
Honesty and ethics	High-caliber management	Flexibility	Flexibility
Quality products	Quality service	Honesty and ethics	Financial performance
Good value	Quality products	Quality service	Quality service
High-caliber management	Flexibility	Quality products	Honesty and ethics
Concern for employees	Clearly defined goals	Clearly defined goals	Clearly defined goals
Flexibility	Good value	Staying power	Quality products

Source: *Winning*, A study by Brouillard Communications

with certain issues becomes knowledgeable and then deals with them in its communications.

Several companies have employed opinion polls as part of the content of their corporate advertising campaign. LTV Corporation sustained a corporate ad program for years that dealt with various national issues, such as trade policies and defense spending, and each ad presented opposing views by respected spokespeople. In addition, the results of an opinion poll, conducted specifically on the point in question, was presented. The ads also included the opinion of the company's chairman. It was an interesting campaign that received wide praise at the time.

It should not be forgotten that these spin-off communication uses of opinion polls are secondary to their primary use, which is to guide and direct a company's own handling of public thought on subjects vital to it. Periodic repolling acts as a yardstick for learning about the progress being made.

A number of the research firms, such as Harris, Gallup, and Roper, have become household names because they handle highly visible public issues so frequently. The Roper organization offers a continuing service that provides insights into how the public feels on changing national, social, and business topics. Subscribers may tie in their own questions for a fee.

Morale Studies

Polling employees can be a fruitful way of uncovering trouble spots in communication. Discovering the views, attitudes, contentment level, and the basic knowledge employees hold about the company is not only a valuable asset to the human resources department and an aid to the management of productivity, but it is also an important check for communications. Employees are one of your basic media. They represent the company in their day-to-day contact—not just during working hours but also in their community lives. Obviously, care is required in conducting employee surveys to avoid any union or personnel problems. On the other hand, such considerations should not be used as an excuse for not doing periodic checks. When done correctly, such checks can actually improve employee relations. The very act of inviting the views of rank and file employees on industry situations, company conditions, social concerns, and so forth is a clear statement of management respect for their opinions. It can be a morale builder.

The low cost and ease of conducting such surveys, usually sent out in interoffice memo form with a "no need to sign" type of questionnaire, makes them tempting to handle unaided in-house. Avoid the temptation. At the very least, get expert help on the form of the questionnaire and be sure the appropriate groups are aware of what you are doing.

Employee surveys may also be conducted on a blind basis by outside research firms to determine opinions on more sensitive issues relating to the company. Attempt this only if you feel it is absolutely necessary. It is difficult to keep the employees completely unaware of who is doing the research. Employees talk to each other and the coincidence of several employees receiving the same survey makes it all but impossible to do these studies completely undetected. The backlash resulting can be embarrassing. Think it through carefully first.

Qualitative Depth Interviews

Qualitative depth interviews bring together the schools of psychology, social science, and marketing in sophisticated probing interviews to uncover the deep feelings and underlying motivations, as well as the opinions and ideas of selected respondents. Conducted by highly trained specialists, usually with master's degrees or doctorates, the interviews frequently last an hour or more. Usually they are conducted in the office or home of the individual being interviewed. The intent is to analyze and understand a key group's real feelings, perhaps even motivations its members do not fully understand themselves, concerning some important issue. The interviews are carefully planned, particularly with a view to relaxing the subject and encouraging candid responses. Checklist questionnaires play practically no role. Interviews resemble nothing more than probing by a psychiatrist. As you might expect, this process is expensive, and as a result, it is usually confined to uncovering insights into issues of vital importance to the corporation, such as how key customers feel about major changes going on within the company or industry, or why the best candidates for the company's new research facility are turning down offers.

This approach was developed primarily as a marketing tool but it can apply to corporate communication work as well. For instance, during corporate restructuring or when contemplating a name change the underlying motives of divisional executives may be explored. It may be useful too in searching out the real strengths and weaknesses of other companies being examined as possible acquisition candidates.

The companies of Omega in Philadelphia and Harlan Brown in Baltimore are two specialists in this kind of depth interview and analysis. It must be remembered in any work of this sort that the interviewer influences at least half the result. The sensitivity he or she brings to the respondent's body language and silence can be as revealing as the actual answers.

Focus Groups

Small groups, with between six and twelve people recruited from the desired target audience, focus on a subject under the direction of a moderator. The purpose is to probe and explore the opinions, attitudes, and ideas concerning the subject. This was originally a device for discovering new creative directions in marketing products such as flavor variations, packaging designs, and advertising, but the relative ease, speed, and low cost of the method made it increasingly popular in the advertising field for pretesting commercials and printed ads. Today more than half of the corporate advertisers in the previously mentioned ANA study use this form of research. Focus group studies are qualitative and, strictly speaking, should not be used as a quantitative way of evaluating finished ideas. This is frequently done, although everyone admits it's wrong and has obvious shortcomings. It is, however, usually capable of uncovering problems of comprehension and credibility and is often referred to as a type of C&C research.

Whether the group is focusing on a new store promotion, a new product idea, or an ad concept, some physical point of focus is essential. This may be as simple as a paragraph stating the premise under discussion. The premise may be anything from statements on public issues to business strategy, or corporate positioning statements. The groups may consist of the working press, the general public, or portfolio managers and analysts. The most common use of such groups in corporate communication is probably in connection with screening ads or ideas for ads. Typically, three to six ads or commercials will be presented one at a time by the moderator of the group. The group members will first be asked to write their reactions to the advertisements. Next, each ad is discussed in open roundtable. Led by a moderator, the questions will cover the major points of concern. The groups are recruited by the research firms or by independent moderators. Usually businesspeople find it most convenient to meet in the evening. It is desirable to hold at least two sessions with two separate groups. This can be done conveniently in an hour or an hour and a half in one evening. The use of two separate groups overcomes one of the problems of the technique which can occur when an unusually vocal and opinionated individual dominates the discussion in an unreasonable way. Although the majority of discussions are surprisingly well rounded, it does occasionally happen that a totally misleading bias is introduced by a personality that controls the meeting. A good moderator can usually control this or at least allow for it in interpreting the results.

The key to the success of this technique lies in the ability of the moderator. Because most work in this field tends to concern consumer products whose target may be "housewives," it is important to check the credentials of the moderators to be sure they understand the subject matter under discussion and have worked with your target audience in the past. Though the moderator need not be an expert on the issue or the financial subject under discussion, he or she needs enough experience to control the meeting. Don't be shocked by one device used by some moderators. They may deliberately pretend to be somewhat uninformed. They will tell their group they don't normally get into these things and don't understand it and can the group shed light on the subject for them. This seems to work.

Where possible, it is desirable to hold these focus groups in facilities specifically built for the purpose. These facilities include a one-way mirror that allows clients a chance to sit in an adjoining room and view and listen to the proceedings. It is usually worthwhile to attend for a firsthand impression. When the work needs to be done in various locations, hotel rooms are sometimes used and the sessions taped.

The moderator should be expected to provide a written report of the results. His or her experience is invaluable in evaluating the groups' sessions. Discounting stray observations and reactions that may crop up in a session, good moderators know how to focus on the more meaningful dialogues and can add a great deal to the interpretation.

It should be restated that the results of the focus group method are qualitative. It is valuable to generate ideas and elicit interpretations of the material being examined and to eliminate approaches that are clearly faulted. The method should not be used, however, to select or rank the quality of the material. The numbers of responses are too few and the chance for influence by a single dominant personality are too great for it to be used as a final determining method. In fact, virtually all research must be tempered with your personal judgment and interpretation. To substitute research for judgment is the way to arrive at the bland and mediocre.

It is essential that a preliminary meeting with the moderator be set up so that a full understanding of the material and the questions of concern can be determined in advance. Although it is possible for clients to interject thoughts and raise new concerns that arise as the session is viewed from behind the glass, this process for obvious reasons has to be limited or it will disrupt the flow of the groups' discussions.

It is customary in recruiting from the more sophisticated target audiences to pay them for their time. In some cases, such as those involving financial analysts, one hundred dollars a session is fairly common. In other cases, samples of products are sufficient. Take your lead on this from the moderator.

One-on-One Research

Interviewing with specific material, such as ad concepts, copy, and other things that might be used in focus groups, can be done on a one-on-one basis, thus eliminating any chance of a group's bias. Generally this is the preferred method for C&C (comprehension and credibility) studies. It is an excellent method for discovering any misunderstandings or troublesome negative implications that may not have been evident in the preparation of the material. This is usually qualitative in nature, but if a large enough sample is used, the result can be quantitative, provided the sample is representative of the desired target audience.

Many of the focus group moderators do this form of research as well, but they may also employ somewhat junior people because a more regimented line of questioning is usually employed. Because group interplay is missing and because they are more structured, the interviews do not elicit the creative additions that may be generated by the focus group. However, with probing—the repeated restatement in different ways of substantially the same question—additional interpretation of material may be drawn from the same respondents.

Generally this type of survey work is not audited by a client. Interviews may be conducted in a variety of locations by the interviewer, occasionally fitting the convenience of upscale respondents with interviews in their offices. More frequently, hotel rooms or conference rooms are used. The responses may be taped, but listening to the repeated questions over twenty or thirty interviews can be time consuming, to say nothing of boring. You may well find it better to depend on the "verbatims" that will be selected by the interviewer in a representative way to offer the client a rounded view of the results.

In considering any kind of research two questions should always come to mind. First, will the results of the study be actionable? Make sure it won't be a research project that's merely interesting but won't actually affect the program, the work turned out or decisions.

The second question is whether it's cost effective. Will the results of the study be used on projects important enough and expensive enough to warrant the research cost?

Finally, keep an eye on new research techniques and methods being introduced by research firms. For instance, some research firms are examining the possibility of continuous tracking in which interviewing is going on all the time. Theoretically this can provide a picture of the continuous ebb and flow of a company's reputation as a result of various communication activities. It could even show the damage done as a result of a bad breaking news story concerning the company.

New companies and new ideas arise all the time. Keeping up with research possibilities, particularly if you have no research director, should be a part of your public relations function.

6
Public Relations—An Overview and a Few Ideas That Work

Public relations now involves more management participation. Unlike product publicity, corporate public relations/affairs involve the presentation of a changing, dynamic subject whose actions and activities must be interpreted differently to different publics.

These publics may have very different views on what a company does. The message concerning a plant closing, for instance, may be well received by the investment community but may present problems in local communities. Every news event, therefore, must be examined and interpreted to see how it will be received by each audience.

The amount of ink is not the criteria for successful corporate relations. Rather, it is the contribution each story makes to building a cohesive company identity, which is important. At times the story that does not appear may contribute most to the communications program.

Why planning is essential and its effect on management and budget are examined. Plans are not instructions to yourself but are an outline of what needs to be accomplished, with only sufficient detail to make clear the approach. They are not for impressing management with how well you know your craft but are written to help management relate its activities to the effect they will have on communications. More than two dozen ideas are offered, ranging from how to protect the company name, to how to use retirees for everyone's benefit, to how to use advertising space representatives to advantage.

A one-liner made the rounds in 1987 that today's management considers corporate public relations too important to leave to public relations people. If that's true and executives without public relations backgrounds are running corporate communications programs, this chapter may miss its mark. It is written assuming the reader is a professional in public relations and can already write a release, edit a company newsletter, and conduct a news conference with some competence. The basic skills of public relations will continue to be essential for anyone conducting the corporate communications effort. Acquiring these skills will require more education than any one chapter in a book can provide.

One element of truth in the joke is that management people from other disciplines are becoming more involved and are paying more attention to corporate communications than ever before. In general this is good. Executives from other disciplines bring with them an understanding of the other operations within the company and may have a good grasp of the company's mission and objectives. They frequently know what needs to be accomplished, even if they are not too well equipped to know how to do it.

Many of the public relations skills required to conduct product publicity are the same as those required to promote a corporation, but there are some important differences. These should be so well understood that they become part of your normal mind-set in day-to-day corporate public relations work. Corporate public relations is far more complicated. It involves presenting a constantly changing living entity, the corporation, to a variety of different audiences, which have different interests. This is in comparison to a product's relative stability. Barring occasional improvements and line extensions, true news about a product is rare. A company is doing newsworthy things all the time. The public relations audience for a product is usually limited to consumers and the trade. Public relations for a company often addresses not only consumers of the company's product but legislators and investors too. You may find that messages ideally suited for one audience are not just inappropriate to other audiences but may in fact be counterproductive. The rosier the picture you paint to the financial community of market dominance and profitability, for example, the more you may risk consumers' skepticism as to the value they receive for what they pay for your products. The more you stress to the financial community your company's efficiency and the steps it has taken to cut waste, the more local plant communities might see this as a lack of social responsibility.

These conflicting interpretations put on news stories by different audiences, each viewing the same story from its own vantage point, are a fact of life in handling corporate affairs. Don't assume that careful media selection can solve the problem. In today's information-inundated society you must accept the reality that anything sent to one medium may be picked up and reworked to play on local interests and biases. The more sensitive the alternate interpretations may be, the more likely the story will be picked up and used in an unwanted way.

This need to watch communications constantly for their potential for adverse interpretation brings us to the most important difference between product and corporate public relations: namely, "ink ain't everything." With the usual limitations of truisms, the more ink the better for rock stars and product; what is said is less important than how often it is said. In the case of corporate public relations, however, that's just not true. The success of public relations efforts for a corporation cannot be evaluated by just weighing the clipping book. In fact, some of the most important work may be in the clippings that aren't there, the negative stories that might have been written through misinterpretation or from ill-conceived news releases. If the clipping book doesn't add up to a cohesive, generally positive story of a corporation with a single personality, if it doesn't have a thread of continuity going through it, then the company's public relations efforts are less than they should be.

Recently companies have begun to clamor for change in the way they pay for outside public relations counsel. With seeming good logic they would like to pay for results, not just efforts. This sounds well and good, but paying for public relations by the amount of coverage could aggravate the already existing tendency to evaluate performance simply on the extent of coverage. Evaluation should instead be based upon the effect the total public relations effort has had in moving the corporation's reputation from where it was to where you want it to be. In order to do this, you need a plan. If you don't have one, you will just be drifting.

Planning

The public relations plan should focus more on what needs to be done than on the details of how to do it. You will need some details for budgeting determination purposes, but the plan should be written in terms of what needs to be accomplished for the corporation, rather than as instructions to yourself and your staff on what specific public relations activities will be required. This difference in viewpoint is essential if the plan is to communicate to your management. Management wants to know what you want to do and why, not how you are going to do it.

Starting with your company's goals, relate in simple language what improvements must be made audience by audience in the perception of the company in order to help the company meet these goals. For example, a chemical company that wishes to reposition itself more in specialty chemicals than in commodity chemicals should show in its plan what specialty chemicals and related services and accomplishments will be selected as a basis of stories to demonstrate the company's move to higher value–added chemicals. Only when this has been made clear in the plan should you deal with questions of audiences and techniques for reaching them, and then only in a relatively simple way. Management people will expect you, as a professional, to know and use the right techniques. Explaining them all in a plan will only bore them, not impress them. Give them enough of the details to instill confidence, not enough to turn them off.

Your plan document will be competing with plans for other company activities from other departments and divisions for management's time and attention, so be brief. This shouldn't mean completely abandoning English prose for an outline. Most of these plans are only comprehensible when presented live. Simply presenting hard copies of a visual presentation may seem modern and efficient, but it is no substitute for cohesiveness and for a short, well-written explanation of what needs to be done and why.

Techniques you plan to employ to accomplish the plan need only be explained to the extent necessary to justify the expenditure.

This will depend to some extent on how knowledgeable your management is with communications. Don't tell them what they already know, but be sure they understand what it is that requires the expenditures.

If your plan calls for sharply different approaches in handling the same event to deal with different audiences, it is probably a good idea to give specific illustrations of how entirely different approaches with different audiences will not only enhance the chance of good pickup on the event, but will also ensure correct interpretation by publics whose views and interests may be quite different. For example, if your plan anticipates the introduction of a new, lower-priced line of products, show that this new line will be interpreted to the trade as an opportunity for greater volume; to consumers as a saving or as a better-grade product at a lower price; and to the financial community as a serious effort by management to enter a new, higher-volume category or to gain an increased market share.

The plan should include a timetable that takes into account the long editorial closing dates for key publications. Relate these closings to anticipated company activities.

Consider the plan as a tool to show how management's activities relate to the press in both positive and negative ways.

If your company has traditionally provided a public relations budget first, and you've developed a plan to fit, consider submitting two different plans: one to fit the budget, and a second one, developed on a task basis, which item by item explains what should be done to meet company goals and what each communication activity would cost. This is different from just submitting two plans at different budget levels. The plan developed to fit a predetermined dollar figure should make clear those objectives it will probably attain and the degree to which they will be met. The other plan, at a higher level, would be more specific and activity related, as well as clear in the degree to which its objectives would be met. It then becomes a management choice of what it wants to achieve, and a dollar evaluation can then be made on the difference in attainment levels.

Ideas That Work

Provide the press with your company lineup, key people to communicate in the event of a breaking story. It can be in the form of a card that you update for them every time there is a change. Even a sticker would work to show there has been a change. But don't ask the press to do it; you put it on.

Merchandize your best stories. Many publications, particularly trade and industrial magazines, are happy to provide reprints of sections of their editorials at low cost. Depending on the nature of the story, reprints can be made available for the sales department to use with customers or by the investor relations department for use with analysts, portfolio managers, or stockholders.

Invite editors of key publications to visit your plants and offices at least once. If you have an idea for them, so much the better, but they will appreciate knowing your company a bit better, and they rarely let such a visit go to waste.

It's fundamental, but *check that mailing list before major releases.* There is nothing more insulting to an editor than getting his predecessor's mail who has been gone "lo these many months."

Use product news wherever possible to promote those of your company's characteristics you are interested in highlighting. People relate to products and services they use better than they do to companies.

Get close to the head of R & D. This is where some of the best news about the company *should* emanate from.

See your advertising space representatives when they call. The business and trade press periodically devote issues to a single field or subject that may be of particular interest to your company. The magazines sell space against these special interests, making the rounds to all the likely companies. Even if you don't have an advertising budget, listen well and be polite but honest with the salesperson about the chances of running an ad in the issue. After the meeting, armed with the knowledge of the special section or issue coming up, you should send an appropriate package of industry information, company releases, photographs, and so forth to the editor of the publication. Keep the two contacts separate.

There are also such things as advertorials, which regularly and quite openly charge for editorial-looking advertising. They have become generally accepted by many publications, but this writer still thinks the reader is being conned into believing he is reading more than an ad, in spite of the disclaimers to the contrary in small type at the top of the page. You'll have to decide those case by case, on individual merit. It may come down to needing to be there because the competition has signed up.

If you are in charge of a corporate advertising campaign and public relations as well, develop the habit of thinking about them independently. The practice of trying to exchange an ad campaign for a more favorable acceptance of your stories and press releases, and possibly more favorable handling of your company's activities in the community, is a mistake. Not only is it unethical, it doesn't work. The publications that engage in it are usually the weaker ones to begin with, and if you are known to engage in the practice you will hurt your own reputation as well as the company's.

Get personal. If you are sending material to a particular publication, add a short handwritten note with your home phone number, in case there are questions. It is assumed your office number is already on the material. The more personal invitation recognizes the fact that many writers and editors take their work home with them and may want to contact someone after hours. The number won't be used very often, but it does say you are trying to be helpful.

Release bad news on Fridays for Saturday's newspapers, which are generally lighter—the best chance of pickup is still Monday's. Know your closing dates, at least for the publications that are most important, and consider timing carefully.

Be obsessed with returning telephone calls.

Read the press with which you are most concerned. Find out the kinds of material that interest them. If this is unclear, ask them. Why guess—they will know you are trying when you go to the trouble to ask.

If a publication runs even an especially bad story about your company, don't pull your ad campaign in reprisal. Unless getting even means more to your management's hurt feelings, stay with the campaign. Continue to tell your positive side to that audience. Don't leave the field of battle. On the other hand, there is no sense in starting a campaign in a publication that has been unjust—that looks as though you are trying to soften them up. Complain firmly but politely, provide the usual letter-to-the-editor rebuttal, if it is called for, and go on with your program.

If you want something off the record, don't talk about it. Nothing is more discouraging to a reporter than being given the most interesting part of the story as "off the record." It also cuts down your worry load.

Make use of industrial trade shows. Although industrial trade shows are usually the responsibility of the sales department, they may offer an opportunity for corporate relations as well as product publicity. Depending on the nature of the show and the industry, the trade show may be of interest to analysts, portfolio managers, government officials, or the general press. Judiciously selected editors, who might otherwise not attend, may respond well to invitations and hostings through such events. This may work especially well if this provides them an opportunity to view you in context with your entire industry.

Use a public relations firm with a foreign office if your corporate relations program calls for international activity. News coming from the United States without local processing can be a disaster. It is not just translation; it is the difference in mind-set and local mores.

Think of your internal employee communication program as a first-line media resource, not just your target audience. These employees are unique in representing your company with the highest credibility in face-to-face contacts on a daily basis. As such, they require special media consideration. They are a communication resource.

Coordination between the personnel department or human resource activities and community relations are essential. There are always natural joiners and community activists working in every company. Find them and support their community projects. What they can accomplish for the company, increasing community goodwill, is only half the benefit. The other is the improvement in employee attitude. This improvement is contagious and will spread from these natural activists. They will need some searching out and require some encouragement and direction, but they are there. Use them.

All community relations are local. Don't handle them from afar. Encourage the local plant manager to spearhead key relations projects. Encourage participation in the most logical areas, particularly those affecting employees' lives—for example, improving commuting and road conditions, reducing crime, improving schools. Encourage original contributions to the community, not just Little League uniforms. Work toward initiating local activities that will eventually become self-sustaining.

Size up your executive talent as communicators. Then consider which industry and trade associations and which roundtable groups would be natural forums. Some executives may be happy to get involved in professional and community clubs, but the idea has never occurred to them or they may not be familiar with groups. Encourage them and even act as a matchmaker, bringing appropriate executives and associations together.

Work to get your executives trained as communicators. Executive training of this sort is available from many companies today, such as Compuspond, and from the larger public relations firms that offer this service. It is a form of insurance for plant managers and other executives likely to be on the firing line when there is breaking news about the company. See that they are prepared to meet the crisis. But the payoff needn't wait until something goes wrong. Armed with their newfound confidence to speak, these people can make excellent extensions of your communications effort.

Special events are usually more appropriate at plant level as part of community involvement; however, even major corporations can hold *headquarters events,* which help tie together a sprawling company. The Allied-Signal Corporation, for example, holds a regular technology fair dubbed Texpo. It features many of the company's more exciting technological advances from the research and development group as well as from the company's many subsidiaries. The fair gives Allied-Signal's own people a chance to familiarize themselves with the activities of the other divisions. It is also an opportunity for the press and the investment community to get a close-up view of the company's more exciting projects.

Events are not an unmixed blessing, however, and whether it is a marathon, an auction, a charitable benefit dinner, a photographic exhibit, or a concert, evaluate beforehand the anticipated community relations value, the event's internal value with employees, and its press potential. The event should also be evaluated for its downside risk if it proves a dud. Make sure the event doesn't overshadow the news you are hoping to highlight by the event. If the event is in connection with a new line of products or a major R & D breakthrough, focus on this. Be sure the news isn't lost in the circus.

Stay in contact with retirees. In the less cost-conscious past, some large corporations viewed their retirees as a separate constituency that helped portray the company's place in the community as a caring citizen. Depending on the longevity of most employees, the number of employees, and the relationship with them, today's companies may want to reexamine the devices used to cultivate this frequently loyal group of vocal senior citizens. "International Harvester—a good company. I helped build it"—whether the day of such bumper stickers will return is questionable. But continuing contact through special newsletters, retiree club sponsorships, and company news encourages retirees' continuation as stockholders, and it shows the current employees that retirement from the company is not necessarily the end. Occasionally, retirees can be used in special situations as plant tour guides, or to augment staffs during community field days or even peak load periods. For instance, there are currently a number of public relations retirees who serve as consultants handling their companies' underwriting activities on public broadcasting.

Protect your name. What do you do when your company or a brand name becomes so synonymous with the product and its function that it starts to slip into a generic term? Did you know there was a Photostat Corporation and that the photostats you use today should really be called Photostat photocopies? Well, Xerox Corporation knows, and it, along with dozens of other companies, works hard to protect its registered trade names. Not only are Xerox Corporation people careful in the way they use the term *Xerox* themselves, but they monitor the way others use it and warn them to use the ® mark and never to use it as a verb, as in "Please xerox this." In addition, Xerox, Coca-Cola, Caterpillar, *TV Guide,*

Muzak, Rolodex, and many others run ads to alert the press to use their names correctly.

There is no reason why a name has to become a household word before such efforts to protect it are made. In fact, at the first sign that the name is subject to misuse, alert the press. After all, how better to show that the name has a reputation and value than to demonstrate that you are interested in protecting it. Don't be silly, of course. There must be some legitimate concern or the motives behind your actions will be transparent.

Incidentally, the ads developed for this purpose are some of the most original used anywhere. *Editor and Publisher* has a yearly supplement devoted to this purpose. Get a copy and look it over before joining in. After all, you have to look as good as the competition.

Rip the adhesive tape off fast. Faced with the need to close outdated plants, General Motors once announced that they would be closing nine plants over a two-year period. The result: major headlines for a short period. But the company got rid of all the bad news up front. From that point, if the company decided to close only eight plants, it is a success story.

Leave renegotiation room. A new TV station erected its new antennae in a previously quiet, wooded location. It installed inordinately bright airplane collision lights on the tower. Public indignation focused on the lights more than on the tower, so when the station's management agreed to reduce the intensity of the lights, they became good guys. Sometimes it pays to put your worst foot forward.

Run regular surveys in the employee publication. Feed the results back in later issues with comments. It helps set up a dialogue rather than a monologue.

Move into the computer age. If the specialized business press is important to your company, begin to provide article manuscripts in computer-readable form. A recent survey found that the majority of technical publications prefer to get their longer manuscripts in this form. As many as half of the submissions they receive are computer readable. Don't bother doing this with news releases, since they require rewrite anyway. When submitting features, check first by phone on the suitability of the feature and find out whether the publication prefers its computer readability in disk, modem, or OCR form. Submit the manuscript first, but mention in the covering letter your ability to provide it in computer-readable form.

Set up a hot line for employees. Find out about the nasty problems before they show up on a news show. The "ombudsman" that answers may be able to handle whistle-blowers and set things straight before they get out of control.

7
Investor Relations

The efficient market theory may work fine for the top one hundred companies, but the average company needs to do a lot of work to spread the word about is values.

The stock market bases stock prices upon all known elements relating to the company. Areas of the company that are unknown are put on the minus side of the price equation. A steady flow of information about the company therefore helps reduce the risk in the minds of analysts. A continuous flow of information helps build credibility. It eliminates analysts' feeling that they are just being told the good news.

Fear of appearing aggressive is unfounded. Even if earnings eventually prove disappointing or industry events prove enthusiasm unrealized, your credibility will not be hurt, providing you have told the whole story in the first place.

Wall Street hates surprises. If you see trouble ahead, point it out, along with your plan to avoid it. Paint a picture of the real world, problems and all, and your management will look realistic and credible.

Focus on tomorrow. You may be undervalued because investors don't know the good things you are planning as well as you do.

The advantages of a balance between portfolio managers and individual investors is discussed in this chapter.

Finally, a number of specific ideas are offered on a variety of subjects, from the president's letter to the use of data bases and closed circuit television.

T he concept of investor relations (IR) as a separate business activity is quite recent. GE is usually credited with developing the discipline as a separate function within the company about thirty years ago. Slow to catch on at first, IR has grown very rapidly in the last decade. Growth was stimulated in the 1960s by an SEC ruling that made it clear that a company's responsibilities could not be met by management's simply saying nothing. Management people would be held responsible to communicate both good and bad news that might have an effect on stock. Since it had become necessary to communicate investor news, like it or not, companies began to develop a breed of IR specialists. These specialists had much of the expertise of the financial officer and the communication skills of the public relations executive. By 1969, these company-grown communicators (business schools, at that point, had not recognized this discipline in their curriculums) formed their own association, the National Investor Relations Institute (NIRI). It has grown rapidly and is now one of the most active business associations in the United States and Canada, with a membership of more than three thousand. In part, this group was formed because of the need of these newly created "experts" in the new discipline to learn from each other and to keep up with an explosively changing investment climate.

Articles and monographs on investor relations of only a few years ago universally pleaded with CEOs to recognize the value of addressing the investment community on a regular basis with a planned program of communication. It is easy to see how far the IR discipline has come. Today, it is a rare CEO who is not committed to the importance of maintaining a flow of substantial information to investors and analysts. The argument that little effort is required to do this, based upon the efficient market theory, is slowly disappearing.

Just how much validity the once sacrosanct efficient market theory will still have when you read this is unclear. This is the theory that most information about a stock is reflected quickly and uniformly in its price. Even prior to the October 19, 1987, market crash it had been under attack for some time. It has even been questioned by its foremost proponent, Barr Rosenberg, former Berkeley professor and considered the guru of the modern portfolio theory. Although academics may still be fighting it out, most IR professionals will agree that it takes a considerable amount of effort to disseminate even the most pertinent news to the investing community broadly enough and in such a way that it affects the price of a stock. This is particularly true if you are with a small company not closely followed or widely held. With roughly three thousand analysts who write reports and ten thousand companies to write about, maintaining a steady flow of positive analysis and company recommendations requires leg-work.

Maintaining a Consistent Flow of Information

The effect good investor relations work can have on a company's price to earnings (P-E) ratio has been demonstrated often enough to create its own doubts as to the accuracy of the efficient market theory. Certainly, the market responds better to those companies that openly provide a consistent flow of information. The logic behind why this is so is very clear. Information reduces risk. The stock market, as a process, arrives at a stock price based upon all known elements relating to the company. Some of the known factors add to the price, others subtract. Areas about the company that are unknown usually contribute to the minus side of the price equation. If the capability of a new management is unknown or if its new product development program is completely hidden behind locked doors; if its depth of management is unclear and a replacement candidate for the CEO isn't in sight; if it's a company likely to make unpredictable moves—these unknowns will all register on the negative side of the stock price evaluation. If it were possible to have two identical companies that were both sound investments and one was known in depth by the investment community and the other was not, the better-known company would enjoy the better price. It is really that simple.

Not only does the increased flow of information help eliminate the unknowns, but it also serves to raise the "top-of-mind aware-ness" of the company in the investment community. Coming quickly to mind is an asset when consideration is being given to purchasing anything, even stock in a particular industry. While this ceases to be much of a factor among the largest blue-chip compa-nies, just developing a presence in the investment community for the new issue or the smaller company becomes a top priority of investor relations work.

The flow of investor information should be more or less continuous. The IR mind-set should be one of "keeping analysts and portfolio investors informed," not "let's tell them something when we have good news." This simple difference in point of view makes a big difference in the relationships that are built with professional investors. When investors have confidence that they know what is going on, it helps eliminate that "black hole" when making an investment decision—that is, "What's *really* going on inside that company we haven't heard from lately?" Akin to this is the fact that continuity in the flow of information helps build credibility. It eliminates the feeling of an analyst that "we are just being invited in to be told some good news."

Don't fear that you will appear too aggressive because of frequent news conferences related to company activities that might affect stocks. Analysts and investors know that companies must compete for equity dollars. They also recognize that in this competitive world, aggressive companies do better. Showing the aggressiveness of a company through its investor relations program, within, of course, legal bounds and good taste, is today more likely to reflect positively on a company than negatively. Don't fear being enthusiastic and aggressive in presenting the company's story. Even if earnings eventually prove disappointing, or industry events later prove your enthusiasm was unwarranted, it is unlikely that any real damage is done to a company's credibility just because it had previously been optimistic. The key to this paradox is that the investor must have been told the whole story in the first place.

There is nothing worse than surprises to Wall Street. If you can avoid them, do so at all costs. This can be done by explaining the problems that must be overcome to achieve goals. By explaining even the internal difficulties that had to be overcome in order to reach the position you are in currently, you gain credibility. Don't leave out the problems. When you do that, you paint a picture of an unreal world. Paint the whole picture, but do it with bold, strong colors, appearing aggressive and enthusiastic.

In discussing aspects of the company, don't just focus on the stronger, obvious elements, although that is important, but spend time giving evidence that management is aware of its weaknesses and describe the logical, strategic plan you have in place to correct those problems. Often, if you describe the specific problems faced by weaker segments of the company and the actions management has taken to achieve even modest results, a presentation will come off as the reflection of a strong, flexible, and innovative management that performs well even in adversity.

Finally, focus on tomorrow. The CEO who complains that the stock market undervalues the company frequently does so because he or she knows the good things that are coming and hasn't told the investment community anything but the things the company has done. It is essential, of course, to provide analysts with the figures in as many ways and forms as they are likely to want. Most will claim they wish to do their own analysis. Few, however, will object if you do some of their homework and go beyond the minimum to provide long-term achievements and an in-depth view of the performance of each individual company component. Although you need this historical data, the investor buys on the basis of what he or she anticipates the company is going to do more than on what it did. It is essential, therefore, to talk about the future. This advice, unfortunately, frequently runs into two forms of objection, the first usually coming from the CEO. It goes like this: "Forecasting is foolish and can reduce our flexibility, and if we are wrong, it will hurt our reputation or hurt our credibility." Other executives, frequently those with a marketing orientation, want to reveal as little as possible of their plans for fear of tipping their hand to the competition.

Writing eloquently on this point of achieving higher appraisals of a company's values by revealing more of its future plans, Theodore Pinkus, chairman of Financial Relations Board, Inc., a large financial public relations firm, said in an article in *Fortune,*

> Treat the investor audience as if it were a single individual thinking about buying the entire business. The key questions they want answered are: What is the competitive position and the market outlook for each of the company's business segments? What are the company's weaknesses? What are management's goals and strategies to achieve them? How adaptable is management to changes in its markets?

Managers do not have to make promises or issue absolute predictions on next year's earnings per share. Nor do they have to worry about losing credibility; they are free to update their public forecast as often as necessary. And they are in no danger of running afoul of the Securities and Exchange Commission [SEC]. Section 26A of the Securities Act of 1933 encourages companies to make responsible projections of future results. What matters most is persuading professional investors that management really has a plan and is not just sitting there waiting for the phone to ring.

The highly publicized insider-trading investigations of 1986 had a chilling effect on the willingness of many corporations to speak candidly to portfolio managers and analysts about their company activities. Hiding behind a "no comment" may seem safe, but it certainly is self-defeating. Obviously, you cannot disclose nonpublic material information selectively. You either tell the truth to everyone or keep to the "no comment," or, more likely, avoid answering the phone.

Under conditions where major news breaks are imminent, such as mergers, acquisitions, or important product announcements likely to affect the price of the stock, such reticence can be in order. But for day-to-day situations, such as dealing with analysts who are probing for upcoming earnings figures, a more open policy can serve both investors and the company's interests best. After all, the SEC is not looking to reduce the amount of information investors are privy to—the more the better—it just wants the information spread out equally.

In practice, setting analysts straight on upcoming results is a basic duty of investor relations people. If most of the analysts appear to be misinterpreting estimates of the company's future earnings, the IR executive should certainly make efforts to correct this error but should do so evenhandedly. On the other hand, if one analyst is obviously making an error in his calculations he might well be taken aside and shown the error of his thinking through the questioning method: "Are you sure your figures have taken into account our sale of the XYZ plant?" Probably the best solution is one offered by Thomas Daly, a partner of IR consultants KST & Company. He believes the best way to stay out of trouble is to maintain an open flow of information at all times. A steady flow of information is more likely to mitigate the effect of only one piece of news on the value of the stock. That's good advice, but when it becomes necessary to turn off the flow of information during merger talks, the "no comment" will raise its own suspicions because of the contrast to your former easygoing relationship with the analysts. The solution, if there is one, is common sense, knowing the ground rules of the SEC, vague as they are, and maintaining personal, scrupulous integrity. Lying won't solve the problem, even if you're tempted. The SEC has come out against that in its 1985 Carnation decision in which denial of merger rumors was judged not acceptable but in itself led to false presentation of the company's position. Do the best you can. Later you can patch up your relations with the analysts you avoided. They'll understand.

Priorities

The size of the company, as well as the number, size, and pattern of stockholders, will dictate to a large extent the IR priorities and, to a lesser extent, the success a new investor relations program will have. A company that has coasted for some time with a few quiet, large investors may make spectacular gains by just alerting a wider field to its stock availability. Job one, in that case, is to have at least some analysts write reports. This action alone produces quick first results.

If you are simply modifying a mature IR program, one in which a company is already well followed by a group of portfolio managers and analysts who are kept abreast of the company's activities, the greatest gains are likely to be made with stepped-up activity with the actual portfolio managers, the ones who make the buying decisions. Obviously, if their analysts are telling them no, you have a different problem. But if you are listed as a buy or hold, the potential is quick with the institutional investor.

Meeting the Investment Community Personally Pays Off

This can mean a road show, but do give the analysts who follow your industry and the more likely portfolio managers a chance to meet you and your CEO. Particularly if your company is located in the hinterlands, you can't do it all by mail and telephone. The psychology of meeting face to face and giving an analyst a chance to say that he has met the CEO personally or has had lunch with him or her is valuable. In some way, give the analysts the feeling they have received, if not inside information, at least fresh, firsthand information, even though technically all they got was straight news. Analysts like to feel that they have great knowledge about companies they recommend. Nothing affirms this feeling more than the chance to meet and ask questions face to face.

Individual Investor versus Institutional Investor

Many IR professionals have operated successfully in recent years by concentrating virtually all their effort on twenty or so portfolio managers. The philosophy is that these are the buyers who have shown interest in the company in the past and control the major share of the company, and efficient use of their time dictates selective concentration against these key investors. To some, this even includes relegating analysts to relatively routine handling. The small individual investor may even be looked at as a nuisance. Many companies have made the pragmatic decision to buy out the small investor in order to save the servicing and handling of the fractional holder. This practice was not uncommon among telephone companies following the AT&T divestiture, in which eight companies were left with tens of thousands of small, private investors. The New York Stock Exchange reports there were 40 million individual investors in the United States in 1983, while a lot are in mutual funds; it is no wonder they are more difficult to reach economically. Where phone calls and meetings and lunches can provide an effective one-on-one tie with key institutional investors, the individual investors, to be reached effectively, require at least a modest corporate ad program or consistent direct mail. But don't write off the individual investor too quickly.

The advantages usually cited in making the effort to seek out individual investors are well known. They act as a counterbalance to institutional holdings. Many consider a 60/40 relationship to be ideal. Private investors tend to keep their stock for longer periods. They are not subject to the quarterly reviews, which have been blamed for the tendency of portfolio managers to make massive shifts in their holdings to provide an attractive appearance at the quarterly review. The individual investor, while sometimes viewed as capricious, actually is far more likely to hold stocks through difficult periods. The value of a broad base of private investors is not lost on the institutional investor, who will consider this when adding it to his or her own portfolio. The more broadly held a stock is, the more marketable it usually is.

What often may be forgotten in today's focus on the efficiency in concentrating on the portfolio managers is the reservoir of public goodwill stockholders can provide. Certain companies also view their stockholders as customers, sometimes offering them product discounts. But at a minimum stockholders are a channel of goodwill to their friends and relatives. Such value, of course, varies with the industry and products involved. The individual investor is not infrequently a customer in his own right first. Pharmacists are heavy private holders of drug stock; so are doctors. Jobbers, wholesalers, and industrial buyers all get to know companies through the products they handle. Where a conflict of interest is not a problem, they are frequently more likely to buy a stock from their suppliers, whom they know firsthand. If their experience has shown them the company is well managed, has high-quality products, and appears to have a bright future, they are likely to invest. In turn, their purchase of stock is likely to help protect their continued interest in working with the company and its products.

Just how unsophisticated is the private investor? According to a study by D. F. King and Company, in collaboration with the National Association of Investors Corporation, private investors are more sophisticated than most people believe. They read the annual report for an average of twenty-five minutes, hold stock for more than three years, and tend to vote proxies for management. In those cases where they represent a large percentage of the shareholder body, they provide greater price stability.

Encouragement of individual stock ownership will take different forms, depending on the group: individuals who already own the company stock may, of course, be reached through reinvestment programs; the employee through stock purchase plans; other potential individual investors through financial publications; and people with vested interests in the company, such as customers and buyers and communities where the companies work, through trade and local publications and mailings.

Ideas to Consider

The Letter from the President

Try to think of the letter from the president to shareholders in the annual report as one of the most important, influential pieces you will write all year. It is not an exercise in futility, nor, as it's been called, "an exercise in saying nothing beautifully." For years, studies among analysts and portfolio managers have tended to show a disregard of the president's letter as puffery. This is probably because analysts wish to appear more professional by stressing their reliance on the quantitative, statistical portions of the data. A new study, summarized in the October 1986 issue of *Financial Analysts Journal,* suggests there is more value to this portion of the annual report than has been suspected. Remember that this letter provides the principal opportunity in the annual report for a company to stress the qualitative side of the business and to talk about future plans and directions. Remember too that, as was stated earlier, people who buy stock do so based more on what they expect a company to do than on what it did in the past. If that suggests that the company letter should look ahead instead of backward, you are right. A content analysis, conducted by Dennis McConnell (College of Business Administration, University of Maine), John A. Hasslen (College of Business and Management, University of Maryland), and Virginia R. Gibson (College of Business Administration, University of Maine) suggests that companies that are winners tend to send out signals that astute investors would do well to pick up. By the same token, losers send out their own negative signals. Although these researchers admit the results are far from conclusive and need further follow-up work, the implication to writers of presidents' letters is worth noting. Companies that expressed confidence about the coming year, projecting good growth and imminent gains, and referred positively to the plans for the year ahead did better in their stock prices in the following year. By contrast the president's letter from companies that performed poorly the following year tended to discuss neither gains nor losses. Furthermore, when the letter mentioned imminent losses, subsequent stock prices declined.

If this qualitative method of analyzing an annual report catches on among investors, it will add a new dimension to writing the president's letter. In the meantime, continue to emphasize the positive about the year ahead. Discuss your plans and look forward with confidence to growth. Don't get bogged down in explaining the dismal past.

Summary Annual Reports

The Securities and Exchange Commission's 1987 clarification on the rule that companies aren't required to publish the traditional glossy annual report raised a storm of criticism as investors faced the prospect of a reduction in available company information as a result of shortened summaries. A survey by Hill & Knowlton, at the time among twenty-five analysts, showed sixteen against the practice, several of them outspokenly so. One analyst stated that a company's adopting the practice of preparing only a summary report without an analysis of its business will make him unlikely to follow the stock. Another described a company that did not do a traditional annual report as showing contempt for the typical shareholder because many clients don't look at the financial details in the 10K's.

Whatever the outcome of this debate, consider the logic of Richard Homan, the publisher of the *Wall Street Transcript*. He views the annual report as representing "the product." He points out that few if any people will buy or invest in a company without having looked at its annual report. If you don't get the report into their hands, it is unlikely an individual investor will buy. And it is even less likely that a portfolio manager will chance investing in a company if he or she might, at some future date, be asked the simple question, "Did you even look into their Annual Report?" and has to say no. Even in this electronic information age, the annual report represents the company as the investment "product." Not surprisingly, Mr. Homan suggests that one of the ways to broaden the availability of the annual report is to run it as an insert, in its totality, in the *Wall Street Transcript*. An interesting idea, and one with a limited but apparently successful track record.

The "In" Industries

One of the standard questions a major research company asks the investment community is for a ranking of the attractiveness or unattractiveness of various industries. The research companies have been doing this for a long time in their shared cost studies, whose results are proprietary to the subscribers. It is fascinating to see how industries rise and fall in their popularity and to watch some companies' ability to reposition their mix of businesses in such a way that they better fit the current popular classifications. Some diversified companies can do this easily by emphasizing the particular businesses that are riding the wave of popularity and by de-emphasizing the ones out of favor. In fact, diversified companies (as opposed to narrowly focused ones) go in and out of favor in their own cycle. Currently, conglomerates are out. But they may come back. Going into a recession, conglomerates appear safer because of the hoped-for countercyclical nature of their various businesses. Generally, each type of business goes into its own recession cycle. This at least slows the corporation's drop in sales to a longer, more acceptable period. Because conglomerates are also slower to rebound, as each business comes out of the recession in time to its own industry, they are usually less in favor when things are going well.

Beyond these chameleonlike games of showing the color that best suits the customers, a certain amount of gerrymandering of what you call a business and how you position its components can be done. For instance, a company that makes a terminal may consider itself an electronics company, or if the terminal is part of a computer, it might consider itself part of the computer industry, or if the computer is part of an aircraft, part of the aerospace business. It may also consider itself a high-technology company, or if the computers are linked up, part of the information systems, communications, and telecommunications field.

Obviously, there is a limit to how far this game can be played. The quantitative dollar returns from the various business units keep the technique within legal bounds. Making incredible claims for being in industries in which you are only marginally involved can affect your credibility and ruin reputations pretty quickly. But at the same time, it is necessary to make a decision on how and where the company is to be perceived, and how you see it yourself is the first step in positioning how others will see the company. For instance, if you see yourself as operating in the automotive field, even though a good portion of your sales are electronics to many other industries, you may be tying yourself to a cyclical industry's performance unnecessarily.

Data Bases

Data bases are now available that list analysts and the companies they follow, as well as the growing number of portfolio managers, both institutional and pension. This is good basic homework and essential information during proxy fights.

Closed Circuit TV

The growing diversity of companies, the globalization of their operations, and their sheer size has added to the impersonalization of management's communication to the thousands and, in some companies, tens of thousands of employees scattered around the world. Although chain of command and conventional internal communications can and do provide a degree of uniformity in the various parts of the corporate body, there are times when speed and the dynamics of direct management communication to employees is highly desirable. Private satellite communication from headquarters to plants worldwide is now relatively routine. One company, Private Satellite Network, Inc. (PSN), installs, manages, and maintains point-to-multipoint one-way video and two-way audio networks in a kind of business television. Routinely, buyers at J. C. Penney have used a companywide system for viewing merchandise.

The current costs and company commitment to such systems require a careful examination of a company's real needs to benefit from such a system. Whether the system will be used on a one-time basis or on a semipermanent basis will depend on the application. PSN has provided a three-way discussion among financial analysts meeting via satellite for financial discussions in London, Edinburgh, and New York. Clearly the drama of such meetings can be capitalized on for special events.

The potential of business television has not begun to be realized. Business television's use for stockholder meetings, for analyst and portfolio manager meetings, and for employees, customers, and the trade is likely to become more commonplace in the future. The use of such a system has been brought to virtually "the routine" by IRN (Institutional Research Network, an arm of PSN), which makes possible broadcasts to select investor groups, presenting strategic announcements of investor importance.

An Investor Newsletter

If the pace of developments in your industry warrants it, a monthly newsletter to analysts can be an effective means of keeping them informed not only of your own company's activities but also of events within your industry. Following the breakup of AT&T, the Southwestern Bell Corporation used this device successfully in the scramble to hold on to the investors it inherited from AT&T.

Investor TV Programming

With the success and popularity of business programs on PBS such as "Wall Street Week" and "Nightly Business Report" the early 1980s saw a rash of business and investor news shows that were hoping to capitalize on the wave of public interest in business and investment news. Predictably, some were ill conceived, and the shakeout in the mid-1980s was extensive. A leader, if not the leading, survivor of the group is the Financial News Network (FNN), which provides all-day programming of interest to investors. It and other shows provide stories of their business operations, hoping to attract investors. At this writing, these five-minute or longer "interview commercials" are generally atrocious. In fact, their appearance gives many of the companies a fly-by-night image they may not deserve. Apparently in recognition of this fact, FNN plans to offer production of such commercial programming directly. Previously, producers working with brokers and investment houses lined up new issues and smaller companies for this kind of instant investment exposure. Overall, the effect has detracted from the image of the investment news shows. Though the use of such programming has a place in today's electronic communications, care should be taken that the end result is production that lends credibility to the corporation and attracts investors with some measure of sophistication. Many of the existing commercials (and they should be called that) and the offerings of off-beat financial newsletters carry with them the distinct aura of "con artists." One can only hope that this valuable form of communication will mature in a direction that will encourage the kind of confidence investors seek.

Finally . . .

One old pro controller who oversees investor relations for a major corporation described the IR job function with beautiful simplicity: "You are really dealing with relaying the chairman's ideas to the investment public." Even so, have a plan. Don't just respond to the chairman or the CEO. Part of that plan should include reliable feedback to the boss. After all, the chairman's ideas are the result of what he or she knows. It's your job to make sure the chairman knows what Wall Street is really thinking about him or her and the company. That can be the hardest part of your job, but that's why you're getting paid all that money.

8
Communicating through Philanthropy

Enlightened companies today recognize that their own health can be no better than the health of the society in which they operate. Contributing to that health through a variety of charitable means is good business.

Philanthropy, carefully planned and related to the company's own self-interest, is not only a valuable communications tool but sensible community relations.

Subjects discussed include matched gifts, corporate foundations, cause-related marketing, contribution of executive time, underwriting public broadcasting, conducting community projects as part of community relations, and the importance of educational grants.

The roots of corporate philanthropy go back to the first industrial barons who gave back earnings through foundations with names like Carnegie, Fisk, Rockefeller, and Ford.

This tradition of corporate giving was brought into question during the early 1970s when the economist and professor Milton Friedman drew wide attention (notoriety, in some circles) with his view that an executive who spends a large portion of his company's income on social purposes is, "in effect, stealing this money from the shareholders." Friedman thought that nothing would work to destroy the private enterprise system more than a real acceptance of the social responsibility doctrine—that is, the concept that corporations have an obligation to participate in a positive social way in the community and country in which they live and work beyond simply making a profit.

The professor's simple logic that a company's management did not have the right to spend money for purposes other than making a profit had a certain appeal. Part of this appeal may have been its shock value, daring to suggest that doing good was bad. No doubt some of the meaner-spirited executives found justification for their natural instincts by embracing the philosophy. One client at the time, no longer with that company and no longer a client, was eloquent in his support, claiming that the only moral and ethical stance an executive could take was in the making of profits for the stockholders and that it was immoral to give any of this away. Incidentally, he had a sign on the wall in back of his desk which read, "Shoot the wounded." It was not unusual at stockholder meetings during this period to have advocacy groups question the propriety of such expenditures for social purposes.

The argument against corporate philanthropy was further rationalized by some people who pointed out that the corporation was nothing more than a "paper citizen"—a legal invention that enabled the individual to invest without the risk of a failure that could wipe out personal assets. This "paper citizen," furthermore, was free from the mortality of humanity. It could live on and continue to perform its function, which was to earn a profit, providing that this was done in a legal manner and that it was able to meet society's needs. Because the corporation was a legal invention, it was argued, and not a living, breathing citizen, it did not carry with it all the responsibilities and particularly the ethical and moral obligations of real citizens.

Today this view is dormant and will probably remain so, at least until the next recession sends investors into a search for maintaining dividends. The silencing, or at least the muffling, of the controversy, occurred as a result of the presidential appeal in the early 1980s for more, and not less, corporate support for social needs. Corporations have been pressured from many sides to take on more social responsibility, not less. The "paper citizen" has been such a huge success in organizing productive activities on a scale impossible for the individual that much has come to be expected of it beyond making products and profits. And corporations have largely responded. Furthermore, they have done this in most cases with stockholder blessings. This is thanks to the growing realization that corporations can succeed only to the extent that they operate in a healthy, educated, culturally mature, and prosperous society. This much broader and realistic view of the "paper citizen" was expressed thus by the chairman of Quaker Oats Company some years ago: "Making a profit is no more the purpose of a corporation than getting enough to eat is the purpose of life." "Paper citizen" or not, a public entity such as a corporation, which employs thousands of people and affects the lives of so many within a society, and which depends for its existence on the health of that society, had better put back into that society appropriate contributions for its continued well-being. That is exactly what many companies today are doing. Corporate donations amount to about $4.5 billion a year.

Philanthropy should be considered in any examination of the corporate mission during strategic planning and as a communications tool. This is because philanthropy itself is not just a powerful way to communicate, but it is a major component in building a corporate culture. The decision of whether to engage in philanthropy, and to what extent and in what form, will have an important effect on the fundamental personality of the corporation and how it is perceived by its employees, customers, stockholders, and the community.

Compare the culture of a corporation in which the CEO embraces Professor Friedman's view that philanthropy is stealing from the stockholders with that of the more typical corporation that will donate just under 1 percent of its pretax earnings to promoting cultural activities, education, and other good works. (Some contribute as much as 5 percent.) Clearly there is going to be more respect and favorable feeling expressed for the company that is reaching out to help. But that is just a start. People are generous with those who show generosity themselves. People relate to the way a company behaves and this helps form part of their own behavior pattern. People relate to their jobs. If the company they work for is generous, they themselves are more likely to reach out and help others within the company and within their own community life. Put it another way, doing good things is contagious.

Philanthropy in certain forms can also be one of the most effective ways to reach particular target groups. Selected cultural events, for example, can attract particular audiences and can provide an opportunity to position a company so that important groups will feel favorably toward it. These special events, usually cultural events, may take place anywhere there is a key audience, frequently headquarter cities or important plant locations. Washington, D.C., abounds with such events. Within the span of a few months, the Ford Motor Company contributed to the Treasure Houses of Britain show at the National Gallery. Computer companies donated money to set up an information revolution exhibit planned for the Museum of Natural History. Pepsi-Cola sponsored an exhibit of Russian art at the Renwick Gallery; AT&T sponsored a Whistler show at the Freer Gallery of Art as well as a Wyeth show at the Corcoran. The Kennedy Center alone is reported to have 343 companies among its contributors. GTE sponsored an exhibit of Henri Matisse at the National Gallery of Art. In its five-month run it was seen by half a million people, who each received a GTE souvenir brochure. It is often from the collateral events connected to such shows that a corporation gains the most. As part of the Matisse show sponsorship, for instance, GTE was also able to host a series of events in the gallery, including a reception attended by 400 Washington leaders, and the opening dinner for 380 included the secretary of state, the secretary of defense, four Supreme Court justices, and top administration and defense officials.

Begin with a Plan

As any public relations director knows only too well, there are hundreds of worthwhile causes, each with a more or less legitimate demand on a corporation's always limited philanthropic budget. Responding to these haphazardly, based upon the emotional content of the latest appeal, results in a hodgepodge of donations of varying merit. They may individually be good things to do but not terribly productive in accomplishing the most good for the most people. Nor does piecemeal contributing contribute what it should to the communication aims of the corporation. A proper plan for philanthropy can produce more good not only for the corporation but also for those to whom the philanthropy is addressed.

The plan should identify which areas of social need are closest to the corporation's own activities and best match its natural ability to help. It should consider too which areas of need, if affected through contributions, are likely to produce short- and long-term gain for the corporation. Pure, unrelated giving with no chance of return is admirable. It has its place, but frequently it is short lived and the subject of occasional donations. In contrast, when a corporation takes on a cause, that is in some way related to its own interests, the relationship is far more likely to be long lived. Companies committed to specific philanthropies work to seek improvements and continue to enhance their contributions over long periods of time.

The logic of a food company's attacking world hunger and of pharmaceutical companies' contributing to community health care adds focus to the philanthropy. The public can accept the sincerity of such logical areas of philanthropy and accept the company's dedication to its field more readily than it can in cases of unrelated philanthropy. Any plan should also consider how the company size and position can be used to add further contributions to the cause. Matched donations are one example and the most popular.

The Practice of Corporate Philanthropy

Matched Gifts

More than 1,200 corporations engage in the practice of matching gifts to help meet education and community needs through charitable contribution programs. According to the Council for Aid to Education, Inc. (CFAE), located in New York, approximately three out of five of the Fortune 500 largest industrial companies and two out of five of the largest service companies have regular matching gift programs. By far the largest beneficiary of matching gifts is higher education, with primary and secondary schools, arts, culture, hospitals, and other causes receiving lesser amounts.

The practice of matching not only acts to increase the amount of the donation, but it also highlights the corporation's interest in the community among its employees. It presents a picture to the general public of management and employees working together for the common good. Usually plans for matching gifts are based upon employees' participation, but frequently they are extended to directors, retirees, and perhaps those on leave for military or other purposes. Usually the connection is an educational affiliation. Other restrictions may be used to help assure that the contribution is indeed a donation, not payment for a service, and that it is coming from the employee, not from some other group or organization to which the employee belongs.

When a corporation first considers starting a matching gift program it worries over the obvious financial exposure this seems to present. For example, with a ceiling placed on matching gifts of, say, one thousand dollars, a small company of 250 employees could face a potential quarter of a million dollars' outlay. In practice, however, studies have shown that three-quarters of all gifts are under one hundred dollars, and it is a rare company in which as many as half of the employees participate. CFAE suggests this formula for establishing a budget for a new program:

$$\text{cost of matching gift} = .05 \times \text{number of eligible employees} \times \$100$$

Following a year's experience, this fairly safe guideline can be adjusted for future budgeting. If directors and retirees are included, the level of giving will increase somewhat. Expect that such programs will grow as more employees hear about it and their own personal economics improve. You may also wish to consider establishing a cap for the program, at least in the early years. One way to do that is to establish the understanding that you will prorate all matching gifts based on the total demand. For example, if gifts total twenty thousand dollars and the matching budget is fifteen thousand dollars, the company would match three dollars for every four given. Forms and specific methods of handling the mechanics of such programs are readily available from the CFAE, which can provide all you need to know to get started.

Corporate Foundations

Some companies, particularly where the philanthropy is unrelated to company activity, prefer an arm's-length relationship between the corporation and the group making the donation. Today about 20 percent of the $4.5 billion given by companies is through corporate foundations. The principal advantage is that the foundation helps stabilize giving. It helps ensure that the philanthropy does not increase and decrease depending on annual or quarterly earnings. For instance, when AT&T was broken up, it continued its long history of Bell System corporation giving by establishing a new foundation with a $140 million portfolio through which nearly $30 million is given away each year. The foundation also provides the opportunity for a professional level of cause evaluation and an isolation helping to assure that selection is based on a set of criteria not subject to transient corporate policies. That is not to say that such funds cannot have a positive effect on the image of the corporation, providing the fund's title is similar to the company name.

Cause-related Marketing

Even the most demanding stockholder could not complain about using company profits in some of the donation "schemes" that have developed with great imagination in recent years. Because many of them encouraged sales, the corporation can afford to give virtually without limit, except for that set by the customers who participate. The cause of charity, on the other hand, benefits from what is usually a highly advertised promotion that harnesses the natural giving instincts of the public to the company's product or service. It has a multiplier effect that can result in record donations to the recipient and in improved sales for the corporation.

Perhaps the largest and most successful of these campaigns was the American Express Company's effort to raise $1.7 million for the restoration of the Statue of Liberty. The company donated one cent to the Statue of Liberty Foundation for each purchase charged to the American Express card or Travelers' checks. The company also made an additional one-dollar contribution when each new American Express card account was approved and whenever a customer purchased a travel package valued at five hundred dollars or more. American Express benefited from goodwill and the new business. The American people benefited from the restoration.

Such plans can become more than a one-time event. Take, for example, McDonald's Corporation's Ronald McDonald houses. These accommodations for parents and children who are attending nearby hospitals for treatment provide an innovative and useful service with special appeal to the young family, an important McDonald's audience. The high identity level carried by the clown character also serves as a warm welcome during a difficult emotional period for parents and children alike. Periodically, specific product promotions are coupled with company donations to the houses, which serves both to stimulate sales of food items and to promote and reinforce the philanthropy itself.

Cause-related marketing programs can take a variety of forms and may involve special media events. For instance, GTE became the official telecommunications supplier to the National Football League. As part of that contract, donations were made to NFL charities. GTE in turn gained exclusive rights to the sponsorship of both the Super Bowl and the Pro Bowl. GTE was then recognized by the league and the television commentators as the official telecommunications supplier. This builds enduring relationships with each team in the league. These teams also often need telecommunications systems and are therefore logical customers of GTE. It is a good cause-related marketing communication package. GTE benefits from the actual sales to the league teams and also gains the positive awareness and image attributes of being linked with these sporting organizations. In turn, the NFL benefits through the GTE promotion and its advertising, and the charities benefit from the GTE donation.

Cause-related marketing ideas abound. They are created every day by the media, ad agencies, public relations promoters, and charitable organizations. Many of the larger ad agencies and public relations firms have specialists who search out and originate likely causes and events with marketing applications.

Giving More Than Money

Donations can take many forms, including used equipment and products. IBM and other computer companies have contributed equipment to in-class educational programs. Consumer products of all types may be donated to charities that either use them directly or for raffles and prizes in their own fund-raising drives. Sometimes of most value, however, is the donation of executive time. This means not only employees' working in their own community on charitable drives or as internal organizers for United Funds, Red Cross and the like, but also executives' giving time over a protracted period in order to fulfill specific full-time tasks for particular charities. One company, for example, devoted the executive time necessary for an expert in human resource management to help the National Urban League develop its own personnel system.

Underwriting Public Broadcasting

A 1987 study by the Association of National Advertisers among its members concerning their practices in their use of corporate advertising revealed a significant increase in the number of members underwriting PBS—38.4 percent, according to the survey, up from 12 percent just the year before. A number of reasons for this increase were suggested, among them the wider scope of programming with which corporations can identify, the desire to avoid the clutter of regular commercial television, and so-called enhanced underwriting. It is no secret that with reduced government funding public broadcasting has had to scramble for private dollars. In addition, the extremely heavy funding once provided by the oil companies has also been cut back to some extent (at one time, oil company expenditures were so great that PBS was jokingly called the Petroleum Broadcasting System). Part of this scramble has involved providing more commercial opportunities for companies in enhanced underwriting, which offers much greater freedom to present a more nearly commercial message than in the past.

For corporations wishing to make a simple statement about their business without attempting to sell a specific product, there is ample leeway to deliver a substantial message under the new underwriting rules. In addition, stations have come up with programming that in some cases is so closely related to certain businesses as almost to represent an extended commercial for some companies. Although this to some degree spoils some of the purity of the medium, for a number of business categories it offers an excellent opportunity (see table 8–1).

Undoubtedly more company interest–related programming will follow as the competition increases that PBS faces from growing numbers of cable stations specializing in various audience segments.

The cost of underwriting whole new shows can run into the millions of dollars for the national system, but opportunities exist for nationally shared participation. On a local basis, costs can be very low for sharing in the underwriting of these and repeat shows. Many local shows are available at costs well within even modest corporate budgets.

Community Activities

Community relations can be both the most time-consuming and the most rewarding form of corporate charity. It is best achieved through employees who themselves wish to contribute time to their community.

Table 8–1
Underwriting Public Broadcasting

Program Subjects	Logical Underwriters
Camping and outdoor activities	Sports clothing and equipment manufacturers
Automobile mechanics and car repair	Automotive replacement parts manufacturing
Old house restoration	Building materials, lumberyards, Household appliances, and equipment manufacturing
Financial news	Investment houses
Sports lessons	Sports equipment manufacturing
Health and Medicine	Pharmaceutical companies, hospitals, health insurance companies
Cooking lessons	Food companies, utensils manufacturing appliances manufacturing
Science and technology	High-tech and chemical companies seeking a high-tech image
Woodworking	Tools and equipment manufacturing, lumberyards
Painting and crafts	Hobby supplies and equipment
Travel	Airlines, hotels, credit cards
Aerospace	Aerospace companies

An excellent first step is to have these employees talk to community leaders. This is a technique that GTE uses, according to Edward C. MacEwen, vice president for corporate communications. As "the telephone company" operating in thirty-one states, it has an extensive community relations system. The company takes the results of these individual community leader interviews and shares them with others in the community. The company then targets both its community relations programs and its philanthropy to those areas most often identified in the survey as requiring assistance. This assures the company that its efforts are in areas that need the most help and that those efforts will therefore have the most impact. This procedure also builds the goodwill of the leaders in the community. Those who participated in the survey have seen the results and are kept abreast of GTE's activity. At the heart of the effort are GTE's employees, who act as volunteers for the community organizations. GTE makes their time available to the institutions and groups selected for help. GTE views this as part of the American tradition of volunteering, which, as the company likes to say, goes back to the "barn-raising bees" when neighbors helped neighbors. To support this, the company has established the Volunteer Initiatives Program (V.I.P.). It encourages employee involvement in community organizations by linking grants of up to one thousand dollars to any voluntary effort as long as the employee's involvement is meaningful and substantiated by the community organization. A committee of employees analyzes each grant request and assigns the amount of money to be awarded. A GTE check is issued to the agency and given to the employee to deliver. GTE arranges for news and photo coverage of the check delivery so that both the employee and GTE receive credit in local newspapers.

This community volunteer system goes deep within the company. For example, of the one thousand or so employees at GTE corporate headquarters in Stamford, Connecticut, almost two hundred do volunteer work. Considering that the corporate headquarters is only one of about fifty locations, the benefit to the corporation of building an image in local communities is really national in scope. The boss is not above a full load of volunteer work himself. Theodore F. Brophy, GTE chairman, at this writing is director of the United Way; trustee of the Independent College Funds of America; trustee of Smith College; member, board of the Urban Institute; member, council of the Brookings Institution; on the board of the Kennedy Center; on the board of the National Gallery of Art; and corporate member of the Greenwich Hospital Association. Incidentally, he is also on the board of three other corporations and a member of the Business Roundtable. He does all this while acting as a very full-time, hands-on CEO.

If this suggests the kind of activity level required by successful CEOs today, good.

One of the advantages gained by CEO involvement at a high level within many groups is the opportunity for contact with peers. It provides a chance for the CEOs to exchange views and discuss, in a neutral environment, social, economic, and business concerns. While it is not a direct opportunity to "do business" and the position should not be abused, it is an opportunity to build a network of friends with similar interests which can make future contact for more direct purposes easier and more fruitful.

Some cities have formed permanent groups of local businesses and representatives from schools, civic organizations, and government agencies to bring together in a more or less formal working relationship private and public sectors to develop solutions for problems such as housing, education, youth employment, public safety, and economic development. Such a partnership was founded in New York City in the late 1970s to provide a mechanism through which the private sector could work with government at all levels for improvement and change. The group is in fact called the New York City Partnership. Its list of well over one hundred members on the board of directors is virtually a who's who of the city.

Educational Grants

U.S. corporations donated about $1.80 billion in 1985 to education according to the Council for Aid to Education, Inc. (CFAE). Like the matching gifts previously mentioned, these donations may be given at different levels in combination with community programs, cause-related marketing programs involving scholarships, and outright gifts, either directly or through company foundations. Used office and lab equipment and products, particularly in technical areas, are often especially functional donations. This strong emphasis by corporations on educational philanthropy is particularly appropriate because businesses depend on a constantly renewed pool of talented young people for employees in each location where a company is a major employer. Businesses rely on that community's ability to turn out educationally and culturally whole graduates who can help the company compete and prosper nationally and worldwide. Contributions to local education are often a must. Creating a pool of world-class graduates for a world-class company should become an important long-term objective for major corporations.

In order to make a meaningful impression rather than scatter activities over many fields, some companies concentrate on some aspect of education. Math and sciences receive particular attention from many companies because they themselves are technically oriented corporations and value the contributions these disciplines offer to their own future growth. Schools from which companies recruit frequently get extra attention in terms of grants and scholarships. Similar donations frequently go hand in hand with grants. Educational donations can take place at a more junior level as well. Equipment, buildings, and special needs of private schools offer many opportunities. One interesting variation is to tie local high school sports, which usually generates considerable local interest, to scholarships. Those athletes who perform well academically as well as on the playing field are eligible for college assistance.

The more imaginative the method of donation and the more focused the donation is on the interests of the corporation, the more likely it is that the corporation will realize an important return for its charity dollar and will, in fact, turn it into an investment for all.

9
Changing the Company Name

Changing a company's name is the most serious change you can make in its identity. It can effectively reduce awareness of the company back to zero.

Common types of name changes are reviewed with their associated problems. The elimination of an industry designation from a name, for instance, may at first seem a safe change, but in reality it can totally destroy a name.

The use of initials and anagrams are discussed, along with the possibility of using an existing brand name as the company name.

The advantages and disadvantages of hometown names are reviewed, along with the use of family names.

The process of computer-generated names is explained, with an outline of common name linkage systems.

Finally, some advice is offered on how to work successfully with name change consulting and design firms.

A total of 1,041 American companies of all sizes changed their names in 1985, according to Anspach Grossman Portugal, Inc., a New York- and San Francisco-based identity consulting firm specializing in name change work. This firm has been keeping records of this sort for some time, and it reported that the figure for 1985 was only the second highest, falling short of the 1,055 name changes made in 1983. In contrast, a hand count of the Fortune 1000 industrial companies made by the author some years ago revealed that fewer than 2 percent of these larger companies underwent a name change during the decade of the 1970s. On the surface, at least, it would appear that the spectacular pace of diversification and business expansion by so many large companies has made name changing a popular corporate sport.

There is no doubt that where once it was a rare experience for a communications executive to conduct a name change project, it is now a process he or she is likely to go through several times in a business career. In fact, however, most of this difference is attributable to interpretation of what constitutes a name change. In spite of the rapid pace of diversification and business expansion, most large companies today wear the same recognizable name they did thirty years ago, according to another study by Lubliner Saltz, Inc., a New York communications and design firm also specializing in name change work. Its study of leading industrial giants showed that only 6 percent of those still on top have opted for an entirely new name since 1955. Murry Lubliner, president of the firm, differentiates between a real name change, such as Esso's switch to Exxon, and simple realignments that eliminate or replace a descriptive word in a name, such as R. J. Reynolds's dropping "Tobacco" for "Industries."

Whatever the actual number may be, judging by the cynicism of many who have been through the process, changing the company's name is not something that should be entered into lightly. It is almost always a longer and more expensive process than anticipated and one that will consume the time and attention of management for months. According to the previously mentioned study by Lubliner Saltz, Inc., over 72 percent of the respondents said that a significant change in a corporate name should be considered "only when there are no other alternatives." Furthermore, 68.3 percent agreed that "most names can be made to work" and "it is what you do with the name that counts."

These findings are in complete accord with an informal survey by the author among fifty large companies that had undergone a name change. Most viewed it as a process to go through *only* when necessary. That survey searched for but failed to find any pattern or technique more likely to be associated with success.

Companies that handled the change without the aid of a consulting firm were about as pleased with results as those that used a name change firm, perhaps a bit more so. Those with a special task force were no more successful than those that handled it as a regular corporate communication function. In fact, those who didn't even employ research seemed to have been about as happy with the results as those spending far more time, effort, and money on the project. Perhaps in those cases ignorance was bliss. In fact, it's the nature of the change that dictates how difficult the project will be.

Changes involving only simplifications of long, awkward names but which retain one strong identifiable name appear to be fairly simple, straightforward, and successful. For instance, changing the name Olin-Matheson to Olin was just a natural simplification and gave the company an opportunity to say in their advertising, "Now you can call us by our first name." At this writing, Baxter Travenol Laboratories is planning on a similar simplification to Baxter.

Important Considerations in a Name Change

Avoid Dangling Adjectives

Even apparently simple changes, however, can present problems. Caution is needed to ensure that the remaining part of the trimmed-down name continues to convey who you are. It doesn't work when the remaining part of the name is some common adjective such as National, American, United, Continental, General, Allied, and so forth. Sometimes such half names have been used internally so often that they become shorthand among employees. A kind of myopia results that can lead to thinking that everyone knows which National or which American you are referring to— your employees may know which American or which National you mean, but the rest of the world won't.

This problem arises most frequently when companies try to escape the narrow confines of a product or industry designation that is attached to their names, such as Continental Can, United Aircraft or Allied Chemical. Each of these companies changed its name in a different way. Continental Can became Conoco, United Aircraft became United Technologies, and Allied Chemical was for a while Allied Corporation. Research studies make it clear that the immediate effect of uncoupling the industry designation from such names is instant anonymity. Unless the remaining adjective is coupled to a substitute term, such as United *Technologies,* or a clear contraction is used, as in the case of Conoco, the company may be plagued with a nondistinct name for years. Consisting of a dangling adjective, such names leave the public unsure just which Allied or General is being referred to. In these cases, a totally new name may be the best answer. The decision to make a change under these circumstances is a difficult one. Names that include a product class in which the company is no longer involved can constitute a troublesome misrepresentation. Under such conditions, making a name change, even though it may still be worthwhile, will reduce recognition to near zero. Time and money will be needed to rebuild company recognition to its former level of awareness and familiarity.

Avoid the Alphabet Soup

A frequently used approach to escaping a name that is confining or too long and cumbersome is to use initials. Despite warnings by most consultants and writers on the subject, companies continue to take this route, often because of internal myopia. Companies may have called themselves AMF or GTE internally for so long that they think everyone knows the code, so they drop the full names American Machine and Foundry and General Telephone and Electronics. This may be fine for an International Business Machines and a Radio Corporation of America, which years ago were household names. In their cases the switch to initials was a formalization of the reality of how their publics were addressing them anyway. But for most small companies it's a sure way to get lost in the crowd. After all, if people don't know your name, how can you expect them to know your initials?

Some managements say they like the sound of initials because it makes the company seem bigger. In a way, they are right. It is generally the larger corporations, the AT&Ts and ITTs, that have taken the route of using initials. What some people forget, however, is the millions of dollars and years devoted to building the awareness and positive associations with these well-known initials. There are countless small companies that try it and are just lost in the alphabet.

If you are considering initials after all that warning, don't overlook the possibility of using numbers, as in 3M or 7-Eleven. The potential exists, for a while at least, to salvage from the alphabet soup approach some element of distinction.

Be Specific

Because of business growth and diversification, there has been a recent trend toward names that are broad enough to encompass a wide array of company activities. As a result, many of today's names fail to contribute what should be their principal function— that is, to communicate the kind of business the company is in.

If a company is small enough and sufficiently well focused it should take the opportunity to be specific, to include the company's "competency," as design firms like to call it. Certainly "General Tire" told far more about the company than "GenCorp." "International Harvester" said more about the kinds of equipment the company made than does "Navistar."

Sacrificing the ability to communicate a company's activities may be necessary for a conglomerate, but this should be avoided in a company's early developmental stages. At that stage the company can well afford to be specific for near-term gains, even though you may know full well that the useful business description will probably be dropped as the company grows. For example, Alpha-Portland Cement Company changed its name to Alpha-Portland Industries, Inc., and Texas Gulf Sulphur became Texas Gulf, Inc. In the meantime, the company has enjoyed the specificity it communicated. The trick is to be sure the first part of the name has enough character to stand on its own some day.

Using Shortened Forms

One of the more involved routes name changing can take is a formation of a new name from pieces of the old. Thus, American Climax becomes Amax, Inc., and American National Corporation becomes AmCorp. If used correctly, this technique can shorten a long, cumbersome name and yet keep the essence of the old name for recognition purposes. A good example was First National City

Corporation's becoming Citicorp. The danger in this approach comes in getting lost in the game of using suffixes and prefixes and letters from the old name, and losing sight of the basic requirement that the new name be clear and distinctive in its own right and not dependent upon associations with the past name. Sometimes too these new names are so obscure in their origins that they are understood only by the people involved. How many people today remember that Cigna was an anagram of Connecticut General and a company called INA? In that case, the company was fortunate and a good name resulted. Further, the name acted as an excellent compromise between the two giants, which merged as presumed equals. The new name helped signal exactly that to both sets of employees as well as to the outside world.

Using an Existing Brand Name

Consolidated Foods adopted as its company name its far better known brand Sara Lee. That might appear simply to be doing the obvious. In fact, it takes rare courage for a corporation to make such a move. Sensible as it is to adopt and appropriate the high awareness and familiarity of a better-known brand, companies tend to avoid this route. In part, it comes from a fear of seeming to narrow the scope of the company's operations down to a single brand. It may include a fear of tying the company's future too closely to a single product. It is an approach that should be considered when possible, however, because it is one of the rare situations in which a name change can immediately *improve* awareness levels rather than bring them back to zero.

It is even more unusual for a corporation to adopt one of its subsidiary names. If the subsidiary has been acquired as a result of an acquisition takeover, the chances of the boardroom's adopting its name are about on a par with a country's adopting its conquered enemy's flag even if it is better known and better looking.

Using Hometown Names

Names that include a city or geographic area can be highly distinctive and useful on occasion, but they can also be limiting, depending on the industry. Long ago the railroads began to change from names like the Chicago, Burlington and Quincy Railroad Company to names such as the Great Northern. Airlines went through this phase as well; Allegheny, for example, becoming USAir. In the past decade, members of the banking industry have been busy removing the geographical limitations in their names in anticipation of their broadening activities.

Though these changes are justified in certain industries, most other companies with established names that include the name of a city or region do not find this represents a communication handicap. Certainly, no one thinks that Cincinnati Tools are used only in Cincinnati, or that the Boston Consulting Group consults only with people in that city.

In fact, the solidity of having a hometown in a corporate name can be a plus and a popular factor with the hometown chamber of commerce. A regional term too can suggest that the company has specific merit for people within that area. If expansion beyond an area is not expected or likely to occur, this is certainly an acceptable route to take.

Using Family Names

The old fashioned approach of naming a company after its founder had a lot of merit; it left no doubt about the reality of the company. There is nothing more distinctive than a genuine surname—Ford or Firestone, for example. But this route is taken far less frequently today, perhaps because entrepreneurs know that most new businesses fail and that if your name is associated with it you become enmeshed in that failure. The other drawback is that when the founder dies the family name may present a problem with the heirs who no longer wish to carry the company association around with them. Where ties exist to a historic industry inventor, however, and the name is available, this can still be a good approach. When Automatic Sprinkle Corporation found its new name A-T-O wasn't any better, management decided the company was better off using the chairman's name, Harry Figgy, and calling the company Figgy International. This is a nice idea sometimes, but the namesake must take a bit of kidding and ego jokes. The current impersonalization of companies suggests, though, that there is real opportunity for real names that suggest humanness and warmth.

The Hyphenated Name

This is a growing trend in brand names, but in my opinion for company names it's TER-O-BIL. The artificial and the cutesy just doesn't fit comfortably on stock certificates.

Computer-generated Names

Several computer programs exist to aid in the generation of newly coined words and names. There are two basic types, each addressing a somewhat different problem. The first takes word fragments chosen by the user and recombines them at random to make new words. The key here is to select fragments that relate in some way to the company's activities or products, or convey the kind of feelings and image the company is looking for. You frequently see syllables such as *Tech, Bio,* and *Comp* being fed into these systems in an effort to come up with company names that sound contemporary. The operator sets in the parameters, which include the number of letters, syllables, and the variety of word parts the computer is to play with. Pages of mostly nonsense are spewed out. However, this process may also produce exactly the right combination of word parts to convey a desired meaning.

This can be a particularly interesting and sometimes profitable exercise when a company is searching for a new name following a merger. The resulting name may be just the peacemaker required to make both parties to the merger feel they have been treated fairly. As a practical matter, such names may also be poor long-term investments. After the short-term political benefits have been absorbed, the name may haunt the company for years. In a difficult merger situation, however, the approach is well worth exploring.

The other computer-generated name approach is based on using individual letters. In this case, the computer functions best when it is part of a brainstorming session in which the team interacts with the system to produce and refine sets of names. The best known company name generated this way is Exxon, formerly Esso. Because of these programs' potential for generating astronomical numbers of names, a number of limitations or ground rules must be set up in advance. These include the preselection of those beginning consonants and vowels, middle consonants and vowels, and final consonants and vowels that seem most desirable and that seem to provide the kind of sound you would like the name to have. Programs may also establish a precise number of letters or form words starting only with consonants, ending only in *y*, or ending in a consonant.

Clearly this approach is not for amateurs. It requires someone familiar with the preselection process to come up with something meaningful. It is also possible to combine randomized letter programs with word part programs. For example, you might wish to combine a list of prefixes with endings that are formed from the randomized letter programs.

The number of decent candidate names generated by these programs can be surprisingly small. Probably 90 percent of the words will be ones you will never want to see again. The trick is to extract the 10 percent that hold the most promise and review them further. A good approach is to employ several people with knowledge of the assignment to go through the printout first, leaving in only the names that they think have a reasonable chance. This final group of names should then be treated the same way. The resulting list will probably drop another 90 percent, leaving you only about 1 percent of the original list for evaluation and testing. This may still be a handful.

Name Change Consulting and Design Firms

In the last decade or so, an entire industry has grown up to service the identity needs of changing business. Growing out of design firms, these companies originally did work that was largely confined to graphics. To a certain extent, this background still exerts an influence in the emphasis many of these firms place on good graphics, even sometimes at the expense of the way a name sounds. Everyday business communication is actually more verbal than written, so a good name must be easy to pronounce, even at first sight. Try pronouncing Unisys and you will understand why that company (the result of the Sperry and Burroughs merger) received such negative press on its name selection. However, as in most cases, if the company sticks with the name, people will get used to it and it will work. UAL did not fare any better when it changed its name to Allegis. While it lasted, it was a great looking name but one that needed to be spelled out on the phone.

It is also vital that sight and sound be locked together in the name. Consider, for example, the problem the German chemical company Hoechst has in English-speaking markets. English is the dominant language of business worldwide and should be of major consideration when companies in any country select a name. Hoechst has explained in its advertising that the name is pronounced something like *Herkst,* while visually it looks more to many Americans as if it might be pronounced something like *horse!* In this case, if national pride permitted, it would be so much simpler just to change the spelling to *Herkst* or perhaps to a distinctive *Herxt.* That would largely keep the identity while solving the pronunciation problem. Interestingly, at this writing, following its acquisition of Celanese, Hoechst elected to stay with the German spelling and combine the names: Hoechst Celanese.

The better design firms have of course recognized this need to serve the ear as well as the eye. They stress that corporate names must communicate quickly, uniquely, and easily in print and on the phone, as well as in person. These companies can offer the experience and guidance a company usually needs quickly.

Companies should be aware, however, of just what is involved in the name change process before signing up. This can be a vulnerable period for a company, not completely unlike that during which a bereaved family needs to make rapid arrangements for a funeral. Anxious to get on with the name change, companies may enter into agreements without realizing the amount of time and expense involved later in the process.

Design firms suffer from a perception that they are frightfully expensive, and indeed some are. But considering what the design firms are often called upon to do, they can be a good investment. To the uninitiated, a name change assignment would appear relatively simple: "Come up with a new name that is acceptable to management, that is legally available and protectable, and provide attractive graphics." In actual practice, however, the design firm needs to do a great deal more, which escalates the cost and can produce truly astonishing final bills.

The account representatives of design firms are usually high-caliber business executives capable of working one on one with corporation principals. Consummate salesmen, they can be of great assistance in keeping a project moving. Their principal role is to act as guides through the maze of steps that may be required as illustrated in figure 10–1 on page 143.

About a third of the cost of most design firms' work lies in the predesign stage. This is largely research, both internal and external, to develop the criteria for the company's name and to examine the communication requirements of the firm and its subsidiaries. This background work will determine how existing divisional names and brand names will be linked with the new corporate identity. An entire system of identity needs to be developed. The actual name selection and basic design, which is the next stage, usually represents less than 10 percent of a design firm's effort. The remaining 55 percent or so of the design company's work, and frequently its greatest profit, is generated by the postdesign application work. This involves developing an identity manual that lays out the proper use of the name, with all its permutations in combinations with subsidiary and brand names for all signage, stationery, advertising, packaging, and so forth. Gaining a full understanding of this whole process and its cost before you engage a design firm can help you avoid the feeling described by one communications director of "having gotten on an escalator that just kept going up and up and up with no end in sight."

It is worth examining your own in-house capability and that of your existing ad and public relations agencies to generate at least some portion of the work required. Independent research firms are available that are at least as competent to conduct the background information search and do the comparative name evaluation work later as design firms. Other firms specialize in name generation and can be engaged as a separate effort. Firms such as Corsearch in New York or Thomson and Thomson in North Quincy, Massachusetts, specialize in conducting the state-by-state name searches necessary to be sure the names are legally available. You may first wish to check quickly the *Trade Name Dictionary,* published by Gale Research, to eliminate the names most obviously unavailable.

It may also be important to have an outside expert resource help deal with the variety of internal political sensitivities that usually crop up during a name change. It is a particularly sensitive time for executives in the subsidiaries. Concerned that their own division or brands may lose out in the hierarchy of the company, or afraid that they will be saddled with an additional logo that they view as an unnecessary burden, they are frequently resistant to change. The executives of design consultant firms are old hands at dealing with this. As the "experts," they can be used to push through identity programs on the strength of their past successes. Where a home-grown, in-house identity system might not survive the slings and arrows of the internal detractors, the outside consultant firm can add the necessary clout to make it a success. Sometimes what you pay for is more highly valued than the "homemade," although intrinsically it may be no better.

Another criticism of corporate design firms (besides cost) involves the sterile sameness of the short, precise names churned out in Gothic type. The sans serif look has certainly taken over in corporate names, and there is validity to the charge that many names lack flair and originality. Alan Peckolick of Peckolick + Partners, a New York design firm, has been very outspoken in this regard. He views any design that does not set itself apart from other similar companies a failure. The design should ideally look and "feel" like the very business the company is in today and, more important, where it wants to be ten years down the road. Certainly for the average company, and particularly for smaller ones, all efforts to look distinctive and to capture a visual niche should be applauded.

Michael Wright, head of strategic marketing for Peckolick + Partners, stresses the need for assessing a company's audience, the perceptions of its marketplace, and tying them together in the creative process.

In the case of many multidivisional giant corporations, however, the design criteria may actually call for the bland. Use of the "corporate blue" and the contemporary look of sans serif type can be viewed by such companies as making the statement "We're a giant corporation, we're a member of the club, we're not trendy, we're solid and sedate."

In many cases it comes down to a trade-off between high visibility, to be set apart from the crowd, and lower visibility, to appear to belong to the blue chips. The case for "vanilla logos" is further strengthened for corporations that have multiple subsidiaries and divisions whose own names must live with the parent company's logo. It can be easier to join a more eye-catching and descriptive division or brand logo with a more austere corporation name. There is merit in both points of view. Where a company can afford to be different and stand out, it certainly should. For the large corporation requiring an identity umbrella for numerous, more flamboyant names, the plainer route may be more practical.

Linkage Systems

Linkage will not be a problem for small companies with single names and brands that carry that name. For companies in multiple businesses, however, and those with several company and brand names, the question of the most practical system for linking these names to the parent company must be given careful consideration. To a large conglomerate this can become a major time-consuming area for study and decision. It is often here that a corporate name change consulting firm can be of greatest assistance. Elaborate hierarchies can be set up showing how to use the divisional and parent company names differently under varying conditions. A corporation that owns a company well-known in its own right may elect to show their relationship in relatively inconspicuous ways. In that case, a small base line that simply says "a Blank Corporation Company" is all that is required. The blank corporation may, however, have other subsidiaries that are not as well known which can benefit from the support of the better-known parent corporations. In this case the linkage system will be much stronger in favor of the parent company.

It is necessary to have a good understanding of the relative strengths of the various names involved to develop a successful linkage system, as well as an understanding of the future plans for the divisions—a subsidiary that may someday be sold must be treated very differently from one that will be the hope of the company's future.

In some cases, the parent company's name may be so weak that a holding company posture in which the parent company's name is left out may be the most advantageous. In these cases, the parent holding company will probably only want to communicate to investors and the financial community using its own name. Even here some linkage is required, however, to show the financial community the strengths the company enjoys through its better-known subsidiaries and brands.

One of the options in developing a linkage system is a conversion of existing company names to brand names. Particularly following a merger the value of a former company name can be maintained by leaving it as a brand name. This too will require special handling within the linkage system.

International needs, and occasionally even regional differences in names, will all have to be considered within the linkage system. Eventually these linkage determinations will all become part of the identity manual, which will be the guide in the future to maintaining the consistency of logo usage throughout the company. The manual will also provide a handy precedent for handling new names acquired in subsequent mergers.

The changing of a company's name should not be a simple, "decide and do" event. It should be examined carefully as a process. The following flow chart and the next chapter will guide you through the steps.

10
The Name Change Process

The stream of events that take place in the process of examining and ultimately changing a company's name is discussed and diagramed.

An example is given of how to set criteria for a good company name, along with "musts" and "wants" lists.

Finally, verbatims from dozens of communications directors who have been through the name change process are offered as advice. These quotes illustrate the difficult, time-consuming nature of changing a company name and include the frequent admonition to "do it only if necessary."

B y this time it should be clear that the complexity of changing a name can vary greatly from company to company, depending on the old name and the new structure of the company. If you have already looked at figure 10–1, don't panic. You will be relieved to know that the chart would even cover the worst-case scenario of the most complex name change process. It assumes that a consultant, or a consultant firm, is involved and will need background on the company. If you are handling the project internally, you obviously will already be familiar with much of the background information the chart suggests is needed. You will have to organize this if you bring a consultant firm into the picture.

Organizing the Process

A name change firm will rightfully insist that it have direct access to the CEO and/or the chairman, as well as the communication director, in order to get directly to the heart of issues as seen by the ultimate decision makers. Name change programs originated by middle management as a bright idea that ought to be explored are more or less doomed to failure and may indeed be expensive exercises in frustration if outside resources are employed. The desire to change a company name must be present at the highest level or it will all result in wheel spinning.

Whether an action plan is prepared in-house or by a consultant, it should be the first step. In this, the criteria for the new name should be set down, or at least a plan for determining that criteria should be laid out. A rough budget and timetable are needed at this stage as well.

It is entirely possible that one of the options may be to stay with the existing name but to redesign it, in which case the project could move rapidly into the design stage. More likely, however, the development of the plan will raise many questions, most of which can be answered with one form of research or another. Figure 10–1, somewhat arbitrarily, positions communications audits as a form of research, which it is. However, it is so fundamental to planning that it may well be considered as part of the backgrounding process. (For an outline of how a communications audit may be conducted, see chapter 3.)

In a multidivisional company, a communications audit may profitably be combined with internal interviews with the various communication heads of the business segments. It acts as a form of icebreaker for the interviews and alerts the personnel to the project, and gives them a chance to prepare gracefully for the interview. It can also be a clue to how cooperative divisional people will be. The purpose of the internal interview is not only to elicit the communication requirements for each business segment, in more or less mechanical terms (such as packaging, brand usage, divisional advertising, and so on), but also to gain insights into divisional managements' perceptions of their division vis-à-vis the parent corporation, in terms of their current business and of their future growth intentions. Do they, for instance, see a greater or lesser reliance on the parent company's identity in the future for their own division? Do they plan a proliferation of brand names or do they plan to rely heavily on their own divisional name? Do they see the

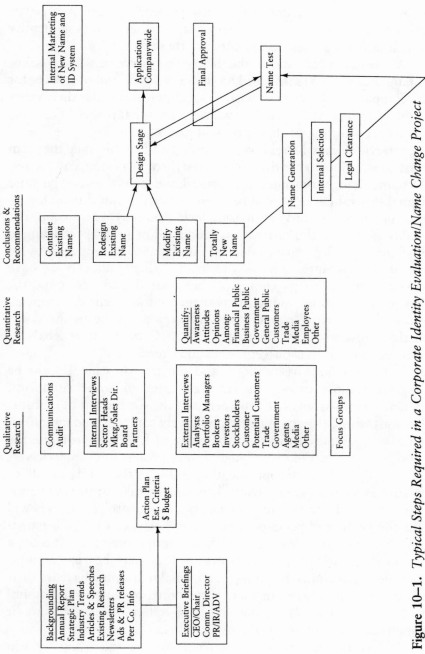

Figure 10–1. *Typical Steps Required in a Corporate Identity Evaluation/Name Change Project*

parent company as a drawback, misrepresenting their own activities, or does it have strengths they plan to use? The new identity system might well be used to enhance these strengths.

At headquarters itself, the interviews serve the purpose of polling the executives involved on their own aims and objectives for the company and how they wish to see it perceived. Get their views of the requirements for their new name and what it should convey. Try to get a feeling of their personal tastes.

Interviews may be relatively informal and should take the form most appropriate to the size and work style of individual companies. If a name change consultant firm is used, the interviews will be more formal. Most interviews will be open and direct. But if troubles are anticipated, particularly at division level, you may wish to consider qualitative motivational analysis, conducted by firms specializing in this kind of in-depth psychological interviewing. Adept at drawing executives out, interviewers who are frequently Ph.D.'s or have master's degrees in psychological behavior dig to determine the dynamics operating among the managers of different departments and divisions. How cooperative will they really be in the name change process? How do they view their own career goals in relation to their division versus headquarters?

If this sounds overly cloak and dagger for what should be simple, in most cases you are right. But in some situations, particularly those involving mergers and the sorting out of multiple divisions with a variety of names, relatively sophisticated interviewing may be required to get to the heart of how best to relate the various pieces of the assemblage. Using professional interviewers capable of this kind of sophistication and with the ability to talk to executives as peers is expensive. It is worthwhile for getting to the real answers, if you anticipate resistance. Frequently, executives will take the posture of pooh-poohing the importance of their separate sector names when dealing with their internal peers; it is almost a macho thing. Meanwhile, down deep, they may be very anxious over the implications dropping a divisional name may have on their careers. The objective outsider, accustomed to this, is also unimpeded by regular day-to-day business relationships, making it somewhat easier to get to the real answers.

Professional interviews conducted outside the company can

contribute a great deal at this stage as well. The objective here is to talk to those outside publics and influences close to the company who have some understanding of the company and how it operates. These may be analysts, customers, or local businesspeople. This informed outsider relationship adds an objective reality that the internal interviews within the company won't quite match. The interviewing should be done by those accustomed to working with the particular publics in question. The interviews may employ the use of some cover by starting with a talk about a particular industry or class of business and then discussing various companies in that business. Later, the interviewer may or may not reveal the client, depending on the nature of the questioning format. It is from such interviews that a company can learn to what extent its current name is a handicap or an advantage: whether the name is considered appropriate to a company in its field; whether the name itself is respected and considered a strength in the trade; whether the name causes confusion with other company names.

Out of such questioning will come a better understanding of the name, and of the company itself and how it relates to its important publics. The interviewing may take the form of one on one or focus groups. The focus group provides a better opportunity for viewing the interaction of the respondents to the company, and it stimulates an exchange of thoughts and ideas. However, it may sometimes provide deceptive results if a dominant respondent sways a group's thinking, causing a distorted picture to emerge. This qualitative stage will determine the likely issues that may then need to be validated through quantitative research.

It is possible, however, that the issues are so clear from the preceding analysis and qualitative research work that no further studies are required, and conclusions and recommendations can be drawn up.

There are then four possible outcomes. You may decide to continue the existing name and logo system. You may decide to keep the name but redesign the logo and perhaps modify the linkage system connecting the parent company name with the subsidiaries, divisions, and brands. The third alternative might be to modify the existing name, perhaps shortening it or changing the competency designation in some way—for example, changing Roberts Aviation to Roberts Electronics. Either of the last two decisions would then be followed by going into design stage. If the fourth option is elected, that of selecting a totally new name, the work on the name change project will really begin. This will start when the criteria for the new name is agreed upon. Names may be generated internally through contests or from a variety of methods, using firms specializing in the process or even ad and public relations firms. From these a weeding-out process must result in a shortened list for internal selections and legal clearance.

At least three or four names should be processed as acceptable candidates at the same time because of the attrition through legal clearance. It is also essential to remember at this stage that new name candidates should be kept highly confidential. There are some people who actually make a living by registering names they find or suspect a company may be interested in using, and then selling their rights to interested companies. Even without these sleazy characters, you might run into some legal snags locally in what must be a state-by-state examination of the names' availability. Be prepared to buy out the rights to a worthwhile name if you can negotiate an acceptable price. When the name or a narrow selection of names has finally cleared this gauntlet, you may still wish to gain the reassurance of further research to be sure the final selection will be trouble free. Frequently this involves repeating the quantitative research that may have been done earlier, comparing the new names with the former one tested. If the qualitative work raised questions or provided hypotheses that need to be verified, then you would have gone into that stage prior to new name generation.

The quantitative research should deal with the connotations and denotations of the name in question as it applies to the various publics. Even if quantitative research is used early in the process, you may wish to include some possible obvious alternative names. This can help to establish the parameters of what different types of names convey about the company.

Following final approval, the name will go to the design stage. This too may require some simple research to select the strongest visual treatments. With approval of the name and final design, application work on the name can proceed. This involves determining the usage of the design in all situations, showing how the name will be applied to stationery, signage packages, and so forth. It will show how the name will be combined with all the other company-owned names. This usually results in an identity manual. Finally, there is the announcement of the name, which should be made an internal event, celebrating, in effect, the new name and the new identity system in a positive way as a sign of a company's movement and growth.

The Criteria for a Good Company Name

Musts

- Available for use—protectable wherever it will be used.

- Unique and distinct to set the company apart. Unlikely to be confused with other companies' names.

- Easily pronounced at first sight in the language of the countries in which it will be used.

- Readily understood when heard, particularly over the telephone.

- Devoid of unfortunate connotations or denotations in all the languages in which it will appear.

- Memorable.

- The graphic design must be readable in small sizes, in black and white, not just color, and in line art as well as continuous tone.

Wants

- Short—one, two, or three syllables. If possible, a name with one word is better than two, two is much better than three. Works well in combination with subsidiary and/or brand names.

- Good potential for strong graphics. A vertical edge to the first initial is helpful.

- Easy to spell.

- Descriptive of the company's principal activity, but flexible enough to allow for company expansion.

- Positive connotations in the minds of customers and Wall Street (not overly clever if you want to live with the name over the years).

- Free of geographic limitations.

After looking at the list of criteria, you may well believe that the search for a new name can be endless. So it may, for companies that are half-hearted about the effort. If there is only a vague discontent with the current name and no compelling reason to make a change, the project can go on in fits and starts for years. If the project is only an attempt to find something that appeals to the chief executives, it is probably doomed to failure.

Don't even consider changing the company's name without first determining that problems stem from the name. It is likely that the company itself needs reworking before a name change should be considered. And if it is simply a question of looking for more visibility and recognition through a better name, be especially careful because the first result of any name change is that all the equity in the existing one is lost. A new name is really a move back to zero as far as awareness is concerned.

Free Advice

A survey was conducted in 1983 by the author among major corporations that had changed their names, and these companies were invited to offer advice to other companies contemplating a name change (see the author's article in the *Public Relations Journal,* August 1983). Their suggestions were frequently helpful, if at times contradictory. You can sense in some through their pithy eloquence that the corporate communications director had undergone an unforgettable experience.

Do it only if absolutely necessary.

Be careful you don't give away important equity in a name you have established for some new type of logo or creative direction.

Be sure the advantages outweigh disadvantages.

Use a good consultant to absorb the emotional heat. Allow plenty of time; two years is about right.

Avoid the big name corporate identity specialists that charge incredible amounts for nonsense research. They want to redirect your corporate strategy, interview all your executives in great depth, etc.

Research, but don't get too complicated.

Retain a corporation trust company to make all the state and foreign filings, and assign one person, preferably an attorney, to coordinate very closely with the corporation trust company.

The biggest problem will be maintaining interest in the name change project after it is well along, before it is completed.

Conduct research before making the change decision. Particularly to determine the meaning of the new name in other languages, and to avoid any other embarrassments. Also be prepared for it to cost more than you expected.

Do internal as well as external research.

Put one man in charge. And make sure you pick a name the CEO likes.

Choose a phonetic name that comes across clearly over the phone.

Main problems will come from older people in the company. Particularly marketing and sales people, who are afraid of loss of reputation with their contacts. Shareholders can be a problem, too.

Be prepared to buy out name rights from small local companies. There are always one or two with a similar name.

Decide, first, whether you are really going to change the name. If you try to find a suitable name first you'll never satisfy anybody, or make a decision.

Assign one person with overall corporate identity responsibility only.

Don't announce name change until all suppliers for items such as stationery, signage, decals, etc. have been assigned.

Must have complete support of top management. Establish a very strict policy policing the use of the new logo.

Have a sound rational reason to change your name. Don't use initials.

There is no right or wrong in this business; only being in or out of sync with company culture and personality.

Go with the president and chairman's gut feelings—do not spend large sums on consultants. Do not get caught up on graphics.

Build on existing name values. Correct existing name errors and avoid complexity of analysis and implementation. Avoid costly promotion unless it achieves other marketing objectives.

Get professional help. Do legal and semantic research to avoid future problems. When you've selected a good name, implement it with good graphics.

Hire the best, pay the most, and don't look back. Be sure there is a real, clearly defined objective for making the change.

And Finally

Don't be afraid to be different. After all, the whole purpose of a name is to set you apart from everyone else, not to make you blend in.

Shakespeare said, "A rose by any other name would smell as sweet," and the essayist James Russell Lowell countered with "There is more force in names than most men dream of." In a way, they are both right. A good name is to be treasured beyond great wealth. But by itself, that good name isn't likely to sell many products or stock either. What you do with that name, the reputation you make for it, is what will give it worth and value in years to come.

11
What to Do When Disaster Strikes

Damage control of company images is better understood than it was a decade ago. The high visibility during times of company crisis must be planned for in advance.

The type of news disaster, be it sudden, catastrophic, ethical, environmental, or sustained embattlement, has a great deal to do with how it must be handled.

Stonewalling no longer works. Maintaining a steady flow of information to the press and maintaining a credible, concerned posture is the first fundamental.

Tell it like it is, but "don't speculate" is a warning that should be given to all employees.

Specific advice is offered on dealing with many of the problems that arise, both in catastrophic disasters and in protracted community confrontations.

The press is offered an insider's view of the effect it has on a company's reaction to disasters. The chapter explores the effect of the increasingly adversarial position taken by the press toward American institutions, including businesses.

I n one sentence, "Put into effect the program you have carefully worked out and rehearsed in the months and years preceding the crisis."

If an unexpected disclosure (as one gentle business writer euphemistically referred to the Love Canal disaster) catches you totally unprepared, you are probably in big trouble. The best you can do is hope and be as candid as you dare. Even a modest amount of preparation can make a big difference in how you survive the event.

Business today probably commits fewer social transgressions than it did in the past. Certainly it is more skilled at avoiding accidents and disasters. Business has had to become more knowledgeable about product safety and more conscious of the ethical standards expected of it. In spite of this, we seem to see more companies caught up in crisis situations that can destroy a reputation of long standing. Crisis management has become a distinct discipline and for many a separate and seemingly ongoing management function.

These breaches in conduct by companies are often very revealing of the company's real culture. Analysts, investors, and consumer groups have learned to judge companies during these periods when the spotlight of the press reveals their warts and blemishes. The general public too forms images when the heat is on. If the problem is handled well, as in Johnson & Johnson's handling of the Tylenol tamperings, a company can actually improve its image during these periods of intense press focus—providing, of course, the company and its management are relatively blame free.

In part, the growth in bad business news is caused by the public's increased interest in business. More than 40 million people now own stock in companies in one form or another. The activities of companies have become news. There is more extensive business coverage by the press, and the press itself has grown more competitive because of its need to fill the evening news with excitement and drama. The battle for viewers contributes to the perseverance of investigative reporters in finding the tidbits and the sensational. Grown more sophisticated since the days of Watergate, the press is not only more suspicious but more skilled in digging out stories than ever in its history. Gone are the days, if they ever existed, of avoiding adverse press by simply saying nothing. Gone are the days, as one (possibly apocryphal) story goes, of an old time public relations man's rushing to the scene of a train wreck to paint out the name of the railroad before press photographers arrived.

Today, even legitimate delays in answering the questions of the press, let alone stonewalling, may be interpreted by reporters as a sign of guilt. The press can smell coverup even when none exists.

During the period when management is rushing to sift through the facts and assess the damage, the press will already be looking to determine who is at fault. Even the Soviets apparently learned from their Chernobyl disaster experience that you can't hide behind a "no comment." Some months later, following the explosion on a nuclear submarine and its subsequent sinking, they were quick to respond in comparative openness.

To the press, accidents don't happen—they are caused by someone "guilty." It can be human error, criminal neglect, company greed, or bad management but guilt is almost assumed. The assumption seems to be that if a company were run properly, nothing would ever go wrong.

To deal successfully with this frequently antagonistic attitude, a company must react to events forcefully. It must do and say the things that will make the press feel that the company's management is, if anything, even more deeply concerned over what has happened than the public is likely to be. Furthermore, management must convey the convincing impression that it is making extraordinary efforts to correct the situation.

The demands are such that crisis management has been added as a separate subject to public relations school courses, and it is offered as a special service by many of the large public relations firms. Companies such as Ruder and Finn, Hill & Knowlton, and the Richard Weiner Division of Doremus Porter Novelli offer complete programs that include training of personnel to handle crisis situations, developing complete contingency plans, and conducting fire drill rehearsals in communication damage control.

Being Prepared

The first step in developing these crisis management plans is to assess the company's area of vulnerability. This follows industry patterns. Airlines, for instance, have had crisis teams for decades to deal with crashes wherever they may occur. Most airlines train the city managers who represent the companies at each of their airports to deal with the immediate frontline responsibility in the event of a nearby air disaster. In addition, most airlines have special disaster task forces set up that are ready to fly to the city at a moment's notice. One typical company employs such a team, headed by an executive vice president. Members carry beepers and can respond quickly to the call from a communication center dubbed the "war room," which is located in the headquarters city. Such a team is far more than just a press relations group. It includes people with extensive industry experience. Familiar with the policies and practices of the company, its equipment, safety standards, maintenance practices, and so forth, they are empowered to deal with the immediate problems resulting from the crash. This same knowledge and authority also enables them to deal with the press intelligently in a reassuring manner, which shows they are in control of the situation. The task force is even knowledgeable enough to field many of the insurance and liability questions.

The relative predictability of this kind of disaster makes the airlines a somewhat special case. However, pharmaceutical companies, chemical companies, and financial institutions each have their own particular areas of vulnerability. But virtually any company can be subjected to some unpleasant, unexpected crisis. In fact it is not unusual for a company well prepared for one type of crisis to be blindsided by an entirely different but equally difficult situation. Whether it is an unexpected, catastrophic explosion or the criminal prosecution of an executive involved in questionable business practices will change the specific handling of the situation, but almost any preplanning will improve a company's chances of riding through the problem with less damage.

Along with the assessment of company vulnerabilities, the formation of a task force usually takes place early in planning. The task force is composed of employees with the skills and experience to handle anticipated problems. This group must be headed by an executive at a sufficiently high level to speak and act authoritatively for the company, who is empowered to make on-the-spot decisions without going through long lines of internal communications. All members of the team should be judged not only on their individual skills and experience, but also on their ability to work well under stressful conditions. Good endurance and a stoic nature can help people deal with the often round-the-clock work involved. Public relations firms that offer such guidance will work with this group, setting up situations to test their ability to handle the communication aspects of the disaster. They will conduct simulated press interviews with members of the crisis teams, often surprising the team members with unexpected additional events and revelations designed to add a lifelike quality to the crisis drill.

Classifying the Disaster

Although many press relations principles remain constant for different kinds of catastrophes, there are some differences. It is well then to identify the exact nature of the problem early in the course of the event and to notify top management immediately. This is particularly important in order to avoid the common fault of underresponding. There is a tendency on the part of some employees and managements to underestimate the extent of a catastrophe in its early stages. What appears to a plant manager to be a simple leaky pipe within the plant, which causes a few sore throats and an afternoon off, may, when viewed from an outside perspective, seem far more serious, and, in fact, the incident may well escalate in a few hours to a major news story. This can occur on the strength of what "could" have happened even when the event itself caused little real damage. In other words, potential disaster counts as news too.

The Cataclysmic Event

When disasters are characterized by considerable loss of life, are of an unusual nature, or are a first of a kind event, such as those at Bhopal, Three Mile Island, or Chernobyl, they will make headlines around the world. When these disasters involve community and employee casualties, their horror and drama, and the physical and emotional suffering all contribute to major and sustained news coverage. The long clean-up and settlement time and the resulting litigation can easily extend the problem for years. Such events are as catastrophic to the companies involved as to the community, not only through directly related costs but also in management's all-consuming involvement. The disaster takes precedent over the company's regular activities, which will suffer.

Such events establish their own ground rules. Precedent setting, they frequently bring new legislation, product changes, plant and manufacturing modifications, and new employee training programs, as well as changes in organization structures and management.

Some forms of catastrophe occur often enough to be almost routine. Airplane crashes, train wrecks, and highway and mining accidents would all fall into this category. Most fires, floods, and, increasingly, chemical leaks are no longer surprises and have lost a lot of their newsworthiness. The intensity of the press coverage depends largely on the extent of the damage and on the slowness of the news day. Should a cycle of similar events be taking place (for instance, the third crash in a few weeks), expect more coverage than modest damage might otherwise warrant.

Product Malfunction

When resulting in death or serious injury on a widespread or potentially widespread basis, product problems can be just as dramatic as cataclysmic explosions and accidents. Once again, the unusualness of the problem contributes to the newsworthiness, as does the degree to which the problem is bizarre. Such a problem was caused in the early 1960s by the drug thalidomide, which resulted in grotesque infant deformities. The fascination with the horror added to the unprecedented press attention.

In this type of disaster it is not just a question of the number of accidents and deaths involved, although that is of course important, but rather of the potential for damage the product malfunction presents. Contamination of a widely used analgesic or food item is much more newsworthy than a similar contamination of a less frequently used drug or an exotic gourmet food, particularly if the item is distributed only in a small region of the country. A distinction should be made between product malfunctions that are inherent in the product, such as poorly designed cribs that allow entrapment of a child's head, and product malfunctions caused by malicious tampering, such as razor blades or broken glass in candy or foods. The manufacturer who finds his products have been sabotaged in some way is, of course, ultimately in a much stronger position. While the initial impact of the news may be extremely detrimental, the role of the company "as also a victim" makes the rebound from the problem easier. The customary and correct reaction to this type of situation is usually to recall either all shipments of the product in question or by specific coded batches. Such an approach is expensive; it should not be made even more costly by overreacting or by making the recall seem to be an admission of product failure if it has not been. If it is clear from the outset that tampering has occurred and that it may be widespread, then there is no choice but to recall until more facts are in hand. Then react as strongly and forcefully and quickly as you can afford.

Compare two different successful handlings of two tampering crises, those of Johnson & Johnson's Tylenol analgesic and of Gerber's Baby Food. The Tylenol tampering was the earlier case, and it struck the public as virtually a new form of terrorism. Several deaths were traced to cyanide-laced capsules. Tampering had clearly occurred somewhere between the manufacturing and retail level. Throughout the incident, Johnson & Johnson reacted quickly, taking the lead in removal of the product, advertising to replace unused product or refund money, winning sympathy and respect from the public and the trade for what obviously was a very costly but highly ethical method of handling the incident. Later, tamper-proof packages were introduced. After a second wave of tamperings more than a year later, Johnson & Johnson abandoned the capsules in favor of tamperproof capsule-shaped tablets, known as caplets.

Gerber's was faced with complaints that glass was found in its Baby Food. Complaints were reported to have reached 250 in thirty states. Gerber's chairman was quoted as terming the problem largely a "media event." The company did not rush to remove all the product. It carefully analyzed the manufacturing and shipping process. Working in close cooperation with the Food and Drug Administration, it determined that the complaints were unfounded and that many were false. In the meantime, the governor of Maryland, Harold Hughes, acting on the strength of the earlier public complaints, had ordered the product removed from the shelves. In response, Gerber filed a $150 million suit against the governor for damages. The FDA's Commissioner Frank Young was quoted as saying, "We've been through the plants with a fine tooth comb and found nothing to suggest any glass was introduced in manufacturing." Gerber's resistance to the panic was justified. The authoritative third party endorsement turned the tide.

Gerber's strong resistant position, so different from the Johnson & Johnson action of quickly removing the product, was prompted in part by experience. A similar problem had occurred at Gerber's in 1984 to which the company later felt it had overreacted in removing the products. At that time, it recalled more than a half million baby food jars and then began to advertise that the products were indeed safe. It was later discovered in that case that there were actually instances of glass breakage that occurred in shipment far down the distribution chain and possibly in the home. The extensive press coverage was blamed for many fraudulent complaints. Consumers were shown actually to have added glass themselves to bring suit.

It is clear that the more rapid the evaluation of the product problem, the better because this allows for a more appropriate response. Such an evaluation must of necessity take into account the size of the corporation. For instance, Procter & Gamble, with extensive product lines at stake, acted quickly and dramatically to remove Rely tampons from the market without question, although there was considerable controversy about whether an actual relationship existed between the product and toxic shock syndrome, with which it was associated. A smaller company might have had to think twice about withdrawing an important product that would represent a major part of its revenue.

In contrast to these more dramatic cases, the recall of automobiles, trucks, tires, and even airplanes for modification have become relatively routine. Damaging to the maker's reputation, yes, but today no longer the headline makers they once were.

Specters from the Past

Whether as a result of avarice, innocence, or ignorance, waste contaminants buried in landfill years ago are seeping out to confront scores of manufacturers in today's environmentally conscious society. Asbestos, which once seemed such a benign protector against fire, now is considered a villain. Though it may not be entirely fair, society judges the past by the standards of today.

Undoubtedly, advancing technology will someday reveal the foolhardiness of many seemingly innocuous products and practices of today. Again the newsworthiness of these disclosures will be almost in direct proportion to their novelty and the horror and human suffering involved.

These cases tend, however, to be slower-breaking stories, somewhat more within the control of the company than the events discussed in the preceding section. Although the liability implications of these problems can be tremendous, the company at least has a better opportunity to take the lead in handling the story properly. Knowing their areas of vulnerability, their own technologies, and their manufacturing processes, companies are frequently in the best position to see where future liabilities may arise. By dealing with these before they become newsworthy, getting their facts together, and positioning themselves correctly, companies can minimize the damage to their reputation. In short, discover the problem yourself and announce it quietly, *but* announce it along with a clean-up plan—or an environmental restoration program. Don't present the problem without the solution, and put the emphasis on the positive actions the company is taking.

Criminal and Unethical Business Practices

"Once trust is lost, it's like a bird that has flown out the window—very, very difficult to get back," says Kent Druyvesteyn, who was hired by General Dynamics as part of its long battle to regain public confidence. He likens the effect of charges of dishonesty in a corporation to the empty feeling many people have experienced when someone for some reason no longer trusts them.

Large, well-established corporations that have been successfully following the same policies and practices for years seem most vulnerable to this form of disaster. Certainly the better known the company is, the more a criminal charge will be headlined. An executive for General Dynamics was quoted years ago as not being concerned about the company's public image. After all, as he put it, the company has only one customer and that's the government. Somehow it had been forgotten that the government is responsive to the public, not only through the legislative body but through the military as well. All that has changed at General Dynamics, which is now making a major communications effort to restore trust.

The very success of companies in following long-established practices may lead to these practices being carried to extremes. This can turn an acceptable if somewhat sharp practice into an unacceptable, unethical, or even criminal act. The practice of giving a corsage or token souvenir to an admiral's wife at a launching can graduate into extravagant gifts that are viewed by the outside world as a payoff. What may start as using the time it takes for a check to clear as a minor advantage (not an uncommon practice by much of the public when considering the "float") can, when carried to extremes, become the subject of criminal charges, as it did in the case of E. F. Hutton.

Up until the 1970s multinational companies often quietly and grudgingly accepted the fact of life that ethical business standards in other countries were quite different from those in the United States—that payoffs and bribes were as natural in parts of the Orient, South America, and Africa as taxes. The American public disagreed, and legislation specifically addressed to that point backed up this improved moral stance. Consciousness-raising situations such as the Watergate affair have raised the level of ethics in the business community. So too have the more fishbowl-like conditions in which companies work. Although undoubtedly new dirty tricks are being invented all the time, many of the old ones seem to be disappearing.

When these malpractices are part of a corporate culture, the companies get no more than they deserve. The best advice to you, dear reader, if you work in such a culture, is to consider a career change. Usually, however, these transgressions are of an individual nature, not condoned by management. In fact, they often are a shock to management when they come to light. Executives under pressure from quotas and lulled by the rationalization that others do it can be caught up in practices that they feel are in the company's best interests as well as their own. Some of the most painful interviews in business occur when management confronts an executive whose criminal actions were taken more on behalf of company interests than his own. What should the company stand be when it is faced with this kind of misguided loyalty? The company will pay an extremely high price in almost every area of its activities if it allows itself to be put into a position where it seems to condone the offense of an employee. There probably is no "disaster" that can strike a company quite like that of appearing dishonest. The lack of trust of customers, the community, and employees that this engenders is devastating.

Quiet dismissal is usually the only choice management really has in dealing with a dishonest executive, one who is in a position to have "known better." The American Ethic still requires that the guilty be punished for their sins. This does not mean creating a scapegoat—that approach can be quite transparent. A quiet dismissal, with a financial severance commensurate with the real transgression in human terms, relative to the standards under which that management operated, is probably the fairest solution and is adequate for most transgressions in the public's mind.

When the ethical problem appears to be more widespread as a company practice, singling out and dismissing the perpetrators may be impossible or impractical. Instituting an ethics training program, as General Dynamics has done, has much to recommend it. Although the press may at first depreciate this activity as window dressing, nevertheless when reporters are invited in to see the extent of the training programs themselves, they lose much of their skepticism. This comes not only from the sheer effort the company is making, but from a better understanding of the subtleties involved in exercising good ethical judgment under various business conditions. Once again, candor plays a big role. In this case, a willingness to accept the reality of past transgressions and evidence of the sincere effort being made to change will, given sufficient time, allow the damaged reputation to heal. But the scars can be very long lived, much as the criminal record of an ex-con is lived down only through continued aboveboard living.

In situations where the transgression is clearly unanswerable, a technique unheard of a few years ago seems to be taking hold—a public apology. Contrary to the old, cynical view of never apologizing, in the summer of 1987 Toshiba and Chrysler both did just that in ads that ran extensively in the American press. In an ad headlined "Toshiba Corporation extends its deepest regrets to the American people," and signed by Joichi Aoi, president and chief executive officer of Toshiba, the company apologized for the serious impact of its TMC divisions' actions on the security of the free world. The Chrysler ad was headlined: "Testing cars is a good idea. Disconnecting odometers is a lousy idea. That's a mistake we won't make again at Chrysler." This was signed by Lee Iacocca. Both companies seem to have recognized the American characteristic of forgiving those who have made mistakes if they admit those mistakes. Much of the damage to company reputation comes from protracted attempts either to cover up or excuse what is clearly inexcusable. The public anger is more often directed against the attempts to wiggle out of a situation in what appears to be a dishonest way than against the event itself.

In such situations, it is probably best to admit that a mistake has been made, be contrite, and explain what actions have been taken by the company to assure that such transgressions don't happen again. If the legal liability situation allows for this type of open-handed handling, it has great merit in its ability to end a painful period for a company quickly and to allow the company to go on with its business.

Rumors

If you don't think rumors can be an expensive disaster for a company, ask Procter & Gamble, McDonald's, Warner-Lambert, Squibb, Xerox, and Lifesavers. Each has had to deal with unfounded rumors involving either the company or its products.

Some rumors can be traced easily to malicious competition. For instance, when Stroh's beer was rolling out its distribution from the Detroit area into the Southeast in the early 1980s, the company discovered that its product was being referred to as that "nigger beer" from Detroit. Competitive brewery truck salesmen were apparently spreading the rumor in groceries and redneck bars that the company was owned by blacks. A different bigotry rumor was used against Molson's of Canada, where in the West the company was being characterized as the Arab beer company. Responding to such rumors directly is to dignify the rumor, which it certainly doesn't deserve. On the other hand, the approach by Stroh's was choice, subtle, and very convincing. The company quietly ran a newspaper ad that had existed for some time but that coincidentally showed the Strohs family standing next to its firebrew kettles. The family members still own the brewery their German ancestors founded.

The Sun Myung Moon Unification Church has figured in a number of rumors concerning ownership of Genesee Brewery, Procter & Gamble, and the Entenmann Baking subsidiary (which at that time was owned by Warner-Lambert).

Management's initial reaction to many of these rumors is frequently to ignore them as ridiculous. In fact, many of them are so ridiculous as to be funny. After some months of trying unsuccessfully to squelch such rumors, however, management finds that they are no longer a laughing matter. At least one product owes its demise to rumor, namely, Spud cigarettes. Back in the 1940s, rumor had it that they were produced in a plant that had a leper worker. After a short battle they were removed from sale, even though there was no truth to the rumor.

Rumors should be examined in two phases. First, try to read the pulse of the rumor, check on its extent and how it may have started. Don't spread it or add to its creditability by fighting it in the open until it appears that the rumor probably won't just die on its own. At this early stage, responding by saying that the rumor is completely irresponsible and not worthy of comment is acceptable. However, even the most ridiculous rumors don't always go away. Take, for instance, one of the funniest but one not so funny to the company. It involved the Lifesavers company. The rumor arose in New York City among the junior set that Bubble Yum chewing gum contained spider eggs. Wisely the company monitored through telephone surveys the extent of the rumor. Eventually, the trade began to call the company for reassurance that the product was indeed spider egg free. When the press picked up the rumor and played with it in humorous articles, Lifesavers acted quickly and forcefully by presenting a classic advertisement headlined, "Someone is telling your kids very bad lies about a very good gum." Characterizing the rumor as absolutely ridiculous, the ad helped turn the trick. Characteristically, the rumor attached itself to the market leader, Bubble Yum. This is frequently the case—the number-one company or product in its field seems to become the target for rumors. In the case of a recurring, popular, fast food rumor—that "the hamburgers contain ground-up worms"—the rumor will change according to which is the locale's leading fast food chain.

One of the most publicized and persistent rumors centered on the idea of a satanic connection to Procter & Gamble. The evidence, according to the rumor, was the firm's logo, which showed the moon with a face in it and thirteen stars. Obviously witchcraft, said the rumor. Phone calls of protest threatening boycott poured into jammed switchboards. Presumably encouraged from fundamentalist pulpits, the flood continued for months. To track down the rumor Procter & Gamble used private detectives. The company sent personal letters to editors in the states in which the rumors occurred. It threatened lawsuits if these satanic accusations were continued. All this brought some relief; the problem would die down for a time, but in a few months it would arise again.

It is interesting to speculate what would have happened if the logo had been changed at the height of the rumor. Handled one way it might have appeared to be tacit admission of the satanic connection. Handled properly, however, it could well have ended the problem by presenting the change as a gracious act, simply changing something that was troublesome to some particular religious sect, making light of the accusation. Could fighting it have actually reinforced the view that a satanic connection was there, because Procter & Gamble was trying to maintain the symbol?

Some Basic Principles for Handling Problems

Public relations cannot resolve a crisis, nor will the sheer weight of words build credibility. Your management must understand this. You can't finesse the words or hope to write the great American press release and solve the problem. Words alone can't make the problem go away; that requires decisive management action. Nor can you indefinitely run interference for someone who wishes to ignore a situation. Ultimately, decisive management action is needed. You can, however, help management people arrive at the decision to correct the situation by appropriately interpreting the effects of their inaction on the public. You can teach your management personnel that if they want to be seen as responsible corporate citizens, they will need to act that way. The organization must acknowledge the Socratic admonishment to "be as you wish to appear."

Long-range considerations should outweigh short-term costs. I am indebted for many of these tips for Dennis J. Signorovitch, director of Corporate Information Services for Allied-Signal, Inc., who has managed public and community relations in many crisis situations. Regardless of what they may say, a great many American managers still think in ninety-day frames. The short outlook may not only affect capital investments or R & D spending, but it may also influence the way they handle a crisis. The company needs to balance the near-term cost of proper corrective measures with the public relations department's appraisal of the long-term cost in terms of public, community, media, and governmental goodwill if its commitments aren't met.

Deciding what to say in a crisis is not a passive experience. The department of public affairs or public relations must be willing to engage the operating managers, environmental personnel, and lawyers when preparing public statements. Frequently, the public affairs people are viewed internally simply as professional communicators. Certainly that should be the case, but it is not a question of merely putting into words the actions that other functional areas take in a crisis situation. Public relations must interpret for operational units the public implications of their decisions and actions. This is not a passive kind of chore. You have to question and probe and challenge the comfortable assumptions many managers or technical experts may be making. Technically sophisticated people and departments particularly will often fail to appreciate the perceptions created by their conduct or statements in the outside world. Public relations people need to assert themselves in this area.

The company always has the responsibility to communicate with employees. In times of crisis, this can be difficult, but it is also most important. Interpreting the crisis and its implications to the employees is vital because they are also members of the community. They are considered authoritative sources of information on the happening for their neighbors and friends. They are a medium in themselves, not just a public.

It is not necessary to respond to every lunatic accusation made during a crisis. It may even be counterproductive. When a protracted crisis, involving, say, a chemical leak or some form of contamination that threatens a community, normal everyday events may be interpreted as a direct result of the contamination. At such a time, even a dead bird or animal may raise suspicion or start a rumor. A poor crop of tomatoes in a local backyard may suggest environmental damage. Even a family with diarrhea can suddenly become a cause for widespread alarm. Unaccustomed to this phenomenon, you are likely to react and deny each of the rumors. Don't forget what Bismarck said (and he survived successfully for years through his political acumen): "Never believe anything until it is officially denied." Think twice before you add that credibility.

Media coverage of a crisis occurs on two levels: the event itself and then the handling of the event. At first, there is the account of what happened, how it happened, how many people were killed or injured, the reaction of the people to what happened. The second wave of press coverage concerns how the company reacts to the event, the handling of it. At this level the media will hand out grades, making such remarks as "the such and such company generally gets high marks for its handling of the crisis." The media is then likely to evaluate the handling in comparison with Johnson & Johnson's Tylenol case, the event at Three Mile Island, and so on. You have to recognize this, and not just respond to the event itself but strive to ensure that the response is perceived as a proper way to handle such a crisis. The actual response and the perception of that response are not exactly the same thing. There is substance and there is symbolism, or the handling of the substance.

Don't speculate. If you or the spokesperson does not have the answers to what happened, don't offer a variety of possible scenarios. Any one of these can be the basis for a horrific story in itself. Better no comment than to speculate.

Immediately assume the public's point of view. Try to anticipate the social impact, the seriousness to the community, the employees, and the industry. These should all be interpreted from the standpoint of the public. The newsworthiness of the event can usually be a surprise even for the most experienced PR person. The tendency will be to see the event from the point of view of management, downplaying its seriousness. It is safer to err on the side of taking it too seriously than to underestimate what the press can do with it.

Monitor the news. You have to know what the press is saying, so use outside sources, and in local events assign watchers and listeners to key media if you can't keep up with it yourself.

Speed is essential. Timing is all-important. Even a few facts about the problem early in the event will reduce the impact of the news. This is a principal benefit of having a plan and a crisis management team. Any delay in responding may be interpreted as coverup. This will start the company off in a position of assumed guilt from which it is more difficult to establish innocence.

Designate your hitters. Every employee is a potential interviewee for the press. They should all be briefed, with particular stress on avoiding speculation. Obviously the most credibility, however, comes from the highest management in the company. To some degree, the level of response is an indication of the importance management places on the problem. Although the public relations person should be the most adept at working with the press, the title that person holds brings with it certain suspicions that an attempt is being made to manipulate. You must evaluate that factor with the personality and presence of the available players. You may wish to designate a hitter. Avoid someone with the title of legal counsel. Far more effective with the press is a person with a direct knowledge of the products and manufacture of the plants, or of the products and the safety measures that are in place and the reassuring steps that are being taken to avoid problems. Again, such a spokesman should, however, be cautioned not to speculate beyond the facts he or she knows.

A crisis will not run its natural course if social activists are involved. Management frequently expects that the crisis will go away naturally. This reinforces their natural desire to do nothing. In some crises this works, but if activists are involved it probably won't, particularly if you have dedicated opposition. Here is a quote from an associate commissioner of the Food and Drug Administration for public affairs regarding Procter & Gamble's Rely tampon problem: "Throughout the series of events, we made

sure the press was notified so as to keep the story alive. We wanted
to saturate the market with information [on Rely]. We deliberately
delayed issuing press releases for a day or two to maximize the
media impact. There was quite a concerted and deliberate effort to
keep a steady flow of information before the public." Don't assume
the opposition is naive.

*When faced with a choice between saying nothing at all or
expressing the company's position, choose the latter.* At the outset
of a major event, obviously circumstances will dictate your response. You must, if you know them, explain the facts. Let's say
that three people have been injured. If you know that they are in the
hospital, say so. If there is a leak, say so and explain that it has been
stopped. But there may come a time during a protracted event when
there is a desire to respond with answers such as "We are
continuing to assess the situation," "We are waiting for reports,"
"We are looking into that." It is better to continue to give more
specific progress reports that restate the company's position and
dedication and illustrate it, maintaining the position that the
company is aggressively concerned and acting on the problem. To
do this requires the revelation of some findings. Complete candor
on this and your legal counsel's point of view are probably 180
degrees apart. It will be a balancing act. In today's litigious society,
moral behavior and honest intentions are not enough, but they are
still fundamental. Balance between candor and legal caution can in
part be worked out in advance if you have the luxury of time.
Remember, there is as much risk in underestimating what the press
can do with undisclosed information as there is in what the courts
can do with your disclosure.

Politicians respond to public fears. It is a responsibility of the
public relations department to make certain that company management understands this and acts appropriately. Important relations
will not just be with the press, but with local political figures too.
Much of management may be cynical about the motives of politicians. Usually their motives are quite simple and direct, however.
They want to respond to their constituents. Management may
assume that a politician won't listen to its views. This will make
management more defensive and antagonistic when dealing with
the political community. It will be public relations' job to overcome

this initial reaction—in effect, to humanize officials to management and to provide a setting in which they can work together for the public's good. "Negative publicity pushes the government into less flexible negotiating positions and can contribute to the long term costs to a company," says Brandy Mott, key Superfund attorney for the Washington office of Breed, Abbott & Morgan (in *Inside EPA*, January 4, 1985). He explains how difficult it is for a hazardous waste defendant to contain financial exposure without paying a severe price in terms of a public outcry. The attempt to limit the client's liability therefore may become self-defeating. . . . As he puts it, "every tactical move that invites bad press costs the defendant something in the long run."

Finally, *view a protracted crisis as requiring counterinsurgency tactics,* but this grows more difficult as it becomes harder and harder to sustain the effort. A prolonged crisis involves a kind of guerrilla warfare, particularly if activists are involved. The interest of management may wane. It's in part the responsibility of public relations to help sustain an ongoing commitment to corrective actions and a positive, frank, and assertive response at public hearings, with action groups, the press, public officials, and so forth.

A Postscript for the Press

Investigative reporters view their own efforts almost exclusively in terms of the effect their revelations will have on their audience. They are surprised when they are confronted with the effect their efforts have had on the companies they are working with. An interesting example of this was revealed by Neil Hickey, writing for *TV Guide* in their January 24, 1987, issue, on television's failures in reporting the *Challenger* disaster. He quotes Richard G. Smith, head of the Kennedy Space Center at the time, as saying that snide stories about aborted launches had created "98% of the pressure to go ahead with the ill-fated Challenger flight." Every time there was a delay the press would say, "Look, there is another delay . . . here's a bunch of idiots who can't even handle a launch schedule." Smith complained, "You think that doesn't have an impact? If you think it doesn't, you're stupid." Hickey stated that most TV journalists rejected the notion that such reporting and pressure from the press goaded and badgered NASA into the launch on January 28, 1986, that otherwise might have been postponed. He quotes CBS's Eric Enberg: "If somebody is paying that much attention to the press and what it says he is not my idea of the kind of person pushing the button if I am riding his spacecraft."

Similar rejections by others in the press of the idea that their influence could create pressure on a company or organization suggests a degree of naiveté on the part of reporters that is astounding. Press people seem positively amazed following an attack that their former sources and friends, whom they have cultivated for years, suddenly go mum or mutter, "No comment." They seem to forget that these sources have careers to protect and that, as human beings, they feel deceived. The public may eventually forget an incident, but the public relations person will not, and the adversary relationship is escalated. It seems there is an almost total lack of appreciation by the press for the effect some kinds of reporting can have on the subject. A company may indeed be pressured into actions that are not in the community's best interests.

12
Mergers, Acquisitions, Takeovers, and Divestitures

When whole businesses are added or taken away from an existing company, the existing image is immediately outdated. These changes also raise concerns about the future of the company's products, profits, plant locations, and future direction which worry major stakeholders. Just when communication is most essential to the company's new directions, most companies suddenly go mum. A kind of postmerger depression affects companies as employees become concerned for their careers and turn inward to deal with political realities.

The excuse given for the silence is that management is still working on how best to put the new pieces together. The company loses an opportunity to capitalize on the short-lived newsworthiness of the merger itself.

Advice is offered on how to work with the communication people in the newly acquired or merged company and how to get a new program launched quickly. The observation is made that acquired companies are more pliable immediately after an acquisition than they may be later.

While divestitures are usually handled quietly, the possibility is raised of turning this into an attractive news story.

The essentials of the role of communications during hostile takeovers are contrasted with those during the friendly merger.

Techniques for fighting takeovers are also reviewed.

Company halt! . . . About face!

Sound as many mergers, acquisitions, takeovers, and divestitures may be, they have created the confusion surrounding American business images, as they are presently perceived or misperceived by the American public. Every business unit added or subtracted to an existing corporation changes to some degree the reality of what the company is. The old image is, therefore, made inaccurate.

When GE sold its small-appliance business, it changed the reality of what the company was, from the way the public remembered it. Conversely, when that small-appliance business was added to the Black & Decker business, which was well known for hand tools, it changed the reality of that company as well.

Apparent as this simple logic is, it can be forgotten, overlooked, or ignored by companies in the throes of a business unit reshuffling. The fact remains that whenever product lines and business activities of a company are altered in an important way, the old perceptions of the company will be rendered to some degree obsolete.

Usually it is desirable to correct and update those perceptions as quickly as possible. In some cases, such as that involving GE and Black & Decker, continuing to use the former company name as a brand name may complicate the severance and acquisitions story. Although such problems are rare, they serve to illustrate one of the advantages to having separate brand names or business unit names that are different from the parent company—one of the few advantages. The separate branded products or business units are far easier to divest if they should become an unwanted part of the company's line of products. At least one divestiture/acquisition was reputed to have fallen through when Litton Industries could find no adequate solution to the name problem during its attempt to sell its microwave oven business to Whirlpool. Certainly that high-tech, largely defense business would have been more sharply focused without that one consumer product. And Whirlpool would have been a natural home for it.

Lesson number one, therefore, is don't be in too big a hurry following a merger or acquisition to dump the old brand or company names. Though there is economy in communicating a single name, consider holding company names as brand names, and even weak brand names, as possible secondary or promotional lines of products. There is some equity in even a modestly established name which gives it value. It is usually easier to rebuild a name than to start from scratch.

What makes mergers and acquisitions (M&As) such communication disasters in most companies is not that the complexion of the company has changed. It is that with few exceptions, just when the company needs to communicate most, just when the interest in the company is at its highest and the company could register important information about itself most easily, it generally goes silent, or, at best, it issues a few unenlightening generalities to make the press go away. Instead, the period during and immediately after a merger or acquisition should be looked on as a short period of opportunity in which curiosity about the company will make it relatively easy to communicate. It should be remembered too that this same period of time is one of major concern for customers, institutional and individual investors, employees, vendors, and plant community leaders, all stakeholders in one way or another in the company's activities. For a company to go silent during these periods of doubt is, therefore, more than just a waste of an opportunity to communicate. Silence allows serious erosion to take place in the attitudes and confidence levels held about the company by all those related to it in any way.

The reason for the frequently awkward silence by companies going through the M&A process is their unwillingness to say anything that might upset those involved or for fear of saying something that might turn out to be incorrect as the acquisition process continues. It's a period of nervousness. It is true that acquisitions and mergers occur before all the answers are known as to how the newly formed company will be structured and how it will operate. In large mergers, it may be months before all of the pieces and subsidiaries are reshuffled, combined, and the redundancies eliminated, when it becomes possible to make a clear and complete statement about the entire operation. But that is no excuse. No one expects a merging economy to have all the answers, nor would anyone be interested if you were to provide them.

There are usually more than enough clear outcomes of the mergers which can be communicated to provide a steady flow of information. Communication should continue at least at the pace of former communication during and following the merger. To go silent is to raise important doubts among those nearest and dearest to the company—the employees, the customers, and the investors.

What they don't know will hurt you. If you don't believe it, consider the possible scenarios.

> A customer for a high-quality line of products watches as that company is taken over by the manufacturer of a similar but low-priced line that is based on price rather than quality. Is the takeover going to mean a change in quality standards?

> An investor wonders how the debt is going to be serviced that was incurred by an acquisition. Should he or she hold the stock?

> A jobber wonders whether the discount structure he has enjoyed with one of the merged partners will be a thing of the past. Should he go to a third supplier? Or might he enjoy an improved discount from his combined sales of products from the merged companies?

> Will a valued scientist in R & D, concerned about his pet project, decide to take the offer from a competitor who seems more clearly dedicated to this line of scientific inquiry?

> Will a salesman concerned with redundancy decide to take the opportunity and move his close customers to a competing firm?

Make no mistake, mergers and acquisitions are a trigger mechanism for change on the part of employees, customers, and investors. Silence will only make the situation worse.

So important is this need to communicate, just at the time when it is hardest to do, that any company that has an acquisition program should address the issue of how to handle the anticipated communication needs well in advance. Be sure your management understands the need for continued dialogue with the company's stakeholders. If this subject isn't addressed before an acquisition is made, the public relations director may find that he or she is the last to know. For obvious reasons, management people often hide out even from their own executives during these periods, and they may not consider how vital communications will quickly become.

If management is looking for acquisitions, it is probably to their advantage to increase the visibility of the company beforehand. A corporate advertising program should be considered that addresses

investors and customers. When acquisitions are made, those acquired will want to be familiar with their new parent. It is an
advantage if they have a favorable impression of the company right
from the beginning. After all, who wants to be bought by some
upstart unknown that might do heaven knows what. If it is a merger
of equals, there can be advantages to being somewhat more equal
by being the better known of the two companies.

Some companies go silent during these periods to save communications budgets because it is clear from the outset that a change in
the company name after the merger will almost certainly have to be
made. This situation can occur in divestitures as well. This was the
case when Libbey Owens Ford sold its name, along with its glass
business, in 1986. The best solution to such problems is enough
advanced warning to plan and to implement quickly a new name
program, which is just what L.O.F. did. If a name change is an open
question that seems to be a protracted problem, consideration
should be given, in the case of mergers, to an interim name,
awkward as that might be. Usually this will mean simply a
hyphenated combination of names which later can be changed or
contracted. Such was the case when Houston Natural Gas merged
with Internorth to become HNG-Internorth temporarily, a name
that was later streamlined to Enron.

If it is so obvious that a name change will be needed, there is no
reason why communications should not be continued on an interim
basis by putting both names together and explaining it's temporary.
Sperry and Burroughs ran such ads before selecting the Unisys
name. In fact, during the Libbey Owens Ford divestiture, the
company's advertising explained the divestiture and signed off with
the slogan "We're Libbey Owens Ford, for a little while longer."
The result of this campaign was to highlight and make clear what
was happening at the company during a period when the audience
would be most receptive to such news—when the audience would
have its gravest doubts, and rumors would be flying. Later the
company employed a mock contest as a teaser for the name
announcement in their plant communities.

A stepped-up communication program, employing investor-
oriented corporate ads, may also be considered by companies
looking to be acquired or searching for a merger partner. Although

most acquisitions programs are set up to make a logical search of acquisition candidates, based upon carefully selected criteria, in the real world it is frequently the CEO's sudden awareness of a company, possibly through an ad that leads to a closer examination of that company's potential.

A company that has previously been taken private through a leveraged buy out (LBO) has probably also ended its investor relations program and much of its public relations activities with the investment community. It is even more likely to have ended any corporate ad program directed to that audience. If such a company wishes to be acquired again, it should restart its investor activities. If you are an investor, you might take note the next time you see such a private company begin a corporate ad program directed to the investment community. It is a bit obvious but is frequently a successful ploy for finding a buyer or for building interest in the company prior to a public offering.

Acquisitions

If you have advanced warning that your company is likely to make an acquisition, one that will be folded into your present company operation, check your stock of annual reports, fact books, identity manuals, and any other items such as films and tapes that will serve to introduce you, the new parent, to the newly adopted company. If a book exists on the history of your company, it may pay to have additional copies run off. Your most recent newsletter and major clippings concerning the company's more recent achievements will round out the collection. Select the material with the intent not only of introducing the company, but also of demonstrating that it has an outgoing, friendly culture. Re-examine any work you may have done on communication audits and edit a version of the audit questionnaire. This can be given to the new division virtually at the first meeting. The sooner the acquired company can begin to function jointly with you on projects in the communication area, the better. If the acquired company is allowed to function completely on its own following an acquisition, for any length of time, the habit can become ingrained. The acquired company is actually more pliable and usually more anxious to cooperate and change its ways in the beginning than after a protracted postmerger period. After a while, a certain guerrilla warfare mentality sets in to preserve the old ways.

In effect, do the dirty work early. If a name change must be made, an office closed, or people released, do it quickly. The entire process of establishing the new procedures and unifying communication policies should be handled early in the relationship. You don't want to be communicating as two different companies or, even worse, duplicating efforts and sending out diverse news.

At the same time, make every effort to learn. Adapt the best of the acquired company's policies and activities, the things that have worked well for it for a period of time. A nice balance must be achieved between getting the people from the acquired company to do things the way you would like them to be done and not seeming to dismiss summarily major components of their previous culture. Remember, however, if they are to adopt your culture, you are going to have to be a living model of what the culture is.

The communications people of the acquired company should begin at once to prepare stories about aspects of their company that would be of interest to your own employees. A final issue of their company newsletter can act as an introduction to your own company. The concept of continuing both company newsletters should be discouraged, but you could consider a new masthead to celebrate. The objectives should be to build one company, one esprit de corp, and to avoid the continuation of anything that prolongs the "them versus us" syndrome. Work to develop new common interests and shared accomplishments. Feature these in news stories as quickly as possible, reporting on the success of the merger at various levels. This will work well for internal communications and will be highly effective with customers and the investor public. The key is to *build new shared experiences.*

Don't forget the important priority of reassuring the new subsidiary's customers that the new parent will only improve things, and will contribute facilities and resources that will make possible even better products and relationships. Doubts of customers, at this stage, can be very expensive.

Mergers

A true merger in which both companies are more or less equal usually leaves both sides with more questions than answers concerning the communication function—principally, who says what. That must be settled first. Frequently these mergers of so-called equals turn out to have a winner who emerges only after weeks or months of interaction. Lack of clear early direction on who is doing what can be paralyzing, depressing, and destructive. Where the merger deal has been cut by a management that is a very small, tight-knit group, the communications director must insist on knowing who holds which card and where the merger of equals will eventually turn out, if communications are to proceed with some kind of rigor during the early and most crucial period of the relationship.

The initial step in a merger of equals is the establishment of task groups from both companies to work out the hundreds of unification questions that will arise in each business function. The communication function is no different. A task force should be formed to exchange information on virtually every aspect of corporate public relations, investor relations, advertising, and employee relations. If possible, it should be armed with the company background material mentioned previously, plus the results of communication audits, communications research, and advertising schedules.

When both sides have assimilated this information, it will be up to them to hammer out quickly an interim recommendation on how to proceed. The task force should then begin to work on the structure the new communications function will eventually use, as well as sketch out its major features.

It is possible that even before this early task force can begin to operate, stockholder ratification of the merger agreement will be necessary. Special stockholders meetings may be needed if the proposed merger date is too far from that of the next normal annual stockholders meeting. Normally, each side prepares for these meetings independently. However, consideration should be given to a joint document by the investor relations group in which the performance of both companies is shown, combined for some convenient time period, demonstrating how the company might have performed if it had been one company. If both stockholders meetings are held on the same day, consideration might be given to linking them together with closed circuit television to make it a special event.

The interim stage between the announced intention to merge and the actual consummation of it may be quite extended if Federal Trade Commission (FTC) approval is required or other obstacles arise. Continue to generate news. The press will normally be receptive, and indeed curious, about new details concerning the merger. Projections may be made as to how the companies might perform when combined, how the company's size and rank will change, what its anticipated market share should be. These projections can be complete with pie charts and schematics of new organization structures. Use all the material you can think of to maintain a more or less steady flow of factual information to maintain momentum. A number of companies have used advertising during this period to discuss the proposed mergers, with appropriate caveats that the approval is subject to stockholder review. Ideally, if a new name should be required, this time should be spent resolving this issue so that it may be announced in conjunction with the stockholder vote. The more of a special event this becomes, the better. Just be sure you know where the control of proxies lies.

Divestitures

Most divestitures are handled quietly. The news generated by them is usually left to the group or company taking over the company. If it is a leveraged buyout, if the company is being taken private, the group may, at least momentarily, not be especially interested in featuring it as investment news. This is usually handled in the form of a joint statement.

Exceptions to this low-key handling of divestitures exist, however. If Wall Street continues to look favorably on divestitures as signs that management is achieving a narrower focus for its business, major announcements of divestitures may become more common practice. Ways must be found, of course, to avoid injury to the company acquiring the business. What might be welcome news to investors that you have dumped a particularly troublesome and unprofitable part of your business could sound as if the company acquiring it made a mistake.

Takeovers

There is a big difference in the role of communications between a friendly merger or acquisition situation and a hostile takeover. In the former, stepped-up communications will help draw together the new components into a single cohesive company. In the latter, communication more or less ceases until the new management makes its desires known. All too often this will be the shakeup of the company into its component assets, which the raider saw as being worth more than the price of the stock he acquired. In this situation, all you can do is sit tight and see what the new boss wants.

The contribution good communications can make is in fending off an unwelcome raider. Ideally, this process should be started long in advance of a raid, and it means making all efforts to communicate anything that will contribute to the evaluation of the company's stock by the investment community. Raiders like to rationalize their activity as an effective weeding out of poor management that has failed to use assets sufficiently to have the value reflected in the stock, generally implying that the takeover candidate's management has been inept in its operation and in its strategic direction of the company. Often this is not the case at all. But it is entirely possible that a company has failed to impress investors with all the positive expectations that might legitimately be held about the future of the company. Efficient as market evaluation may be, it can only operate on the information made available to it. And if the investor relations job has not been adequate, the company may suffer by being undervalued. It is not just the performance of management but the perception held of the management's performance that dictates the value placed on it by investors. Communications' major function in deterring raiders, therefore, is most effective well in advance of the problem.

The role of communications following an unwanted tender offer for the company's stock will vary and will, of course, be directed by the CEO and chief financial officer in close harmony with legal counsel. But generally the first step, which should be taken as quickly as possible, is a letter alerting shareholders to the fact that an offer has been made and advising them to reserve any decision until you have ample opportunity to respond. At this point, any clearly unattractive aspects of the offer may be mentioned, but remember, the role of the letter is not to clarify the situation. Rather, it is to raise enough cautionary warnings and doubts so as to impede stockholders' precipitous actions. The letter is frequently accompanied by a copy of a press release, saying more or less the same thing. You, of course, alert the press to the company's concerns about the raider's offer.

Usually a second letter is sent out within ten days, and the second press release goes out with details and specific recommendations to shareholders on how management perceives the offer and what action it recommends should be taken by shareholders. The release and press interviews rely heavily on selecting those objections that seem best suited to deter action. If the company is widely held, or if much of the stock is held in street names (by the brokerage house) that cannot be accounted for, it is probably wise to express the problems resulting from such a takeover in an advertisement in the financial press, such as the *Wall Street Journal* and *Barron's,* as well as in key newspapers, such as the *New York Times,* and in local papers in areas where large numbers of stockholders are believed to reside. The employees, who themselves usually represent major holdings, should also be brought into the fray, along with union leaders, community leaders, and other groups likely to be affected by the proposed change in ownership.

As a rule of thumb, remember that the louder the screams of anguish by the target, the more uncomfortable and expensive the raider's job becomes. The more doubts, the more confusion, the better chance for maintaining the status quo. During such periods, those responsible for communication with the financial and public press should be in virtually daily contact and be accessible around the clock.

A Final Perspective on the Results of M&As on Companies' Images

When it is all over, the public and even a large majority of the stockholders will be left confused and unaware of who merged with whom, even of what companies were involved in mergers at all. A study conducted by BBD&O in 1986 among active stock investors asked this question: "To the best of your knowledge, in the past two years was (name of company) involved in a merger or acquisition? If yes, to above: What was the name of the other company involved with (name of company)?"

Nine major companies that had undergone highly publicized mergers were mentioned to the respondents. The study disclosed that on average more than 71 percent of the investors surveyed were unaware of the nine mergers and acquisitions that had all occurred within the preceding two years. For example, 72 percent did not know that Rolm had been acquired by IBM. More than half were not even aware of the Nabisco/R. J. Reynolds merger.

In the same study, it was also learned that even these active stock investors were confused and uninformed about corporate name changes. Ninety-five percent were unaware that Consolidated Foods had changed its name to Sara Lee Corporation. Ninety percent didn't know that Standard Oil of Indiana had become Amoco, and only 28 percent knew that International Harvester Company had changed its name to Navistar.

To go back to the statement made in the beginning of this chapter, mergers, acquisitions, divestitures, and takeovers are truly communications disasters. If you've been through one, don't look back; reshape the identity of the new company and begin projecting the new image you want the company to have. In most cases, you will be starting from the beginning all over again. That's the way it is.

13
Corporate Advertising—What It Is and What It Can Do

Used by about half of the Fortune 500 industrial companies, corporate advertising can be a highly effective tool for a variety of corporate problems and communication needs. Although one of the more expensive public relations tools, it can build recognition of the company and what it stands for more quickly than any other controllable force.

The term *corporate advertising* can mean different things to different people. It is best understood in terms of its major categories: issue, or advocacy, advertising; goodwill advertising; financial, or investor-related, advertising; sales-related, or market-prep advertising; and hybrid advertising. The latter may call on corporate advertising to accomplish any combination of these chores.

It may be used to address the entire population but more usually highly selective groups.

It can be an important cohesive force among employees and far-flung subsidiaries.

Once thought of as "soft kind of advertising," corporate advertising today is more often run for sales reasons than any other, particularly by companies making expensive, complex, or highly customized products that require great confidence in the manufacturer.

Corporate advertising is the major league of company image building. If used at all it will represent the major item in a company's communications budget. To do it correctly requires a commitment of resources that should be fully understood before plunging ahead. Part of that commitment is a willingness to stay with a corporate advertising program for an extended period of time. Except in isolated situations, one or two ads won't accomplish anything substantial. One- to three-year programs are more realistic. Another part of the commitment is executive time for working with an advertising agency in developing effective ads. Generally, corporate advertising requires more top management time and cooperation to develop than does product advertising. As an expression of the corporation's personality it should not be left up to the agency to establish but should reflect management's aims and character.

Variously known in the past as public opinion advertising, institutional, or image advertising, *corporate advertising* is now the general term for a variety of forms of advertising used by corporations for purposes other than the immediate sale of their products and services. Most corporate ad content focuses on the company rather than on its products and services, although corporate ads frequently use some product achievements to demonstrate the company's capabilities. Because advertising is as much a creative art as a science, the dividing lines are often blurred between the different types of advertising. As a result, research in the field is less than exact. However, all studies agree that corporate advertising represents between 2 and 4 percent of all advertising in the United States, and accounts for between $1.5 and $2.5 billion, depending on how you define the ads themselves.

An increased use of corporate advertising throughout the seventies and eighties led to its examination and identification as a somewhat separate part of the advertising business. It is, however, an ad form that has been practiced since the early twentieth century. Numerous examples exist of early bank, insurance, and telephone company advertising which belong in this category.

During World War II, "institutional" advertising, as it was then called, was widely used. Although few peacetime products were available for sale, many companies recognized that if they stopped advertising for several years, it would be difficult for them to regain their old reputation quickly after the war, since a younger generation of consumers would come into the market unfamiliar with their products. Evidence exists that those companies that maintained a public presence by using this form of advertising did rebound more strongly after the war. Apparently they had gained a share of mind that resulted in a greater share of market when normal supplies became available.

The term *institutional advertising* and the technique itself lost favor in the immediate postwar years in the rush to advertise products and services to a hungry market. Gradually, through the sixties and the seventies, the technique found more and more users. Today, just about half of the companies composing the Fortune 500 industrials and the Fortune 300 nonindustrials employ corporate advertising among their activities.

Larger corporations are far more likely to engage in corporate advertising than are smaller ones. Over 90 percent of the 100 largest industrial companies use it, while only about a quarter of the companies ranked from 300 to 500 among the Fortune 500 employ corporate advertising (see table 13–1).

This relationship with size is, as a *Harvard Business Review* article by this author on the subject pointed out in the March/April 1982 issue, not because the bigger companies have more money to spend, but rather because they have more problems and the efficiency of corporate advertising goes up as the scope of a company's operation increases. The more publics a company has to deal with, the more employees, the more diverse its core businesses, its plants, sales offices, and so forth, the greater the need for a

Table 13–1

Corporate Advertisers among Fortune 500 Industrials (1985)

Companies	Percentage Employing Corporate Advertising
Top 50	100
Top 100	96
101–200	52
201–300	45
301–400	26
401–500	16
Top half	73
Bottom half	24
Total 500	47

corporate advertising program to establish, identify, and integrate the company as a single entity with a clear mission in the mind of its important constituencies.

Not only are the larger companies more likely to employ corporate advertising, but their investment in it, individually and collectively, is greater as well. The average budget is about $1 million. Only a couple dozen companies have corporate ad budgets over $5 million. In all, corporate advertising has accounted for about 2 percent of all advertising over the years. Today that figure is closer to 3 percent.

In 1984 corporate advertising increased more than 60 percent over the previous year, a far faster rate of gain than that of advertising in general. These gains were held throughout 1985 and 1986 when it increased at about the same rate as other forms of advertising. Corporate advertising in 1987 showed double-digit growth although other types of advertising was down more than 4 percent.

Categories of Corporate Advertising

The term *corporate advertising* is so vague as to mean entirely different things to different people, even within the industry. For example, people at *Barron's* or *Financial World* magazine think of it in terms of advertising addressed to their financial audience. Such advertising's purpose is to attract and hold investors. The *Washington Post* or the *National Journal*, on the other hand, use the expression *corporate advertising* but think of it as meaning more the kind that discusses legislation and public issues. A third view is held by people at *Business Marketing* magazine or *Business Week* which considers it more a sales tool to be used principally to sell business to business. It is necessary, therefore, to divide corporate advertising into its basic forms in order to deal with it intelligently and to understand its dynamics. It can be categorized as issue, goodwill, financial, sales-related or market-prep, and hybrid.

Issue Advertising

Issue advertising, or advocacy advertising, as it is sometimes called, is used by both corporations and associations to present views on a variety of social subjects. These may be simply informational or they may be a public service, such as a General Motors advertising program that covers subjects like wearing seat belts and how to avoid the dangers of counterfeit auto parts. Similarly, some utility advertising warns of the need for care when working near overhead power lines, and telephone advertising warns that care must be taken during construction not to cut buried cables.

Issue advertising can also be quite controversial, such as R. J. Reynolds's program that argues for the rights of smokers. Some issue advertising is done to prepare the way for product sale. Defense contractors such as Bath Iron Works have advertised for the need of an enlarged U.S. Navy. The degree of controversy varies with the issue involved and the mood of the public at the time.

Issue advertising is actually far less frequently used by corporations than is commonly supposed. Because of its often controversial nature, it may get more attention than the media expenditures for it would otherwise warrant. Less than 5 percent of corporate advertising (that's only 5 percent of the 2–3 percent of all advertising) falls into this category. More companies choose instead to let their trade associations act as the lightning rods and engage in public controversy on behalf of the industry rather than directly attack issues related to their own company names.

Goodwill Advertising

Once far more popular, this form of advertising was sometimes called institutional advertising. That term became almost a pejorative in the advertising community, implying a weak, ineffective type of ad. It was sometimes also called feel-good advertising. It is usually a vague attempt by business to be loved by the public. Its use reached its peak in the 1960s and early 1970s. Today only a few companies such as Philip Morris, oil companies, and a few others continue to advertise in this form. The move away from this form of advertising is the result of more intense focus on bottom-line accountability for all communications in business today. It was the lack of provable benefit that gave this type of advertising a poor name.

Financial Corporate Advertising

More corporations employ corporate advertising to improve their perception among the investment community than for any other single purpose. Much of this advertising is in narrow media, however, so the amount of dollar expenditure against the investment community is not as large as other forms of corporate advertising, which address larger segments of the population. Corporate advertising to the financial segment has increased over the years for a number of reasons, the growth of the investment community being one. In 1986 there were more than 47 million stockholders in the United States. The competition for equity dollars has also increased, not only from other stocks, but from other types of investments too. Brokers who once dealt mostly in company stocks now offer a wide variety of financial instruments. This competition for their time has resulted in many corporations' going directly to potential investors with their messages.

In recent years, the relative importance of institutional investors has increased, but this has not diminished the importance of private investors. Today they are viewed as an important balance to the fund managers because the individuals hold their stock longer. They are more stable and do not have the need for quarterly performance adjustments for which portfolio managers are notorious.

Also included in this category is the stockholder advertising used by both sides during takeover battles.

Market-Prep, or Sales-related, Advertising

Although corporate advertising, by definition, does not feature products for sale, it does have an effect on product sales, particularly long-range. This seeming anomaly has contributed much to the confusion surrounding the subject. An enhanced reputation for a corporation has a decided influence on the purchase of its products. This is almost in direct proportion to how major a purchase the product is. Products that are complex, difficult to understand, expensive, and considered by the buyer a capital investment are sold on the strength of a corporation's reputation as much as on specific product advantages. This can be seen clearly in the continued extensive use of corporate advertising by financial institutions such as banks, insurance companies, and brokerage firms. Dealing principally in commoditylike services with little product differentiation, their success lies in the image they convey to the publics. Some of these financial companies refer to their campaigns as corporate, and others do not, although the content of the advertising may be very similar. Because of this, their advertising is not always reflected in published corporate advertising expenditure figures.

Market-prep advertising generally takes two forms. One attempts to modify the marketplace so that it will better accept the kind of products the company is known for. For example, Campbell Soup Company promotes soup as a nutritious lunch, knowing that a major share of the soup bought will be Campbell's. General Foods has promoted the idea of balanced nutrition, which includes sugar, thus helping make their cereals more acceptable. Issue advertising that promotes the need for a larger U.S. Navy is at the same time market-prep advertising: it prepares the marketplace for the sale of the product, ships.

The other form of market-prep advertising is more common. It attempts to alter the perception of a company to make it more acceptable as a resource for its products and services for which demand already exists or is expected to exist. In this regard, Levi Strauss has attempted to change its image to become an acceptable resource for women's dresses. And the Singer Company, like many other old-line American companies, advertises to change its reputation to become a participant in the high-tech marketplace of today. Overwhelmingly, the bulk of today's corporate advertising expenditure is of such a nature.

These are communication efforts by companies that wish to be perceived as appropriate resources for modern products and services that are in current demand. Some are to correct old images or are efforts to build new images where none existed before, such as that of CSX, the new name of the old Chesapeake and Ohio Railroad, which has now branched out into many other fields. For instance, Colt Industries no longer wishes to be identified only as a gun manufacturer. American Can advertised to become known for its financial services and specialty retailing as well as for its packaging, and finally took the direct action of changing the outdated image by changing the company's name. Coleman wants to be known for products other than just its lanterns. GenCorp (formerly General Tire) wishes to be known for more than its tires and even changed its name with that in mind. Virtually all of the chemical companies have now diversified and wish to be known for their higher value–added, more profitable pharmaceuticals and specialty products.

Although corporate advertising has sometimes been characterized as "optional communications that are dropped during recession periods," the market-prep form of corporate advertising actually appears to increase during difficult economic times. It becomes the substitute for at least some individual product advertising. These campaigns act as a backdrop to other efforts. They are often referred to as umbrella programs.

Hybrid Corporate Advertising

Also on the increase is corporate advertising that attempts to modify a company's image for multiple reasons. Usually it combines investor relations objectives with sales objectives. For industrial companies and those selling to business, this is a natural combination with a high degree of overlap between business and financial media. Furthermore, 60 percent of private stock transactions are made by businesspeople. The creative ad message to both potential investors and potential customers is often similar as well. The same advertisements for Allied-Signal, for example, which position the company as a resource for contracts and subcontract work in aerospace and the automotive field can also help position the company in the minds of the investment community. It reminds them that the company is working in industries that are viewed today with promise and that the advanced nature of the company's work makes it a good stock for future growth.

Uses of Corporate Advertising

Part of the increase in market-prep and hybrid corporate advertising by many of today's high-tech industries can be attributed to complexity of the products themselves. These are often customized and difficult to treat in individual product ads. This, coupled with short life cycles for the products, makes it desirable to sell the company rather than the product, whose features and intricate systems may be difficult to describe. This becomes even more desirable if the product may be outdated and superseded in a matter of months by the company's own new products. Many examples of this can be found in the heavy use of corporate advertising by computer and software companies.

Another pertinent use of corporate advertising today is by companies that want to maintain a share of mind while their new products are not yet available and when their existing product line suffers in direct competitive comparison. This is often the case in high-growth, high-tech fields with short product life cycles. Wang, Xerox, Savin, and the old Sperry company all switched on occasion from specific product ads to more general corporate ad campaigns while they appeared to be revamping their product lines. These corporate campaigns were then switched to new product launch programs when the company thought its products were sufficiently state of the art to compete in the public arena of competitive product advertising. Naturally, this in and out nature of the strategic and tactical use of corporate advertising adds to its image as an "optional form."

Basically, corporate advertising of this sort is used to close the gap between the reality of what a company is, or is trying to become, and the perception held about that company by publics that are important to it. Its use can become critical during periods of change, changes not only in the company but in society, when a company must alter its image in order to deal with the future realities of the marketplace. This problem is, of course, compounded in industries where the company's image dominates the purchase decision.

An example of this is found in the telephone industry. The long lead time caused by the protracted litigation prior to the AT&T divestiture enabled many independent telephone companies to reposition themselves well before deregulation to deal with the new telecommunications environment. Recognizing the drawback they would have with their "POTs" image (as insiders called a "plain old telephone" reputation), most even took the term *telephone* out of their names and reintroduced themselves to appear as exciting high-tech telecommunications companies (see table 13–2).

Following the breakup of AT&T, all seven of the new "Baby Bells" began corporate ad campaigns in their scramble for identity. Their problems at the time reveal much about the kinds of things corporate advertising is called upon to do. In brief, these newly restructured companies, in a restructured industry, first had to announce their existence to the investment community in order to hold on to the vast number of stockholders each had inherited from AT&T. The question uppermost was just how many telephone company stocks investors were willing to have. As of this writing, all seven of the Baby Bells have done quite well in holding on to their important following. These companies also faced a newly structured marketplace with new competitive forces suddenly presenting a confusing array of products and companies from which customers could choose. This proliferation of products, technologies, and companies combined to form an unstable and unclear picture of just how to do business in this new marketplace. The telephone companies with their old POTs image were at a disadvantage.

The seven regional companies at the same time had to form new and separate competing identities as regional holding companies for the smaller, individual state phone companies and to overcome the old telephone image. It was vital for these companies not to lose their major business customers in the transition. Their ads talked about individual company strengths, their capabilities, and the advantages their particular geographical location gave them. Each strove to present its state of the telecommunications art. All of this was addressed to both business and investors. To varying degrees, the success of these companies since deregulation speaks well of the effectiveness of their corporate ad programs.

Table 13–2
Changing Names in the Telephone Industry

Old Name	New Name
Continental Telephone	Contel
United Telephone Company	United Telecom
General Telephone & Electrics	GTE
Central Telephone	Centel

Trends and Current Practices

Although most of the principles and techniques employed in the use of corporate advertising have existed for the better part of this century, corporate advertising has undergone many changes in the last decade. As recently as 1982, the major oil companies were the largest users of corporate advertising, mostly of the goodwill variety. Much of this has stopped. Today automobile manufacturers and electronics and telecommunications companies are the largest users of corporate advertising. They employ it, however, for sales-related reasons. IBM, in fact, is credited with coining the term *market-prep advertising*. The American automobile manufacturers wish to enhance their image as quality makers in the face of the quality competition from abroad which enjoyed a better reputation for advanced technology and careful construction.

Before the oil companies in the 1960s, heavy industry was the greatest user of corporate advertising—for example, U.S. Steel, Bethlehem Steel, National Steel, Alcoa, Diamond Shamrock, Caterpillar, and National Lead. These have been replaced by the high-tech and electronics companies as the principal users of corporate advertising. Companies such as Eaton, Trinova, Parker, and TRW have changed dramatically in the last five years, concentrating on becoming more advanced in dealing with higher value–added products. These changes in their business have been communicated to both their customer bases and investors through their corporate advertising.

Joining the American corporate advertisers are more than seventy global marketing foreign giants, all using corporate advertising as a sales-related marketing tool. These companies use it to establish an identity for themselves in what is usually their major export market, the United States. These companies include Nissan, Toyota, and the other automobile companies, and Hitachi, Mitsubishi, Daewoo, Fujitsu, and Toshiba. Not only Japanese companies, but others such as Krupp, Siemens, Volvo, Ericsson, Northern Telecom, SFENA, and Aerospatiale are regular corporate advertisers.

Corporate advertising has also changed in look and tone of voice. Today it employs a variety of creative techniques that would have been considered too flamboyant for the staid financial and business community of only a few years ago. Today, through use of the New Wave art and animation, companies convey an up-to-date look. There is a somewhat greater use of cartoons and conversational copy to suggest a more human management. Today's advertising is more likely to talk about future directions and interesting innovative activities that reflect the progressiveness of management rather than it is to deal with charts and graphs citing the past achievements of the company. It is more likely to feature a relatively minor product that is exciting and innovative than to feature a company's duller products even though these may be higher volume and more profitable.

Corporate advertisers are increasingly opting for larger, more expensive space units. Several publications report that they carry more corporate spreads than single pages, more color than black and white. Consider these statistics from *Business Week* on the advertising they carry:

- 57 percent of corporate advertising programs are run as spreads, compared with 17 percent for all advertisers.

- 32 percent of corporate advertising programs are run as single-page units, compared with 61 percent for all advertisers.

- 11 percent of corporate advertising takes the form of multipage or fractional-page units, compared with 22 percent for all advertisers.

- 75 percent of all corporate advertising is four-color, compared with 57 percent for all advertisers.

Insert sections are almost commonplace. IBM, Daewoo, the Singer Company, Westinghouse Electric Corporation, AT&T, and several automotive companies have recently used multiple-page units.

Though corporate advertising demands a greatly increased corporate communications budget there is no doubt that under many conditions it is the only practical way to build or modify a corporation's image within a reasonable time frame. Let's explore just what those conditions are and when they may be cost effective.

14
Corporate Advertising—Should You or Shouldn't You

Each form of corporate advertising is examined in terms of conditions under which it is most appropriate. Included are questions to ask yourself about the company, your industry, and current situation in order to arrive at a cost-effective decision.

As a management tool, corporate advertising is highly problem/ objective related. It is not something to spend money on without a good idea of what you expect from it. The situation a company finds itself in at a given time will determine whether corporate advertising makes sense or not. Just as the problems of companies vary so do the objectives of the advertising. The form the advertising should take will be dictated by these objectives. The factors related to the need for corporate advertising may be examined systematically, or they may simply be "felt" by a sensitive management in a kind of visceral reaction to existing conditions. The fact remains that these conditions themselves will determine whether corporate advertising is an appropriate tool to use.

The differences are so great among the basic forms of corporate advertising—that is, issue, financial, image, or market-prep—that an examination of the conditions should be made separately when considering the suitability of each type of advertising. It is also possible that the combination of factors may suggest a hybrid type of advertising campaign.

The Decision to Conduct Issue Advertising

Issue or advocacy advertising is usually considered in response to legislative or other social activity that threatens the well-being of a company. Indeed, the tactical use of issue advertising is an important legal right of corporations that must be maintained. The ability to speak up and present business's side in a controversial situation is important not only for the company, but also for the public. It allows for a more complete evaluation of proposed legislation and social conditions in which all evidence is presented and views aired. Periodically, social scientists, politicians, or the press raise a concern that the deep pockets of corporations will be used to buy a public attitude on social issues which is not in the best interest of the people themselves.

In all candor, as a practical matter, there is little cause for concern. First, there is actually far less controversial issue advertising than is supposed. The ads that do run usually are limited to select audiences and appear only a few times at most anyway. Restraint by directors and stockholders, coupled with the rather tenuous relationship of much of this type of advertising to the bottom line, make it unlikely that any company will put large enough sums of money in back of truly controversial corporate advertising to accomplish detrimental social results. The effect of advertising on behalf of a controversial issue is frequently to polarize people and to nurture an opposition. The end result, therefore, is simply the increased exposure of the various aspects of a particular issue.

Far more prevalent is a kind of pseudo-issue advertising in which fairly popular issues are championed by companies. This is done to gain attention by climbing on a currently popular bandwagon, to give evidence of a company's social concern, or, even more frequently, to champion the favorite causes of the company's customer base.

Consider how noncontroversial most of the issues advertised are. Many are so bland as to be on the blah side and are largely public service in nature. A few examples: drive carefully, save energy, hire the handicapped, promote a clean environment, improve physical fitness, fight alcoholism, drug abuse, crime. Occasionally, what appears to be a nonissue can turn controversial if it seems to threaten the civil rights of some group. For example, encouraging people to wear seat belts seemed innocuous but is now looked on as having controversial overtones. Some consumer groups have fought the legislation in states where use is mandatory as an infringement on personal freedom.

Issues highly charged with emotionalism and controversy are wisely avoided by companies, abortion and gun control, for instance.

Between these extremes exist issues that, while somewhat controversial, are within advertising's capability to affect, even with its relatively low credibility factor. Such issues as deregulation, tax law reform, new legislation, or tariff questions fall into this area. Frequently these are issues the public sees as business related and therefore a legitimate subject for companies to discuss. A company may rightly think it is to its advantage to educate at least portions of the public on a subject matter that affects its business. Advertising can be used to state the company case precisely, giving it treatment that is beyond the regular press coverage. Generally these are subjects on which a company can constructively offer facts, analysis, and research findings. Sometimes companies are in a better position to provide such information than the press or action groups or even the government itself. Frequently, such issues are relatively short-range problems in which the advertising assumes a tactical role. But over the years certain industries, such as forestry products and chemicals, have had long-term social relations problems that they have eased through long-term, strategically designed educational programs that include advertising. One example is the paper company campaign in which wood was repositioned as a crop, a renewable resource, in order to counter the image of the forestry industry as a denuder of landscapes and a depleter of natural resources.

An appraisal of how environmentally sensitive the industry or industries the company is in must be made before the company entertains the idea of using advocacy advertising. On the one hand, if the industry is blessed with few environmental problems and is unlikely to be an activists' target, then there may be less need for corporate advertising than if the company is environmentally or consumer sensitive. On the other hand, it is also safer to use issue advertising under these conditions. Again, consideration must be given to whether the ads themselves may create an opposition group where none existed before or where one was only loosely organized. If this suggests that hiding is usually the safest solution, it's usually not. Advertising that can lay the groundwork to avoid foreseeable problems can be the safer course.

To be most effective, issue advertising should be based on shaping public opinion before it solidifies. This requires a constant monitoring of trends and an interpretation of events likely to occur that can affect the corporation. This can be seen most clearly in the anticipation of legislative problems. The question must be asked, Can educational work, including issue advertising, be conducted well in advance of the legislation in order to be sure that the decision makers are aware of the unfortunate consequences of new legislation or the benefits of new regulation? The timing can be exquisitely important in these situations. In some, a long lead time can allow for a relatively subtle laying of groundwork. In other cases, however, a carefully timed single blockbuster ad on the issue may be a more potent device. The former route is particularly desirable if the press is generally not knowledgeable on the subject. By being the first to raise questions about a specific issue a company can preempt a certain spokesman role. Companies that speak out on issues can anticipate more calls from the press as they express a willingness to share their views and go on record with information that contributes to the discussion.

In essence, therefore, evaluating whether an issue ad program is worthwhile comes down to weighing the benefits that may accrue to the company through meeting the campaign's objectives in terms of favorable legislation or accomplishing changes in social issues against the downside risks that a higher silhouette may impose.

Though the financial cost of running issue advertising can be considerable, it is generally not the deciding factor and is usually not as expensive as other forms of corporate advertising. Frequently appearing in black and white, using op-ed positions, the advertising may need to appear in only limited space addressed to key audiences for short periods of time. Do not fail to include in the equation the additional internal time that will be needed, not only to prepare the campaign, but to respond to the press and participate in a public dialogue on the issues.

The Suitability of Financial Corporate Advertising

Corporate advertising to the financial community can be an important tool for the financial relations officer. Although the efficient market theory holds that information is so broadly and quickly disseminated about companies that their stock values are all efficiently and fairly evaluated, there is little doubt that there are too many companies and too few analysts to assure fair and equal evaluation for smaller concerns. Advertising can stimulate an interest on the part of potential investors to ask their brokers about a particular corporation. These inquiries in turn stimulate the registered representatives to seek an analyst review of the company. The odds are good that an analyst review and subsequent report will be favorable to the company. Some studies have shown that up to 90 percent of such reports are on the positive side. Further, it is clear that when a new analysis is prepared on a company it stimulates action on that account.

It is doubtful that analysts themselves gain much additional direct information from the contents of corporate ads. The type of ad showing financial performance is less frequent in today's more sophisticated climate. Instead, today's ads are more often used to show the direction a company is going in. These feature the positive moves management is taking to make the company a better investment. The very fact that the company is advertising itself, portraying itself as doing exciting and interesting things, is a positive signal to analysts that the company is self-confident. Usually this type of advertising is written to the general investor level. It is assumed that brokers, analysts, and portfolio managers will read over the individual investor's shoulder.

The changing marketplace, which has placed so much more equity in the hands of professional fund managers, has led many investor relations directors to downgrade the need for this form of advertising. This attitude is understandable, particularly from the investor relations directors of smaller, narrowly held companies.

They hold a view that sees the number of influences limited to only a dozen or two pension and fund managers who are close to the company and major holders in it. These relationships are carefully nurtured in frequent one-on-one contacts by the investor relations executives. Since they view their role in these terms, it is understandable that a relatively expensive item such as a corporate ad program would seem far less productive to an investor relations executive than would additional meetings, analyses, or staff. Add to this the widely held belief, nurtured by a desire to seem professional, that fund managers and analysts disregard corporate advertising, and it is clear why so many corporations leave advertising out of their investor relations program. However, they may be wrong.

In the increasingly competitive scramble for equity dollars, it is doubtful that companies can ignore the communications advantages of advertising without suffering a penalty. The vastly increased number of financial instruments offered to investors, and the competition for the registered representatives' time and analysts' attention, suggests that despite the arguments against advertising of this sort, it can be worthwhile when conditions are right. At least a dozen proprietary studies have shown that analysts as well as fund managers read and act upon, and in fact appreciate, corporate advertising that provides the kind of information and view of the company they believe is valuable. The financial publication *Barron's* employed Erdos & Morgan to do such a study of their own, which *Barron's* has published. The relevant finding was that about three-quarters of the top fund managers considered corporate advertising at least somewhat effective.

Despite this positive view of such advertising, it is by no means a remedy for weak P-Es. It must be remembered that the standard financial indicators for a company will outweigh any ad program's effect on stock. In general, you can't drive up the value of a stock past its legitimate worth through advertising. However, the stock can at least be raised to its proper evaluation if it has been suffering from misperception or if it has simply been lost in the maze of offers.

In general, these are the factors that should be considered as influencing the decision to use a program of this sort: if capital formation needs are great, even the relatively small percentage contribution that effective financial advertising may be able to make can be very helpful to the stock price, bond issue acceptance, or credit ratings. When a large number of stockholders is involved or borrowing is high, this contribution can be appreciable.

A corporate program might be considered if an inordinately low price-to-earnings ratio exists, lower than that of peer companies, suggesting that the company has been overlooked.

The health of the company should be good enough to result in positive reports by analysts before starting such campaigns. Once the campaign is running the situation is somewhat different. A continuation of an existing campaign during difficult times is highly desirable if it is affordable. Calling attention to yourself with a new program in hopes of overcoming financial problems may simply be aggravating the problem with more attention.

If the company has changed its direction sufficiently to create a gap between what it is and how it is seen by the investment community, corporate advertising should be used to change the perception.

If the corporation has changed names or stock symbols, this, of course, should be announced. A logical extension of the announce-ment advertising is a series of ads explaining the corporation's new direction.

If the chance of takeover is high and there is a desire to avoid it, there may be a role for corporate advertising. However, beware because it can also call attention to a company and increase its chance of being put into play. Generally, advertising as a deterrent is a long-term tool. A new campaign for a severely undervalued company may have the reverse effect, that of signaling it as a buyout candidate. At least one company known to the author has found a buyer by employing just such a strategy. Remember, as a simple quick fix to drive up the price of stock, it is unlikely to help.

If acquisitions are a consideration, corporate image advertising should be considered as a means of acquainting the business community with the company. Such ads can make clear in advance the advantages the holding company offers as a parent. This may help minimize strain following an acquisition, and it helps famil-iarize employees of the company with their new owner.

Advertising of a tactical nature may play an important role during merger, acquisition, and takeover plays. Obviously during these periods extreme sensitivity exists. It hardly need be emphasized that close communication should be maintained with corporate counsel.

The Decision to Conduct Market-Prep Advertising

If the objective is the immediate sale of specific products or services, advertising directed specifically to that aim is almost invariably more effective and more cost-productive than the more indirect market-prep approach. The market-prep form of advertising described in the previous chapter becomes the advertising method of choice under rather special conditions:

1. *When a product is unavailable or in short supply or for some reason it is desirable to maintain or capture a share of the market's attention in anticipation of future sales when the product becomes available.* These conditions exist during wartime shortages or glitches in production. They also can exist during periods when existing products have become outdated in relation to newer competitive products. In these times of catch-up until advanced products are in stream, it may be desirable to switch from specific product advertising to maintain a presence and to whet public appetite for the new products when they arrive.

2. *During times of recession, when the competition has reduced its advertising pressure, it may be desirable to step up market-prep advertising to gain share of mind in order to rebound more quickly when customers are once again able to buy.* This particular aspect of the effectiveness of market-prep advertising has been noted in several research studies carried on through the different recessions since World War II. Recognition of this is reflected in the most recent recession when advertising failed to dip to the extent it had in earlier recessions. The competition is learning that market-prep advertising may take the form of umbrella campaigns for a wide variety of related products or lines. This technique is favored in recession periods as a cost reducer, replacing separate product ad

programs with a simple, less costly (albeit possibly less sales-effective) umbrella ad campaign.

3. *Market-prep advertising is also appropriate for repositioning a company as a suitable resource for a new line of products not previously associated with it.* Such advertising can extend the identity of a company to encompass other related industries or even entirely new categories. Generally, however, there is little to be gained from this indirect approach if product advertising for the new category can carry the communication assignment on its own.

4. *Another particularly useful form of corporate advertising to prepare the marketplace is advertising directed toward changing the public's buying habits in some general way that will favor the type of products the company makes.* To be effective, the company should be a major, if not principal, supplier of the product type in order to benefit through the increased popularity of the class of product. As was mentioned earlier, the advertising stressing the nutritional benefits of soup automatically benefits Campbell's, which has a major share of this market. Frequently, issue advertising such as that previously mentioned for Bath Iron Works which encouraged a stronger U.S. Navy has the effect of helping to prepare the marketplace and is certainly sales related. The form it takes happens to be issue or advocacy advertising.

The Decision to Use Goodwill Advertising

It should be clear from previous comments about this form of advertising that the author has difficulty in identifying conditions that make this type of advertising a cost-effective tool. Most people wish to be loved and the executives who guide major corporations are no different. Their favorite causes may suggest themselves as the bases for corporate ad campaigns. Companies may benefit from a close association with a particular public service activity, and may wish to further identify with it and encourage others to join through advertising. Such advertising is more a decision of the heart than the head and to an extent of whose heart is involved. Self-serving advertising, however, that sets about stating the altruistic activities in which a company is involved and that has the express aim of making the company more popular is, as far as the record goes for such advertising, surprisingly lacking in results. Such campaigns may generate quantities of mail and win approval from executive peers, but in the author's experience, research conducted specifically to learn whether attitudes toward the company have changed for the better show generally disappointing results.

The Suitability of General Image and Corporate Identity Advertising

The objective of a campaign may simply be to raise the awareness of the company, or to establish a reputation where none has existed before, or otherwise to correct or modify an erroneous view about the company. Sometimes this is done without specific goals in mind. In some cases, it is done for multiple reasons, and a kind of hybrid advertising may be employed. For instance, it may be expected to improve the company position on Wall Street and among its customers and in Washington, or with it, employees and other important publics. These multiple objectives, when added up, can make the corporate ad campaign an extremely productive tool. Multiple objectives, however, can also weaken the discipline that should be used to evaluate the results of the campaign in relation to its specific goals. Nevertheless, goals should still be set for each audience.

The decision to use this kind of multiple objective corporate image advertising may come down to the question, Is an improved image worth the expenditure? That is a deceptively simple question but one very difficult on which to provide proof. It should hardly seem necessary to have to explain the advantages to a company of having a widely held favorable reputation. Perhaps for that reason, relatively little research work exists providing evidence one way or the other.

Two studies have made a serious attempt at proving the case for corporate advertising. Both are tainted somewhat by having been sponsored by interested companies that have used the studies for promotional purposes. Both, however, appear solid in their format and the results are highly credible. The first and more ambitious of these is now a dozen years old. At that time, it was reported to have cost almost a million dollars. It was a national study by Yankelovich, Skelly & White for *Time* magazine, the Phase Two Study. It shows the effect of corporate advertising on sixty-four major corporations. Some of these companies were large product advertisers while some were not. Some were large corporate advertisers and some were not. Familiarity and reputation were both enhanced when corporate advertising was employed, whether product advertising was used importantly or not. Most important, supportive behavior by important publics was improved as well. Specific questions were asked regarding whether respondents would support a particular company on social issues or through legislative changes, whether they would recommend the company to a prospective employee, whether they would purchase its products, the stock, and so forth. Those companies with corporate ad programs consistently ranked higher by impressive margins.

The newer study was conducted in 1986 by Brouillard Communications, a division of J. Walter Thompson Company. It surveyed senior executives in major American corporations and financial institutions. Produced by Yankelovich Clancy Shulman, the research was designed to find quantitative answers to the "what does it get me" question so frequently asked about corporate communications. It determined that when a company is perceived as a winner, its good reputation means increased marketability of shares and that it helps sell the company's new products among this affluent audience. The research showed that the company is more attractive as a business partner, more likely to be recommended as an employer, and more likely to be welcomed into a community. Like virtually all such studies, it found that familiarity breeds favorability. Among all audiences, if a respondent thought he or she knew the company well, he or she was much more likely to rate the company a winner—four and one half times more likely, to be exact. As James H. Foster, president of Brouillard Communications, put it, "A company may have all the makings of a winner, but if that company isn't known, it won't reap the tremendous benefits perceived winners enjoy. After all, without knowledge there can be no informed evaluation."

When considering this type of campaign, some of the questions that should be raised include the following:

1. Is the corporation's present reputation already identified by nationally advertised products carrying the company's name, or is the company more or less invisible, represented only by brands with their own separate identities?

2. Are the company's products low-priced packaged goods, bought pretty much on impulse, or are they high-priced, considered purchased products, which depend heavily on the reputation of the parent company to consummate a sale?

3. Is the company in an industry that depends on securing the absolute top scientists and graduates to maintain its competitive edge? Does the company's current reputation among this group attract or detract? Does it need correction?

4. Is the company a service business in which a corporate ad program can show employees in an idealized work role? Would it help if the advertising set the standards for their meeting the public or for producing quality products?

5. Is the company's current reputation poor because of some past performance that has long since been corrected, yet the old image lingers on?

6. Is the company in an industry subject to unexpected or unwanted disclosures? If so, it may be appropriate to begin a corporate image program in advance so that the public's first introduction to the company is not some unwanted, bad news. An established positive reputation can help companies ride through the difficult time.

Program Announcement Advertising

If you underwrite public broadcasting or provide grants for other public performances it is generally productive to support these efforts with so-called tune-in advertising, which is supportive print advertising giving time and station of the program and featuring the underwriter's name. The rule of thumb encouraged by PBS is generally to spend a dollar on tune-in ads for every dollar of underwriting. This seemingly generous allowance for such program promotion is in fact of double value to the underwriter. Not only is the audience for the show increased, but just as important, the identification opportunities are greatly increased through the use of tune-in ads. Even with so-called enhanced underwriting, which now allows the employment of nearly commercial-like messages, the ability of viewers to identify properly the underwriters of shows is surprisingly limited. This inability of the public to tie show and sponsor together goes back even to the early days of radio and television when it was common for complete shows to be sponsored by one company. The tendency is for large, well-known companies associated with such sponsorship to be played back in this research out of all proportion to their actual participation. As a result, it is not uncommon to see Exxon, Mobil, and Gulf, for example, being credited in research studies with the underwriting of programs they have either ceased to be associated with or in fact have never underwritten.

When the underwritten shows are editorially very compatible with the company's aims and marketing direction—for example, an outdoor show sponsored by a sporting equipment manufacturer, or a science show by a high-tech company—the opportunity exists to use show content illustrations in the tune-in advertising (see chapter 8).

Some caution and common sense is necessary in not overplaying the promotion of clearly public benefit types of shows or celebrations in order to avoid the appearance of milking for the company's benefit what is fundamentally a donation.

Name Change Announcement Advertising

Virtually every company making a name change advertises to its major publics, generally to the investment community, if it is a publicly held company, but at least to its customer and potential customers. These announcement ads in many cases are extended into longer-running corporate ad campaigns. The news opportunity of the name change is often used as a peg for supporting the company's structural changes or for showing new directions that the new name suggests. The advertising can also serve as a kind of pledge of the company's continued commitment to product quality, service, and policies that might otherwise be in question as a result of the alterations the name change seemed to signal. The ads to the investment community may concentrate on the change of stock symbol or may simply include that information in the body of the text.

When the change is a result of a merger, the ad offers a chance to state the mission of the newly formed corporation, its objectives and ambitions. These ads can be an opportunity for a high level of imagination and creativity. There are of course as many ways to announce a change as there are changes to announce. An examination of many of these ads collected over the years reveals a relatively limited number of recurring strategies:

1. The name change is minimized as the least of the changes that are occurring within the corporation.

2. That the corporation outgrew its old name is a strategy frequently used when a company decides to drop the industry designation as well as simply shortening it.

3. The name change is announced as though a brand new company were involved, but already a billion (or whatever) dollars in size or number one in the industry.

4. Announcements of acquisitions or mergers are sometimes positioned as a company's doubling in size or in some way making a giant leap in industry position.

The many uses of corporate advertising can cause confusion. You must continually keep in mind the objectives you are after with your own particular ad campaign. One way to take some of the mystery out of it and to keep your ad campaign on target is to understand the ad strategies that are available to you, which is discussed in the next chapter.

15
A No-Nonsense Approach to Corporate Advertising

There are about fifteen corporate advertising strategies. By combining elements of different strategies you can account for virtually all of the corporate advertising today.

By having a basic understanding of these various strategies, an advertiser is in a far better position to work with an ad agency to develop a distinctive ad campaign.

The strategies are explained and candid appraisals offered on how each works.

I f you start by knowing what you are trying to accomplish with an ad campaign, you will be well ahead of most companies that are considering starting a new program. Be sure these advertising objectives are firmly understood by your agency people.

If they are not certain about what you are trying to accomplish, ad writers are likely just to listen to what you, as the client, want to say about your company. Then they try to put that down in print or on television in as interesting a way as possible. The trouble with that approach is that corporations usually try to tell things to the public that may be important to the corporation—but about which the public couldn't care less. The chief executive may be fascinated with the things he is doing with his company. But unless there is a way to show the reader or viewer what is in it for him, you are going to have a very dull ad.

Tell the agency people, "This is what I want to happen." Not "This is what I want to say." If they are any good they'll take it from there.

Lacking reader benefit, the writer is forced to invent all sorts of copy and visual devices to achieve some interest. When these devices are extraneous to the subject—and they frequently are—the advertising is weak.

One way to tackle this problem is to recognize at the beginning the strengths and limitations of the created strategy you are following. Here is kind of a tool box of creative approaches. You can look over each approach and see which seems to fit what you are trying to accomplish. There may be more strategies but so far fifteen seems to account for most of the corporate advertising that is running today.

Many ads combine features from two or more strategies. You will see that some of them lend themselves to more interesting advertising than others.

1. *"You don't know us but you know our brands."*

This is a favorite of corporations that market a lot of well-known consumer products under names different from that of the parent company. The logic of the approach is irresistible to certain corporations.

As they see it, "Here's our company with all these household name products. If only the world [particularly the world of investors to whom the ads are generally addressed] knew how important we are, it would be terribly impressed. In fact, just the sight of all those familiar packages plus the fact that they all come from us should be news of interest to a lot of people."

Well, it's news up to a point. And up to a point the strategy can work, provided that expectations for the ads aren't too great.

It may actually be worthwhile to acquaint the financial community with the corporation's impressive array of consumer products. But research shows that people are not going to come away remembering the products you make or you the next time they see

---

The identification of these corporate advertising strategies was begun in the author's book *Corporate Advertising, the What, the Why and the How* in 1981 and later refined into an August 1984 article in *Business Marketing*.

those familiar products on the shelf. And forget the idea that this type of ad creates some kind of magic synergy that encourages people to buy other products in your line.

2. *"Look what we're doing for humanity."*

This type of advertising was very popular in the late 1960s and throughout the 1970s. It occasionally produces some very emotional and high-interest ads.

But do they accomplish anything? Few companies today still spend money in an effort to be loved by the American public. Look at the general lack of success the oil companies have had on that score.

The usual criticism for this creative strategy is that it's obviously self-serving and has virtually no credibility. Unless you can thoroughly disguise this technique either as a public service message or as an announcement of an interesting new product that coincidentally also helps humanity, stay away from it.

3. *"Here's what humanity ought to do for us."*

Advocacy, or issue ads of one form or another, usually promote viewpoints of direct interest to the corporation. Deregulation or changes in tax or tariff laws are frequently subjects, but the ads can discuss other public issues, from health to business manners.

The degree of interest these ads achieve is almost directly proportional to the public's interest in the subject itself. The more controversial it is, the more readers the ads attract.

A few companies, notably United Technologies and Mobil Corporation, have made such extensive use of the technique, particularly in its op-ed form, that it has become part of their respective corporate images. They have developed reputations as outspoken corporate citizens.

Be prepared to become pen pals with thousands of readers if the ad subject hits a nerve. If it doesn't, you'll have some of the most boring advertising in the United States today.

4. *"Here's how we're in the news."*

The late Bill Bernbach used to say, "If you have some news, don't get in its way. Put it out there and use it because it's potentially the most interesting thing you can offer a reader."

Obviously, it's difficult to develop a whole campaign around news. But you can look for it and take advantage of it when appropriate. Set up an infrastructure in advance involving the ad agency and key corporate people so they can act quickly when newsworthy events occur. This can lead to one of the most effective forms of advertising there is.

5. *"Here's how we restructured our corporation to fill your needs."*

Ever since chief executives discovered the joys of redeploying their assets, they have been fascinated with the vast improvements they've been able to make in their company's efficiency and productivity. (In fact, U.S. industry is a lot more efficient today than we give it credit for being.) Therefore, it's tempting to advertise that to the world, or at least to the financial community. But if you use this approach, be prepared to wrestle with one of the dullest strategies on the list.

The basic problem is that nobody gives a damn how you built your company unless you can describe it in terms that are meaningful to the reader. In the case of the financial community audience, this means illustrating or in some way demonstrating that your new structure is going to result in profitable growth.

6. *"You don't know us, but we're in everything you use."*

This is a very old technique employed by the manufacturers of hidden products, materials, and components. It's a particular favorite with industrial companies deciding to go public with their message for the first time.

There is one problem with it: Who cares? Another is that if you feature your component as being in a very famous product, readers may remember that product instead of yours.

7. *Featuring company products.*

More and more corporate advertising is taking this route. Companies whose products are excellent in and of themselves promote those products as examples of the quality, service, innovativeness, and potential profitability of the corporation.

The inherent advantage in this strategy derives from people's natural interest in products. That gives the corporation the chance to speak in terms of user benefits. Computer, telecommunications, and other electronics companies, as well as automotive and financial companies, all enjoy an opportunity to use this technique.

Frequently it's hard to distinguish this kind of corporate advertising from product advertising. The difference lies in the ads' underlying intent, something that may be clear only to the advertiser himself. So to make the technique work, the ads should feature products that illustrate important characteristics of the company. They should not feature products simply because of their sales or profit potential.

8. *Featuring laboratory developments.*

You can call this the "our company is higher tech than yours" strategy. And there's little wonder that it's particularly popular at the moment.

Other than through acquisitions, the future growth of most companies largely depends on their ability to stay ahead of the technological competition in their fields. It's a great technique for companies with exciting new product developments on the verge of introduction.

The trick is to feature newsworthy developments without being so predictable and blue-sky that you lose all credibility. Another problem is selecting R & D work that's newsworthy without tipping your hand to the competition.

9. *Championing your customers' pet public issue.*

At first glance, this looks like issue or advocacy advertising. But when you examine it more closely you'll see it's really market-prep work. It supports your customers' own interests and shows them that you're on their side.

The approach is particularly popular with companies that have government contract business. Promote public defense and you make it easier for a weapons appropriation to go through.

If you're selling cement, promote building or road repair. If you're selling housing materials, promote lower interest rates to improve housing starts. There are many versions; this strategy can be very effective. How exciting the ads will be depends on your execution.

10. *"Continuous dividends since 1492" (or the year of your choice).*

Use a lot of bar charts in these ads and you'll be talking to the investment community just the way everyone else did a few years ago. Thank goodness this kind of advertising seems to have passed its zenith.

Sure, having a solid dividend record is important. So are twenty-one other financial indicators that an investor should examine, if he has any brains. He'll get them from his broker or an annual report anyway.

Advertising is simply the wrong vehicle for that kind of data. Ads are better used to talk about future plans, products, and growth opportunities. Look forward not backward when you talk to investors.

11. *Using an outside spokesperson.*

The theory, which was more popular a number of years ago, is that the positive image of the spokesperson can be transferred to the corporation. A well-known face may attract attention, particularly on television, but this technique often is an ineffective cop-out.

The price of good talent and the difficulty of finding someone well known, with an appropriate image, is greater than you think. One version of the approach uses a different spokesperson in each ad. If the person is a recognized expert in a particular field, his or her persona can have the effect of a testimonial for the corporation. But even Bill Cosby didn't pull it off for E. F. Hutton.

12. *Using the CEO as spokesperson.*

Is there a CEO anywhere with a soul so dead that he hasn't wondered if he couldn't be another Lee Iaccoca, or at least a Frank Borman? Just remember that for every Lee Iaccoca there's a John DeLorean who was doing his own sports car commercials before the roof fell in.

The CEO obviously is a powerful weapon, appropriate for very serious problems where great credibility is needed, perhaps to discuss the need for an important rate hike or to speak out on a legislative problem. But if you're not careful, he or she may convey the impression that the corporation is in trouble, which is when most CEOs speak up.

Don't confuse this approach with using the CEO as a product representative, such as East Coast chicken farmer Frank Perdue or ice cream store franchiser Tom Carvel. Their unique public personalities, developed through advertising, transfer distinct images to their products—a far different task from transferring a CEO's image to an amorphous conglomerate.

13. *Featuring an employee.*

Featuring one or more employees can be a better device than using the outside spokesperson, if the employee represents the intended message. Frequently, the employees appearing in ads are engineers or scientists who can illustrate the advanced technology of the company. But Plain Joe employees can work as well.

A peripheral benefit is that in some cases the internal effect of the ads can be worth the price of the campaign. Featuring an employee can generate interest in the company and employee pride. And when the featured employee becomes a role model for work or performance standards, the ads can actually improve productivity.

You may lose a few newly made celebrity employees to the headhunters, but it is rare.

14. *The "don't count us out" technique.*

This is a strategy no one willingly employs. But as more companies have faced bankruptcy or other massive financial problems, they've turned to this approach to instill confidence in their stockholders, bankers, and creditors.

Its effectiveness depends on the content and credibility of the case made. And that can be dangerous. For one thing, you're spreading the bad news among investors who might not have been all that aware of the problem.

Credibility is difficult to achieve because you may be accused of protesting too much. Then too the ads themselves can be used as a weapon by unions and creditors who, in all likelihood, will attack the advertising as an extravagance. They won't recognize that the campaign may in fact be in their own long-term interests.

Whatever you do, don't keep on protesting that everything's fine once the problem is over. Don't remind people of the past. Look to the future and talk about all the good things coming up.

15. *Dazzle 'em with opulence.*

When all else fails or when there just isn't a clean-cut strategy, you'll have to fall back on the same old technique that corporate advertisers have been using for years. If you must tell the readers all those good things about the company which the readers don't give a damn about, use gorgeous photography, luxurious color (silver as a fifth color has been very popular lately), and multipage insertions, at least spreads.

Yes, those techniques do work to a certain extent. You can buy your way into the reader's mind.

But if you have a choice, reexamine the strategy. You may find that a change can make your advertising a lot more effective.

Good luck and call if you need help.

16
Globalization

Globalization is the current buzz word among multinational corporations searching for ways of standardizing their product marketing and advertising throughout the world; it is used in countless articles and books. Everyone knows it's where the world is going—but no one is quite sure how to get there.

It has been observed that the level of standardization is highly dependent on the nature of the products involved. The more universal the product and just how it is embedded into each culture appears to be a primary factor. The more universal, the more upscale the product, the more likely standardization is practical and desirable.

Corporate advertising by its nature presents a universal product, the corporation itself. This must be seen as consistent. Usually addressed to upscale audiences, particularly the financial community, corporate advertising must be standardized in order to present a consistent corporate persona. On the other hand, public relations efforts handled from afar can be a disaster. Local execution of plans originating from headquarters, but well controlled, is a partial solution.

Implementing standardization of communications successfully demands that much attention be paid to the interchange of ideas and information between headquarters and its subsidiaries to form a global point of view.

A generation of business has found success in decentralization— that is, in establishing each of its divisions and subsidiaries in the United States and overseas as a more or less independent profit center charged with responsibility for its own bottom line. With this responsibility has gone much of the communication authority to achieve the necessary sales goals. In general, it is entirely reasonable and proper to allow each subsidiary the freedom of communication to fit best its own local marketing mix. In another trend, a number of worldwide competitive pressures have combined to make greater standardization of products, marketing, and advertising an attractive goal for many large companies.

Much of the popularization of this view of the future must be attributed to Marshall McLuhan, with his concept of the global village, and to Prof. Ted Levitt of Harvard, who wrote a convincing argument for standardization on a global basis in 1983 in the *Harvard Business Review*. Today *globalization* is a buzz word and a subject demanding the attention of marketers worldwide.

Global standardization is an attractive goal and frequently it is competitively necessary for multinational companies because of the obvious economies of scale that result from standardization of product manufacture. It also can make possible the profitable exploitation of smaller specialized products that might not otherwise be able to support advertising and promotional pressure in smaller countries.

For example, the Henkel Chemical Company of Germany had an assortment of adhesives and tapes with both industrial and consumer applications which individually appeared to offer no immediate worthwhile return for any one of the company's European distributors to promote. By tackling the problem of packaging, display, pricing, and advertising as a Pan-European project, the company was able to provide a cohesive line of products, which in aggregate offered good profit to dealers and distributors alike. This would not have been possible if the marketing had been left up to individual subsidiaries. The adhesive products would have been left in disarray, neglected because each subsidiary saw the line only for its very limited contribution potential within its own market. This is really the major incentive for standardization—the goal of globalization is the ability to do things of value to the company and ultimately to its various subsidiaries and divisions which no division or subsidiary would ever be motivated to do for itself.

Globalization—How to Get There

Although large corporations generally agree that globalization is where things are going, they are frequently at a loss as to just how to get there.

This drive for globalization is encouraged at the advertising level by ad agencies that have themselves merged into enormous international giants. They have found globalization a wonderful rationalization for their own merger expansion. In theory, matching a network of company subsidiaries worldwide with ad and PR agency offices worldwide would seem the perfect structure to embrace the global village that everyone agrees lies just ahead. A rationale given for moving rapidly in this direction includes competitive reasons and getting ready for the direct broadcast satellites, which will enable advertisers to broadcast the same message in different languages throughout Europe simultaneously.

A look behind the scenes of this race to globalization, however, suggests that newcomers should move with a great deal of caution. It could be deceptive just to look at some of the few globalization successes such as Coca-Cola and assume that such standardization can follow for your own products. Most successful globalization has taken years to achieve. In the case of Coca-Cola, the initial globalization impetus was massive, in the form of the U.S. Army's presence in Europe at the end of World War II. In effect, that amounted to a successful sampling introduction of an ethnic food on an almost worldwide basis. It was a unique situation, impossible to duplicate today.

There are also limitations on the degree of standardization that is practical for different types of products. Consumer nondurable products, for example, often have to be adapted to local taste. Some products, such as food, are embedded in each culture and are subject to more variations country to country than are durable products that are found outside the home, like automobiles.

The more research and engineering development involved, and the more high-tech the product, the more effort a company usually makes to standardize the product globally to help affect the scale

economies. We find, therefore, durables somewhat more standardized country to country.

When it comes to industrial products, worldwide standardization becomes even greater. It is also true that standardization
becomes more acceptable the more upscale the audience or product
may be. In fact, some products lend themselves very well to
worldwide similarity: airlines, credit cards, banking, and insurance.
All target upscale audiences and by their nature are more likely to
benefit from and, in fact, need standardization country to country.

Advertising tends to lag well behind how standardized the
product itself may be. Obviously the first obstacle is the language
difference. Here we see that industrial advertising enjoys an advantage because English has become the language of business. The
scientific, technical, and most industrial journals, and business and
financial publications have important worldwide English-speaking
circulations. Industrial advertisers often run a basic campaign in the
English-language publications and let it go at that. They know that
English is the language of business today. The decision-making
executives, particularly in high-tech industries, stay abreast of their
field today in English, not German.

Dozens of multinational corporations in banking, insurance,
and other financial fields that wish to tell their story to investors
have campaigns that are largely, if not exclusively, in English. The
Wall Street Journal Asian and European editions, the *International
Herald Tribune,* the *Financial Times, Fortune* overseas edition, and
The Economist can reach virtually all major investing groups
around the world, regardless of the country. Add to this the
English-language editions of *Time, Business Week,* and major
vertical publications, such as *Aviation Week,* and you can frequently
do an important portion of your communication without leaving
the mother tongue. You at least have established a core around
which you build country by country.

The Consistent Corporate Identity

Debate over the degree of standardization that is appropriate for
various products and services should not even exist when it comes

to corporate advertising. A company cannot be a different company everywhere it operates. You cannot change to suit each country. You need a consistent persona.

Whether it's in your public relations effort or a corporate advertising campaign, the identity of the company must be presented as a single entity. Generally speaking, the advertiser should neither hide the company's nationality nor flaunt it. Attempting to be highly national can be as great a mistake as attempting to take on too much of the local color. The corporation must be itself.

This position on the need for a consistent corporate identity becomes very clear when you consider the investing public, which is so frequently a major audience for corporate communications. Investors want a solid, consistent character in the company they put their money into, so do other stakeholders, employees, and professionals.

Nothing demonstrated the close interrelation of the world's investing markets more clearly than the 1987 stock market crash. A look each morning at what had happened on the Japanese, Hong Kong, Australian, and British exchanges was an essential beginning to anticipating the day's activities on the New York market. It is one world as far as investing is concerned today. Even if a company is not necessarily listed on all exchanges, the company's investors may be located anywhere in the world.

The need for consistency can also be seen whenever a corporation's customers and trade consist of an audience that is upscale and highly mobile. Travelers notice ads and signs from their home country when they travel. When these have a similar look and are compatible with what such travelers are accustomed to, it builds respect for the size and solidity of the corporation. When these look different wherever the travelers go, it diminishes the image they carry away.

Though it may be apparent that corporate advertising must be standardized, it is not always so apparent how to go about it.

Investor programs should certainly be implemented from headquarters. The English-language financial press may be adequate. However, you may wish to add local newspapers, which have important business audiences, particularly where the company is listed on that local exchange. This too can be directed from headquarters, but use the assistance of the local investment house, or public relations firm, which can provide both copy and translation assistance.

The Relationship between Headquarters and the Subsidiaries

In cases of corporate ad programs whose objective is sales related, the worldwide campaign should be controlled by headquarters but only with *adequate* input from the subsidiaries.

The decentralization of American corporations has created a provincial mind-set among employees. Those who work in subsidiaries are frequently nationals whose careers and futures are built primarily within their individual countries. Understandably, they have a point of view that is different from that of headquarters. People at subsidiaries and divisions tend to see the differences that exist between themselves and other subsidiaries and between themselves and headquarters. What may be more difficult to accept is that people at headquarters in most American companies are hardly any more global in their outlook than are those at subsidiaries. Decentralization has tended to isolate headquarters from the subsidiaries' local decisions. Depending on fairly formalized reporting systems, people at headquarters seem to focus on the similarities of subsidiaries. At the same time, the subsidiaries are seeing the differences. Gradually, as corporations develop new structures to deal with this problem, a more global mind-set will result. This will need to include career paths that involve experience in other subsidiaries and at headquarters and compensation methods that will reward a more global point of view.

Until this becomes a reality at all corporate levels, the best solution is as full an exchange as possible across subsidiary lines and up through headquarters on subjects relative to communication. To pull this together, frequent exchanges of input at a high level is essential. The executives in charge of communication at each subsidiary must have a good understanding of corporate global objectives. Equally important, they will need to provide the input to the corporation that assures that headquarters understands each market, its needs and peculiarities. This interchange requires effort and plane travel and group meetings, possibly rotated, so that over time, subsidiary personnel become familiar not only with headquarters, but with other major business centers.

Corporate ad and communications programs developed by a headquarters that worked hard to seek out subsidiary input become a response to this input. The ads become a response to the local needs as well as to the parent company's. Subsidiary cooperation and support goes up. As a guiding principle, the amount of cooperation the company is likely to get from its subsidiaries is about equal to their input and participation.

It is also important to understand that part of the decentralized, provincial mind-set includes the well-known "not invented here" syndrome, particularly if a subsidiary has been doing its own corporatelike advertising. The subsidiary is then likely not to support the headquarters' corporate campaign locally. In fact, executives at the subsidiary are likely to say the corporate campaign is a waste of money and inappropriate for their market and to develop what are sometimes amazing rationales for not using it in their own country.

Consider the subsidiary executive working with his local ad agency. He has come to know, trust, and be influenced by his agency. The local agency executive has worked hard to encourage and promote a locally prepared corporate ad program. This local agency support usually dries up when the creative work is done at the corporate level. One thing any local advertising person will tell you is that he can do it better than headquarters. Even though locally placed corporate campaigns prepared by headquarters require less work for the local agency and may even generate more income for it, the local agencies are traditionally resistant.

There are really only three ways that a corporate ad campaign or advertising of any sort will be used by subsidiaries in any way that will conform to the desires of headquarters, at least with any degree of consistency. The first method is through directive. As was stated earlier, not too many managements of today's decentralized companies are willing to tell their subsidiaries what they must do as part of their marketing mix; that would relieve the subsidiaries of too much responsibility. To give them a directive to run a certain campaign allows the subsidiary, in the event of a profit shortfall, to point to the advertising and say, "That's the problem; I couldn't do what I wanted to do."

In its early years, the Polaroid Corporation was growing rapidly internationally under the very strong hand of Dr. Edwin Land. At the same time Land's unique camera and film was frequently in short supply. The company was able to enforce a policy, written into distributors' contracts worldwide, that made it obligatory for distributors to run the advertising provided by headquarters. It is a rare company today that enjoys such a position even with its own subsidiaries, let alone distributorships.

Some companies attempt to set down directives stating that no corporate advertising may be run except that provided by headquarters or unless the advertising follows tightly described rules. Predictably, the subsidiaries will respond by simply not running any corporate advertising.

The second approach that works is of course for headquarters to pay for the advertising, including the local media. The problem here is that it is sometimes to the disadvantage of the company for tax and dollar exchange reasons actually to pay the media bill out of its own budget.

It is usually more practical to take a third route, which is very effective in gaining subsidiary support. This is to allow a subsidiary so-called bottom-line relief, or bottom-line protection, that media expense will be taken into account when evaluating the subsidiary's "performances." It is important that the subsidiary's executives not lose bonuses or fail to make quota because of a corporate ad expenditure. Remember, running the corporate program is as much in the interest of headquarters, and possibly of other subsidiaries, as it is in the interest of the group running the local campaign. Solve that personal financial problem for them and compliance will soar.

In all cases, it is customary for headquarters to pay production costs on headquarters-prepared ads, but this is an insufficient incentive by itself for most subsidiaries to use the ad material consistently.

As the mega-agencies and public relations firms are quick to point out, it is a great help if all the subsidiaries work with local agency offices that are part of one ad agency or public relations network. But do not count on the agencies to be policemen. Expecting local agencies to control what your local subsidiaries do is not as realistic as it seems. A corporation's communications are not going to be any more standardized than what the company sets out and works to achieve through its own structure and policies.

There is usually surprising independence among individual ad agency offices and, if anything, even more rivalry, in which the "not invented here" syndrome flourishes. One major advertiser uses this competitive spirit within his agency's European branch offices by staging a yearly competition in which the new creative campaign is selected from the local work done by each of the agency's subsidiaries.

Normally, for an American company the American office of the ad or public relations agency acts as the agency of record, or lead agency, exercising at least a modicum of control over the branches. An alternate version of this is possible through the concept of regio-centric handling. In this concept a European branch office is selected to act as the focal point for all of the European offices. The practice works similarly in Asia and in South America. Since it uses an office more accustomed to working with branches and companies within its own region, this arrangement can be a practical alternative when standardization is limited to a modest group of countries. This arrangement also works well when there is a lead subsidiary within a region to work closely with the lead agency.

There is only one exception to the clear case for the centralization and standardization of corporate advertising. This is in the very small subcategory called issue or advocacy advertising, which on some occasions may be required locally. Avoid it if you can. It is not used as frequently in Europe as it is in the United States, and it is almost unknown in Asia. It is also tricky to handle for a foreign company, since it may seem to be butting into national issues as an unwelcome outsider. If it does appear necessary, it should be carried out only if the local subsidiary is convinced it is essential, and only with the help of the best local talent you can secure. Don't attempt it from headquarters. On the other hand, local subsidiaries should be warned not to engage in it on their own without clear-cut approval from headquarters of the entire project. It is headquarters' responsibility to be sure that what is done locally in one country does not have an adverse effect on subsidiaries in other countries or on the parent. In today's global village, communication is too universal and interest in business news too widespread for you to assume that what you do in one country will stay put. A business news story can travel very quickly and be seen in an entirely different light somewhere else. This characteristic of business news, by the way, is yet another reason for speaking with one voice as a corporation.

The Language Problem

There are some excellent translation services in the United States. Don't use them. They may be fine for business letters, but they should not be relied on for important press releases, which should be sent out from local offices in all events. Certainly, never use American translations for advertisements. They should undergo local *adaptation*. It is not a question of good or bad translation; it is a question of having to rethink every major business communication within the context of the language and customs and the business marketplace of each country. A whole book of the sometimes hilarious missteps taken by large, seemingly sophisticated companies has, in fact, been written by a David Rick, called *Big Business Blunders*. The linguistic and social differences can create problems of misunderstanding in personal relationships overseas and at any stage in marketing, from naming the product through to its packaging instructions and displays. But it is probably most troubling in advertising.

For instance, the early Volkswagen was affectionately called the Beetle, even in American advertising. Try that name in an African country and you will be calling it the worst kind of bug imaginable. A generation later, an American carmaker ran into an even worse problem when it discovered that the name of its little car in Brazil translated to "man's little thing"—hardly an appropriate term especially in a macho country.

That Americans are so frequently tied to their own language makes them more likely than Europeans to commit these errors. Even the worldly-wise British have their global limitations, however. One multinational advertising agency executive, writing on the subject of careful translation, used the expression that all the local problems should be "tabled." In Britain, *tabling* means "discussing it now." In the United States, of course, *tabling* usually means "postponing it."

The only practical solution to the translation problem is to have it done locally, which increases the level of participation by the local subsidiary and its agency and helps to encourage them to lend their support to the program.

A good starting source of information on intercultural differences is the Society for Inter-Cultural Education, Training, and Research (SIETAR International) in Washington, D.C. A book called *Managing Cultural Differences*, by Robert Moran and Phillip Harris, is a good basic text.

17
Corporate Communications
in a Recession

At this writing we appear to be at the end of one of the longest continuous growth periods in the United States' history. Following the October 1987 stock market crash, it may be prudent to add some of the material on advertising in a recession that first appeared in the author's 1981 book *Corporate Advertising, the What, the Why, and the How*. Also included are results of subsequent studies of what happens when corporate advertising programs are cut during a recession. These first appeared in the *Public Relations Journal* and in a study for the Association of National Advertisers' (ANA) Corporate Workshop of 1984.

A psychology of fear permeates recessions, which tends to make matters worse than they need be. Employment levels, and even sales, are far less affected than is supposed. There is evidence that when communication efforts are maintained during recessions, an increased share of public mind is achieved. This results in a faster postrecession recovery for companies. Despite this, communication budgets are frequently cut, although less so than in earlier years. When this happens, it is preferable to cut back objectives but to fund adequately those programs that are not eliminated completely. It is also frequently desirable to redirect the company position to suit the psychology of the time.

When corporate ad expenditures are cut during this period, it is usually more because of the high visibility of corporate advertising than because of the actual dollar amount saved. During these periods, planning for new programs is usually stepped up, and most companies resume corporate advertising following recessions at even higher levels.

T echnically, a recession begins when economic growth stops for three consecutive quarters, or when the inflationary growth is greater than the overall growth in the economy and real growth comes to a halt. Despite the unprecedented growth of the U.S. economy since World War II, repeated recessions have occurred throughout these years, causing periodic slowdown cycles. Major events affect the cycle and can lend a specific character to a specific recession. There may be strikes, wars, international events, or energy shortages. Crop failures, though rarely considered today, are still a possibility. The 1973–75 recession was largely attributed to the oil shortage, which disrupted the economy in virtually every country in the world.

Government actions can be a significant economic influence and are expected today to be manipulated as a controlling force, to smooth out the peaks and valleys to minimize a recession's effect. The massive U.S. debt is currently being blamed for the October 1987 market drop and undoubtedly will assume major responsibility if a recession should follow. It is interesting to consider, however, that the national debt grew throughout one of the longest sustained growth periods in the country's history and throughout one of the strongest bull markets Wall Street has experienced. The national debt was virtually the same the day before as the day after the crash. Why then the precipitous drop?

A clue to much of what happens in recessions may be found in some of the words that are used to describe them: *depression, recession, panic, slump,* and *crash.* The frame of mind characterized by these terms suggests that there is a deep psychological element, principally fear. Fear is a powerful motivating emotion. It leads to overreaction, whether it is jumping out of a Wall Street window or postponing badly needed capital improvement or even just not buying the new car. Fear inhibits many of the positive activities associated with and contributing to growth. The picture many people carry of these periodic downturns in the economy can be summed up as "a lot of people are out of work and no one has any money to spend." To a large extent, that image is based on experience of the 1929–32 Depression. It is a personal heritage in many family memories. Children are told about what happened during the Great Depression by their parents and grandparents.

The Great Depression was a time when employment fell by 18 percent and the unemployed represented almost one-quarter of the nation's work force. Let's examine the reality of the downturns that the United States has experienced since Wolrd War II and see whether these fears are well founded.

Customarily, our fears are fanned by the well-publicized unemployment rate, the percentage of the labor force out of work, which does rise sharply in a recession. What we rarely hear about, however, is total employment, the number of people working. This figure has actually declined only slightly in modern recessions because it is offset in part by an increasing population. The figures in table 17–1 are those of the Department of Labor, Bureau of Labor Statistics, for total employment, seasonally adjusted.

Even in the longest and deepest recession, that of 1973–75, we can see that employment declined by less than 2 percent. The growing population is just one of the factors that compensate for some of the recessive elements. Unemployment benefits of course are another. Inflation too may have an interesting countereffect, if it is running at a higher than normal rate. In the 1969–70 recession and in 1973–75 consumer spending actually increased by important amounts in part as a response to inflation.

We forget that even if the unemployment rate is 10 percent, nine out of ten people are still employed, and that because of unions and other resistive forces, salary levels tend to be stabilized. The U.S. economy declined only 1.7 percent in 1982 in the depths of that recession. Put another way, 98.3 percent of the buying power was

Table 17–1
Total U.S. Employment
(in thousands)

Recession	Start	End	(Change (percent)
1948–49	58,417	57,269	−2.0
1953–54	61,397	59,908	−2.4
1957–58	63,959	62,631	−2.1
1960–61	65,959	65,588	−0.6
1969–70	78,740	78,537	−0.3
1973–75	85,578	84,180	−1.6
1980–82	99,303	99,526	−0.0

Source: U.S. Bureau of Labor Statistics

still intact. The modern recession also appears to be of short duration. The average recession since World War II has lasted less than a year.

Advertising in Recessions

During this postwar period a number of studies on the effect of advertising during recessions has been conducted—product and service advertising, not specifically corporate advertising. As a result, the old-fashioned response to recessions, that of cutting ad budgets, appears to be dying out. The old reasoning went something like this: (1) People reduce buying during recessions so advertising can also be reduced or discontinued; (2) individual budgets can be reduced because competitors do the same thing. Well, competitors don't seem to be doing the same thing anymore. In fact, in the 1982 recession, advertising expenditures increased 10 percent.

Much of this change in attitude can be traced to research findings, such as the work done by the Cleveland agency Meldrum and Fewsmith, Inc., with the American Business Press, as well as postrecession studies conducted by McGraw-Hill Research Group. All have shown that companies that continue to advertise during recession periods survive them better. More important, these companies bounce back faster and farther following the upturn. The dynamics of this phenomenon are generally explained by saying that recession advertising acts to buy a share of mind and attention for the advertisers' products and services, which are then later realized as sales when the public can once again buy. That a share of mind precedes share of market implies a need to protect existing market share by advertising even during slack sales periods, particularly if this is what competitors are doing.

None of these studies differentiates between product and service advertising and corporate advertising. However, observation of the field over a long period has provided a clear pattern of what happens to corporate advertising during recession periods. Advertising addressed to the financial community to enhance stock value generally drops off. The softer institutional-like advertising, particularly that which expounds philosophies or might be criticized as feel-good advertising, also diminishes. Sales-related corporate advertising, on the other hand, is increased, especially advertising used as an umbrella for a line of products each of which may previously have had its own ad support. Where several products may have been advertised in the past, the weaker products may be left unsupported, except for these corporate umbrella campaigns.

This shift in the pattern of usage generally results in total national corporate advertising expenditures' more or less following the national expenditure levels for product and service advertising.

A case may also be made for the use of regular corporate advertising during recession periods for reasons besides its ability to act as a background umbrella. By definition, corporate advertising doesn't ask for the immediate purchase of a company's products or services. Instead, it builds confidence in the company and its products. It is more likely to talk of things of the future and to lay the groundwork for making sales easier at some future date. This may be a realistic approach to communication during periods when consumers may not or cannot buy. This includes not only recessions, but periods of shortages, such as during wars. In fact, World War II saw a major use of corporate advertising.

Contrast this use of advertising to enhance the quality image and reputation of a company and its products with the usual ad response to recessions favored by sales groups. They typically hope to stimulate immediate product sale in the face of lackluster markets through price cuts and promotions. These can tend to cheapen the image of the product and company and may still not work in a nonbuying atmosphere. To put it concisely, as long as people are not buying today, get them ready for tomorrow.

Sound as this philosophy may appear, realistically it is frequently difficult to implement in the face of quarterly earnings demands. It is likely that a mix of long- and short-term advertising will be used. It is also likely that communications budgets will be as subject to company budget cutbacks as other major functions and department activities. Such cuts, once again, require a re-examination of the objectives to determine what goals can be postponed, rather than some convenient, politically easy to cut activity. With a view that the recession will pass, rethink the program in terms of what activities and objectives may be postponed. In addition, consider and step up the priority on programs that may help you rebound faster following the recession.

You should also attempt to evaluate what is happening throughout the recession to each segment of your market and to each of your audiences. For instance, even in a recession the rich are still rich. Luxury items frequently continue to do quite well with their small but well-heeled markets. If you overreact because your company makes luxury items, it could be a great mistake. Conversely, even though you may have a line of very low-priced products, they may be the most hurt. Why? Because frequently, unfortunately, it is the low end of the work force that is usually hit hardest in a recession period.

While it may appear that changing communication to stress low cost would be the natural route to take during recessions, it has been found that during these periods consumers often give added thought and weight to the quality of what they buy, to product longevity and long-term costs, not just initial outlay. Where products may be substitutes for several other items or may replace items in related categories, whole new areas of marketing opportunity in recessions may be found. A classic example is that people may not simply shift from a high-price to a low-price restaurant when things get tight but may decide to eat at home, thereby changing the whole picture of the food market. Keep in mind that when buying patterns change, they make new opportunities if you are alert.

You will find there are dozens of relatively safe, small economies that can and should be made throughout your communication program, from giving second thoughts to a new company film to considering using black and white instead of four color in advertisements. The most important economies, however, may be in increasing the effectiveness of the programs that you find you can afford. This means rethinking the various positions you are using as you present your company and its products to the various publics. Although it is impossible to explain how each and every product and industry category should approach this, a few product and company examples may start your thinking along these lines.

In the 1980–82 recession, Michelin switched from saying that its steel-belted radial tires were expensive but worth it, and instead stressed how "surprisingly affordable Michelins were."

A-1 Steak Sauce began showing people using the product on hamburger not steak.

Ziploc Food Bags made the point that with food prices so high, leftovers had become worthy of storing in special plastic bags.

Citibank, which had said, "The Citi never sleeps," changed the slogan to read, "When it comes to making your savings earn more the Citi never sleeps."

Arm & Hammer Baking Soda presented itself as an effective and obviously low-cost dentrifice.

In essence, you need to position whatever the company does or makes as a worthwhile investment, with solid reasons for using it in a tight economy. It is certainly not a question of becoming the cheapest guy on the block. It is a question of becoming a financially responsible solid investment during a difficult economic period.

The continuing study of U.S. recessions, a McGraw-Hill Research/Laboratory of Advertising Performance analysis of six hundred industrial companies, showed that business-to-business firms that maintained or increased their advertising expenditures during the 1981–82 recession averaged significantly higher sales growth both during the recession and in the following three years than did those that eliminated or decreased advertising. Figure 17–1 and table 17–2 are reproduced through the permission of McGraw-Hill Research. They show annual sales of 1980 through 1985, with a base index of one hundred in 1980.

Annual sales are shown in figure 17–1 as an index from 1980 through 1985, with a base of one hundred in 1980. Sales indices for selected industries are shown in table 17–2.

Sales indices of industries reflect the positive impact of advertising during recessionary periods.

The six hundred industrial companies were categorized by standard industrial classification. These figures further emphasize that advertising during recession periods has a positive effect on sales efforts.

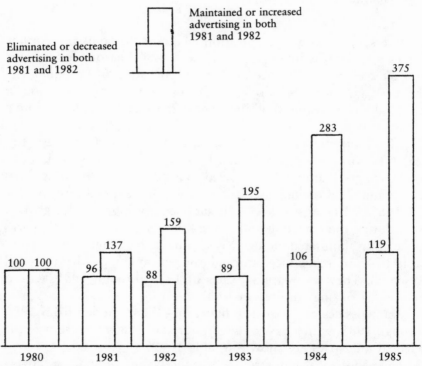

Advertising During a Recession
(1980 = 100)

Source: The Continuing Study of U.S. recessions, a McGraw-Hill Research Laboratory of advertising performance.

Figure 17–1. Sales Indices 1980–1985.   For Companies That Continued to Advertise during Recession versus Those That Cut Back

Table 17–2

Sales Indices by Industry–Advertising during Recessions

| | | | | 1985 Sales Indices[b] | |
SIC No.[a]	Number of Companies	Industry	Sales Index 1980 (Base = 100)	Eliminated or Decreased Advertising in Both 1981 and 1982	Maintained or Increased Advertising in Both 1981 and 1982
20	43	Food & kindred products	138		213
23	8	Apparel & other textile products	—		160
24	6	Lumber & wood products	113		259
25	9	Furniture & fixtures	220		210
26	4	Paper & allied products	—		150
27	18	Printing & publishing	102		213
28	53	Chemicals & allied products	92		839
29	4	Petroleum & coal products	—		104
30	5	Rubber & misc. plastics products	105		238
31	7	Leather & leather products	89		142
32	4	Stone, clay, & glass products	—		150
35	26	Machinery, except electrical	113		205
36	83	Electrical & electronic equipment	86		287
37	10	Transportation equipment	126		157
38	41	Instruments & related products	209		596
39	14	Misc. manufacturing industries	55		444

Source: McGraw-Hill Research Laboratory

[a] SIC industries with four or more companies reporting are shown in this table.

[b] Individual company indices were calculated and averaged to compute indices by industry.

What Happens When Corporate Ad Programs Are Cut

In spite of the logical case for maintaining communication pressure, there may still come a time in the course of a recession when there is no choice but to cut back in major ways. In a program that includes corporate advertising, this is almost certain to be affected because it will represent such an important part of the total communication department budget. In an examination of what happened to corporations that made major or complete cuts in their corporate ad programs during the 1980–82 recession, some revealing findings on the course of events may be helpful.

Telephone interviews and an exchange of correspondence with approximately thirty such companies that had largely discontinued their corporate ad programs revealed, first, that although these cuts were in all cases based on "financial reasons," the term *financial* meant different things to different companies. In very few cases was it a simple cash flow problem. And rarely was corporate advertising singled out for elimination because it was considered an optional activity. No, most of the cuts occurred as companywide budget cutbacks in which all department budgets were cut from 10 to 50 percent and more—and in which advertising was virtually the only expense major enough to accommodate the savings without decimating an entire department.

Only a few companies stopped because they thought they had nothing positive to say in the recession, even those addressing the investing community. Most of the companies studied had had campaigns addressed principally to investors. All of the companies that discontinued advertising of this sort were in industries hardest hit by the recession—like forestry products and metals. Only four of the companies admitted their balance sheets were so bad that they considered it inadvisable to draw additional attention from Wall Street. One of the companies cut back corporate advertising despite a fair earnings record because its industry was considered such a disaster area that the company thought its financial campaign was a waste of money until the whole industry turned around. That company was using the period planning its next ad campaign, which was run following the market upturn.

Three or four companies—again, companies particularly hard hit by the recession—said that the high visibility of corporate advertising left them little choice but to cancel out. They explained that stockholders and unions perceived it as an unnecessary expense, even though management recognized its importance. A few quotes will make this point a bit clearer:

How can you continue to advertise when the stockholders have just gotten a dividend cut to five cents?

How can we close plants, lay off hundreds of workers, and talk to the unions about economies, then continue what they consider a costly ad program that doesn't sell products? Not that the campaign costs so much relative to the rest of our business, it doesn't amount to that big a savings, but it is hard to show austerity when something is that visible to employees and stockholders.

Here's another one, this from a company that maintained its communications budget but switched to less visible tools with this rationale: "We need the exposure, we need to communicate, we just don't want to look like we are doing it."

Only four of the thirty companies said they had cut out just about all forms of corporate communications. A few of them said they maintained their investor relations activities on a smaller scale. They continued with analysts' meetings, press releases, and stockholder notices, but these were either somewhat reduced in number or less expensively produced.

Again and again companies would state that cuts went across the board through all departments and that the only way they could meet the budget was to cut back on the biggest item, which was corporate advertising. None of the companies said that the corporate ad program had been dropped because management thought it was not worthwhile. In fact, a number of them were using the hiatus period to develop new corporate ad strategies. All but four in the study said they planned to resume corporate advertising when things improved. Indeed, by 1984 more than two-thirds of the companies had started new corporate ad programs, many in a big way. Some of the remaining companies were either bought or merged out of existence, so in effect, virtually all the survivors resumed advertising.

As you might expect, there was no immediate reaction from outside when the companies dropped the advertising. Such a lack of response to stopping should be expected. As one old teacher never seemed to learn, you can't ask those who are absent please to stand up. You can't expect to quietly discontinue communication and get a lot of response. Just two companies said that they were asked at analysts' meetings whether they had discontinued their campaigns, but they were unable to say whether the analysts perceived this as a sound move under the circumstances or saw it as a sign of weakness.

In cases where there had been severe cutbacks in the staff, the employees noticed the change. In these cases, the elimination of advertising was considered by the employees as a good company move. Now, with the exception of that statement, everything else that happened to these companies as a result of cutting back or stopping their corporate ad campaigns appeared to be negative.

Here is a quote from a well-known metals company that had advertised broadly for years to the general public and had cut back substantially (this company did, however, shift some of the funds to product advertising): "Everything, awareness and attitudes, dropped about 5%." Another corporation with a well-known household name reported, "There has been no real drop in awareness statistically, but elements and attributes from the study moved around a great deal." This company also said that its image with the public was changing. The lack of a campaign, in effect, allowed the public to free-think the company along lines that were not necessarily the directions in which the corporation wanted to go.

From another company, "The downward effect was pretty much across the board, and it was very noticeable." A longtime corporate advertiser, a conglomerate that gradually cut back its corporate ad expenditures as segments of the business were affected by the recession, reported that the level of response dropped with alarming speed each time the budget was cut. The company's was an issue campaign, accustomed to high reader mail volume.

Another company, which stopped its corporate ads to the financial community, observed, "We follow our stock ownership very closely. When we first started the campaign we saw a lot of new names on the list. We now seem to have lost a lot of individual investors. Our stock is not as broadly held as it was."

From another company, one that had a long-running corporate campaign with multiple objectives, "We know we have lost familiarity and we know that higher familiarity carries a higher multiple."

Hard research data was rare among the companies. However, a forestry products company whose corporate program ran from between $1.5 and $3 million annually in magazines from 1971 until 1981 reported that during that period it had raised its favorable awareness levels from about 33 percent among the target audience to 51–53 percent. The company stopped corporate advertising completely during 1982 and 1983 and researched its standings in the first quarter of 1984. This was one of the few companies to have conducted such research following the cessation of advertising because in most cases when the department budget was cut, the research was cut along with it. The favorable awareness levels dropped fifteen points, or virtually back to the 1971 levels. Yes, there is such a thing as memory decay, and it can happen faster than most communicators think.

A regional petroleum company, whose annual spending varied from $1 million to a high of $3 million just before the oil crisis, reported that although favorable awareness decayed during the crisis years, its customer confidence level held up. Then the company pulled out advertising completely in 1982 and 1983. Its last research sweep at the end of 1983 showed a slight decay in market area customer awareness. The employees and dealers were the first to notice the cutback. The dealers were particularly negative about the lack of advertising support.

Although the lack of statistical results from among this group of companies was disappointing, the quotes were directionally all the same. When corporate advertising is cut, the following things appear to happen: first, a loss of top-of-mind awareness; second, a loss in awareness; and third, a change in the attitudes held about the company, usually a deterioration of those attitudes. How long does this take? It will depend on how well known the company is to start with, and how well represented by brands and products with the same name that continue to be advertised. It also depends, in part, on how old the name is. If it is a very well known household name, people may hold on to the familiarity for years. But their perceptions about the company will shift into different directions. Without advertising to guide the directions, the image of the company may become distorted and different from the one the company would like. If the company name is not so familiar, memory decay can be as rapid as a few months. This point should be considered, especially by companies that have recently undergone a name change. It would not take long to wipe out the work done to establish the new name if a program is prematurely cut.

18
... And Finally, a Word
to the CEO

The chief executive officer will affect the character of the company more than he or she might care to admit. This effect will be influenced by his or her tenure, the pre-existing character of the company, his or her personality, and his or her conscious effort to play a positive role in shaping the company. Only the latter factor is truly controllable. A positive effort by the CEO will help create a broader, more positive reputation that has distinct advantages for the company. A proactive, rather than reactive, approach to communications is shown to be an advantage in dealing with many publics, employees, investors, the press, customers, and even the government.

The effect of a good company reputation varies in degree and kind, according to the product or service category. Though this effect may be more obviously shown in some industries than others, it still exists regardless of industry.

The CEO should take direct responsibility for the proper staffing to accomplish a positive communication program. The CEO must also establish the corporate mission, which sets the style and personality of the company. Finally, the role of the CEO as spokesman is examined in terms of when it is appropriate and when it may be a disadvantage.

As chief executive officer you affect the character of your company and how it is perceived more than any other influence. This is true regardless of your management style. Whether you operate with high visibility, like a Lee Iaccoca, or prefer to operate quietly behind the scenes through others, you are shaping the personality of the entire organization. You do this in a number of ways: through the decisions you make, the priorities you set, your management structure, and, most importantly, through your own personality and style. The latter may be more of an influence on your corporation than you care to acknowledge. Whether you like it or not, this function is an unwritten part of every CEO's job description. Think back and remember how much time you and your peers spent when you were in middle management trying to "read the boss." Where was he leading the company? What were his hot buttons? What impressed him? These were all questions you had to consider in building your career. The next generation is following your signals just as closely.

This influence of yours will be there whether you are conscious of it or not. It won't go away even if you attempt to ignore it. You have a choice of recognizing this role, controlling it, and using it for the benefit of the company, or ducking it as best you can. You can do that for a while by choosing to believe that the character of the company is something you inherited, that it is built into the structure, and that you must accept it. When you first take over direction of a company there is a certain validity to that view, but eventually your influence will prevail.

Your effect on the company's character is modulated by five factors:

1. *Your tenure.* Clearly the longer a CEO is in command the more he or she will have affected the company.

2. *The existing character of the company as inherited.* The influence of the person founding the company is unique. Founders especially build companies in their own image. Some become almost one with their product, like Frank Perdue. This is a very different situation from taking over the reins of an established company, especially one that has changed and been modified a number of times through the years. The more amorphous the company you inherit, the more influence you can and will exercise over it. But if you don't take care, that influence may be to make it even more amorphous.

3. *Outside events that shape the destiny of us all.* Major

changes in the market and social and environmental pressures will each affect and change a company's character and image. Certain industries, such as chemicals and pharmaceuticals, have been particularly sensitive to these influences.

4. *The dynamism of your personality.* Let's face it—some CEOs have charisma and others do not. While either type will affect the end character of the corporation, the charismatic CEO is more likely to become more closely associated with his corporation through sharing his exuberant personality with the company. Conversely, the withdrawn CEO may set the stage for a withdrawn company that operates with a low silhouette.

5. *Conscious effort.* The amount of time and money devoted to determining and controlling a company's image varies considerably from one company to another. The amount of attention paid to this aspect by top management varies as well. The more conscious the concern for a company's reputation, the more it is kept on your personal management agenda, the more you can positively contribute to this somewhat ephemeral corporate asset.

It should be apparent that the first four factors are largely out of your control. The length of tenure, the character of the company that you have taken over, outside events, and even your personality will be factors you will largely have to live with. Only the fifth factor is entirely within your control. It comes down to whether you wish to take command of the role you are going to play or whether you just let your power within the company affect its character willy-nilly.

Hardly a business discipline exists that does not extol the importance of a CEO's involvement. If you were to meet all those demands you would probably be guilty of failure to delegate. However, in the case of corporate personality you have little choice. So as long as you are going to play the key role, you might just as well make the best of it and do the best for the company and its personality at the same time.

Fortunately it's largely a matter of taking an interest in the subject and just being yourself. You don't have to have all the answers. That will be up to your staff, particularly your communications director, public relations, investor relations, human resources, and marketing. In fact, you needn't devote the time to reading this whole book. If you finish the rest of this chapter and scan chapters 2 and 11 you should have the basic messages that apply to your role. If the question of corporate advertising arises (which can be a major investment in image building), you should read chapters 13, 14, and 15 as well.

The Importance of the Company's Reputation

Before proceeding to discuss your role, let's deal with a fundamental question frequently asked by CEOs, particularly those struggling to meet the next anticipated dividend: "Is a clearer, more positive identity among a broader audience of people worth the cost and internal time to achieve?" Does it really make any difference to a company whether it has a good reputation? Does it have an effect on stock prices? Does it affect employee relations, Washington relations, or even product sales if a company is better known and respected? It might seem obvious that it would, but in fact communications officers are frequently at a loss to marshall the kind of quantitative evidence a skeptical CEO might require.

It is right here at this first fundamental question that we see one effect of the personality of the CEO and how it can affect the personality of the corporation. The quantitative evidence of the effect of a better reputation on a company is just not available in terms absolute enough to satisfy a CEO who is by nature highly skeptical, particularly if he or she is reticent about operating in a visible way. The CEO may confuse his or her own ego with that of the company and interpret any effort to enhance the company's reputation with personal immodesty. Although the screening process for reaching the top would seem to eliminate all but those executives with the strongest egos, CEOs are frequently people with a kind of drive that suggests fundamental insecurities. Writing for the *Harvard Business Review*, David Finn, chairman and cofounder of Ruder & Finn, Inc., a well-known public relations company, exhorts corporate leaders to stop hiding their human qualities behind a mask of corporate anonymity. In this somewhat different context, he blames the public's poor opinion of business on corporate executives' failure to present themselves convincingly as persons who care about the state of the world, and he blames this on their diffidence. As he puts it, somehow the business world has taught executives to hide their human qualities behind masks. They should not worry so much about whether their decisions to do business in style will be seen as ego trips.

The CEOs who prefer to operate their company's communications in a strictly reactive rather than proactive way should re-examine their own personalities to see whether they are making a sound decision for the company or simply projecting their own personal character traits.

There are enough examples of successful companies that operate with a low silhouette (Procter & Gamble, for instance) for a CEO who is so disposed to settle the argument quickly to his or her own satisfaction—if not to that of the communications officer. Companies a CEO might cite as highly successful which make little or no effort to project a strong corporate image are usually long established. Through time, product quality, and consistency they have achieved a favorable identity despite a lack of conscious effort in that direction. Or they may be new companies growing rapidly because of new products and innovations in an expanding industry. Make no mistake, whether an effort is made or not, every company has some type of identity. A company may be no more widely known than among its customers, banks, and stockholders. It may have a bad identity, but some sort of identity will exist.

The question comes down to one of control, whether to work to fashion a company's identity, extend its recognition into areas that may ultimately be useful to the company and its operation, or just to let the identity happen.

The effect a broad, positive perception can have on businesses in certain industries is so clear cut that its value is rarely questioned. Banks, insurance companies, brokerage firms, and other financial institutions, all businesses depending heavily on public trust, almost invariably spend considerable effort in building this trust through carefully managed identity programs. These industries were the first to use corporate advertising that devotes the ad message to building confidence in the corporation rather than selling specific products or services. In fact, the interrelationship between their sales and their reputation is so taken for granted that today many of their ad campaigns are hybrid combinations of product, service, and corporate advertising.

Even a surface examination of the effect a good company reputation has on the sale of its products makes it obvious that people are more willing to buy products from a company they trust, one known for quality products and for standing behind the products in the event of problems. It is also apparent that the more a product represents a major investment or commitment by the buyer, the greater the role the reputation of the company behind the product will play. The reputation also grows in importance with the complexity of the products. Where quality is not immediately apparent in the product by thumping it or through simple examination, the buyer must, as with many high-technology products, have confidence in the people who made it.

The role a company's reputation plays in sales can go far beyond this simple commonsense relationship. To look at it we might examine the theory of cognitive dissonance as put forth in a 1957 book by psychologist Leon Festinger, published by Stanford University Press. The dissonance theory is an outgrowth of so-called cognitive balance, itself a theory that assumes people attempt to maintain a state of harmony in their beliefs and attitudes. It follows, therefore, that disharmony is an uncomfortable state that produces tension, which people instinctively avoid. Such discomfort can arise when the source of the product appears to be out of sync with the product category. Acceptable as Ford's reputation may be for automobiles, for example, the company might have difficulty transferring that acceptance to a line of computers. This is only one form cognitive dissonance may take.

Another may exist when the company's image is at odds with the self-image of the buyer. The current scramble among long-distance phone companies illustrates this point. The comfort level of dealing with the familiar AT&T company may be much greater for those who view themselves as conservative and willing to pay for the known past reliability. A self-image of "innovative" would be more compatible with change.

An interesting example of the effect company reputation exercises can be seen among business customers of the so-called Baby Bells. Each of these seven companies, the result of the AT&T divestiture, inherited what was often referred to in the industry as a "POT's image" (*p*lain *o*ld *t*elephones). This was a major handicap in entering the newly formed competitive field, one characterized by aggressive, modern technology and innovation. Competitors purposely contrasted their own images to the telephone company's conservative POTs reputation. In fact, so well known is this selling technique in industrial sales that it has been given an acronym: it is called FUD, standing for *f*ear, *u*ncertainty, and *d*oubt. These are elements that the salesperson attempts to raise about the competitors' products. Surprisingly, this technique is used even more commonly in industrial sales, where the buyer is professional and presumably skilled and well informed. This kind of buyer is every bit as emotionally involved as a consumer buying for himself, perhaps more so because the professional buyer in industry is making a purchase which may affect his or her career. Cognitive dissonance can occur if the company making the purchase sees itself as young, aggressive, and innovative and the buyer visualizes the Baby Bell as, let's say, just a plain old telephone company with black telephones.

Intellectually, the buyer may know that the Baby Bell systems, service, and reliability constitute the best buy but may fear the effect such a decision might have on his or her reputation within the company. Much of this takes place at a psychological level; it is felt and acted upon almost unconsciously rather than clearly understood by the buyer. Interestingly, every one of the seven Baby Bells launched a corporate advertising program in an effort to be seen as a modern telecommunications company, offering advanced equipment and services. The need for this change in image was seen by the independent telephone companies as well. Anticipating deregulation as it dragged through the courts, one by one they changed their names, dropping the term *telephone* from their titles.

Currently the largest corporate ad expenditures are being made by automobiles, aircraft, and business equipment manufacturers. All are makers of considered-purchase, big-ticket items.

The industries in which companies appear most reluctant to control and enhance their indentities fall principally into three groups.

1. Consumer product companies with multiple brands. Frequently these brands are heavily advertised and the corporation vicariously accepts its recognition through them as sufficient. In reality, however, when the brands have names different from the corporation's there is actual little rub-off association.

2. Companies that make hidden products, components, chemicals, materials that go into final products made by other companies. These companies may feel they have a good reputation among their narrow customer base and view that as adequate for their identity needs.

3. Conglomerates formed through mergers and acquisitions which may be in such diverse industries, with such conflicting image requirements that the corporation assumes the passive posture of a holding company. When such a diversified company includes well-known brands or its products are hidden industrial components, the pressure to accept anonymity as the easy way out can be overwhelming.

In fact, broader awareness and greater familiarity for any corporation, even those in these three situations is a decided advantage. The benefit relationship may be less apparent in some businesses, but it is no less real. The benefit may not be as quantifiable for a conglomerate as for a bank, the dollar return may vary with the industry and a given company situation, but the benefit to varying degrees will indeed exist.

The Advantages of a Good Reputation

Just what evidence is there that an enhanced reputation and wider recognition actually constitute an advantage? If you are going to devote time and money to achieving a more positive identity, what will the return on the investment be? The return from the company's various publics will take different forms. Hence it should improve sales from customers, and improve morale and productivity among employees. It should make recruitment easier, particularly in terms of securing the best prospective employees, an important consideration in the scientific disciplines where competition for the top 2 percent can be intense. It should improve credibility and enhance the company's news value with the press, as well as improve its credibility and build respect from among government officials. It is not too much to expect more preferred treatment from among the trade through the company's lines of distribution. Often overlooked is the effect on other companies. Mergers, joint ventures, and subcontracts are all made easier and more acceptable when a company is well known and respected. This factor is attaining global importance as multinational companies seek partners for ventures that are either too large or too risky to tackle alone. This can be seen very easily in the aerospace field. To cite one example, the European Airbus employs products and services from no fewer than five hundred U.S. companies.

The tangible evidence of the value of a reputation surfaces dramatically during mergers. Negotiations involving acquisitions or the divestiture of smaller subsidiaries force management to face up to the value of goodwill.

Judging by questions that arise most frequently from clients, it is the effect of an enhanced reputation on the value of stock, the P-E ratio that drives many corporate identity programs.

If the return on investment in a company's image varies among different publics, we must look for evidence in a variety of different ways from different studies and sources. As of this writing, no complete model exists covering all of the publics, nor is one likely to be produced. Regrettably, but understandably, much of the research and many of the case histories (and there have been a great deal) are proprietary. Even the highly researched relationship (as well as the one most generally accepted), the effect of advertising on sales, is difficult to substantiate because it is largely guarded as competitive information. The effect of an enhanced reputation among employees, improving their morale and productivity, has also been studied and found substantial. But the information is held as confidential. In that case, it has been learned that employees react quite positively to working for a company they are proud of, that an employee's stature in the community goes up when the company's reputation is improved. This affects not only the employees, but their families and friends as well. Studies done by the original Yankelovich, Skelly & White, Opinion Research Corporation, the Strategic Planning Institute of Cambridge, Booz Allen Hamilton, Erdos & Morgan, AHF Marketing Research, and others tell the same basic story in separate studies for individual clients concerning various aspects of the effect of a company's reputation. The evidence is there. If you have a friend at one of these companies he or she can substantiate the positive returns of a good reputation, but results are not for publication.

This lack of published data to a certain extent reflects the acceptance as fact that enhanced visibility is a plus. It is only when there is a need to know, or to prove, that money is spent for research data. Broad-based surveys establishing relative identity levels for a large number of companies has until recently been unavailable in the United States. (Some work of this nature has been done in the United Kingdom.) This has made it virtually impossible to compare the stock performance of American companies with good and bad reputations. With that data available, it would be possible to compare company performance levels with reputations. This would serve not only to prove the relationship's existence, but also to make it possible to attach values to improved reputation. Perhaps one day such a study will be done.

One recent study designed to establish the value of a good reputation that is not only public but highly publicized was conducted in 1986 by Yankelovich Clancy Shulman for Brouillard Communications. This is an advertising agency headquartered in New York City which has made corporate advertising a specialty.

The research was conducted in two stages, first qualitative, then quantitative. The qualitative work involved focus group sessions with affluent adults (annual household incomes over fifty thousand dollars) in Chicago and New York and in-depth personal interviews with senior managers of ten companies. This allowed the researchers to plan the quantitative stage. It also identified the term *winning* as best describing companies with excellent overall reputations. That later became the tag name for the study, "Winning!" The qualitative stage also generated a list of attributes associated with winners and the candidate list of winning companies.

The second stage involved more than 1,000 interviews in four categories: 655 affluent consumers, 217 corporate executives, 62 directors of research for large brokerage firms and institutions, and 104 portfolio managers from the top one hundred institutions. The corporate executive sample all worked for companies with revenues of $100 million or more. Eighty-six percent of this group were chief executive officer, chief operating officer, chief financial officer, or executive vice president of their companies.

The companies were ranked on a six-point scale. Those rated as five or six were categorized as winners. Forty companies were ranked by each respondent. Respondents were then asked questions related to the likelihood of their supportive behavior in relation to these companies, their likelihood of purchasing products, investing in stock, welcoming them as companies into their neighborhoods, recommending them as a place of employment, and recommending them for joint ventures. In each case, regardless of the audience interviewed, the companies that had been judged as winners were substantially better supported. (The Brouillard people later reported that the "winning" companies fared better during the October 1987 market crash as well.) The following questions and responses were reprinted with permission from Brouillard Communications.

"Assume you are shopping for several kinds of new products you've heard about and want to try, but there are different brands of each kind of new product available. How likely would you be to purchase the product from _____?"

Those saying "Very likely" to buy:	Affluent Consumers	Corporate Executives
Among those rating the company a winner	67%	62%
Among those not rating the company a winner	30%	34%

"Suppose you had $75,000 to invest in the stocks of these five companies. How much would you invest in _____?"

Amount invested:	Affluent Consumers	Corporate Executives	Research Directors	Portfolio Managers
When company rated a winner	$21,900	$20,400	$21,500	$21,000
When company not rated a winner	$13,300	$9,400	$11,000	$10,000

"Assume that an industrial park is being built in your area and that companies we have been discussing are interested in locating manufacturing facilities there. How likely would you be to recommend that _____be encouraged to locate in the community?"

Those saying "very likely" to recommend:	Affluent Consumers	Corporate Executives	Research Directors	Portfolio Managers
Among those rating the company a winner	58%	71%	73%	58%
Among those not rating the company a winner	40%	40%	45%	38%

"Assume your nephew recently received a degree from a leading business school and has received job offers from several companies. If the job descriptions and salaries were similar, how likely is it that you would recommend that your nephew seek employment in _____?"

Those saying "very likely" to recommend:	Affluent Consumers	Corporate Executives	Research Directors	Portfolio Managers
Among those rating the company a winner	72%	63%	79%	58%
Among those not rating the company a winner	26%	20%	7%	26%

"Assume that your company has been contacted by several companies about participating in a joint venture and you have been given the responsibility of making a final recommendation. If the advantages and disadvantages were about equal for each, how likely would you be to recommend entering a joint venture with _____?"

Those saying "very likely" to recommend:	Corporate Executives	Research Directors	Portfolio Managers
Among those rating the company a winner	61%	71%	56%
Among those not rating the company a winner	27%	38%	32%

Other studies going back at least as far as 1969 have shown a positive relationship between image and stock performance (Batten, Barton, Durstine, and Osborn, Inc., "How Public Attitudes Influence Corporate Profits," 1969). Akin to this is the effect of corporate advertising on stock values. The major study done in this area was conducted in 1979 by Shoenfeld and Boyd, two Northwestern University professors, who concluded that corporate advertisers (who presumably would have better reputations) enjoyed a 4 percent lift in stock prices after allowing for all other financial indicators. Although somewhat controversal and employing a complicated model, this study has not been successfully challenged. It was based upon the examination of more than 1,600 companies quarter by quarter for three years. The 4 percent lift conclusion would appear reasonable.

A Few Basics

Staffing

Look to your director of corporate communications for the guidance and direction to make the corporate identity program work. These programs are largely a creative process, and so one strong individual can accomplish far more than can a committee. In fact, if you wish to kill the whole idea, assign it to a task force. Based on experience that task force will probably come back with expedient reasons for shelving the whole program. Each member usually has a personal agenda, and this assignment will probably seem to them an intrusion.

Your corporate communications director should have a strong background in public relations but in addition will need a sense of style and taste. Frequently art training shows up as part of such a person's background. The more complex your business, the greater the need for experience within your company, or at least within your industry.

He or she will need the stature of a senior vice president's title and should be a regular member of the management or operating committee or whatever it is called in your company. This should be a direct report. He or she will need the clout of your close association and must learn to read you like a book in order to interpret and shape the character of the corporation you are seeking.

You may wish to consider having your investor relations function report to the director of corporate communications rather than the chief financial officer. In part, this will depend on the individuals. The main consideration is that IR and PR be able to work very closely.

If yours is a market-driven company, there may be a temptation to use the product-marketing staff rather than a corporate public relations/communications officer. Resist it. Important as marketing is, it is only one aspect of the character and identity of the company. Good marketers rarely appreciate the need to court Wall Street, Washington, and plant communities, to say nothing of the press. Their training rightfully focuses their attention on the marketplace and on sales to the consuming public. They might just be willing to trade long-term reputation for a short-term sales hike. Lastly, select someone with whom you are completely comfortable. If you do it right you'll be spending a great deal of time together.

Deciding What Your Company Really Is

This may be the hardest part, particularly after mergers or divestitures and for companies with complex business portfolios. Determining the corporate mission in today's rapidly changing environment can be almost an ongoing exercise. Remember, however, that if you can't determine what the company is and where it is going, your employees won't know. And if they don't know, the outside world won't have a clue. If you follow the usual practice of having a brief company description on the inside cover of your annual report, you will at least have a start on developing a corporate mission statement, but it will need to be re-examined. It must reflect longer-range considerations. You should not merely highlight that facet of the company that currently enjoys Wall Street's favor; the statement must reflect the reality of what you are and what you will be three and five years out. If that sounds as if strategic planning is involved, you are right. But whatever its name, strategic planning involves the shaping of the company, and good identity programs involve the reflection of this strategic plan. In fact, to turn it around, as the process of strategic planning matures, the reviewing of objectives, mission, asset redeployment, cash flow priorities, and the rest should include examining the fundamental character of the corporation and how it is perceived by publics important to it. It is from this pool of opinion that all of your activities must be drawn. It is essential for strategic planning to consider the effect its changes will have on the character of the corporation and to adjust this in the planning.

You may also wish to consider incorporating within the corporate mission a statement on the ethical standards of the company. If that sounds a little goody-good consider this. Such statements increasingly are becoming part of companies' operations, particularly those companies working in industries with built-in potential problems such as chemicals and pharmaceuticals, but financial companies and defense contractors have suffered as well. Employees come from widely different backgrounds and may not all enjoy your own personal ethical standards. Hard pressed to deliver on their career goals, they just may be tempted to cut corners. Make it clear that the company has a standard and that people are judged by it accordingly. You may even want to consider actual ethical training sessions given by specialists in this field. (There is more on this in chapter 2.)

It Works from the Inside Out

The favorite communications truism that "you can only reflect the image of the reality of a company successfully" is at least 90 percent true (which is probably a higher percentage than for most truisms). Clearly false reflections will not hold up for very long. A large corporation sends out so many communications in so many ways from personal contacts made at all levels with a multitude of publics that it is impossible to project less than the reality in a sustained way. On the other hand, that you try to present the best side of your personality should be a given. Furthermore, a slight lead on what is about to be the reality is possible. But for any identity program to work the inside must be taken care of first. Employees should not be caught by surprise but should be treated as in-house family and should fully understand the company and its aims and be marching more or less together. To begin a communication program when a company is in disarray is simply to project a chaotic company. When the house is in order, however, don't assume anyone outside the company will automatically be aware of that fact. It is at that point, when the internal effort has created a company that is superior to the one perceived by outside publics, that a stepped-up communication program makes the most economic sense. It is a question of closing the gap between what you are and how you are perceived.

How do you know when you are at this point? Research. The opportunity for self-deception in your position is great. Myopia or the misinformation given an overly protected CEO can be very misleading. Some form of objective outside appraisal must be made to be sure just what a company's real reputation among important publics is. Just as important, particularly in larger, more complex organizations, is how you are perceived internally. Objective third-party interviews among executives can establish the reality of the company as they see it. Certainly before any consideration is given to major changes in a company's identity, such as a name change, or before major financial commitments are made to corporate ad programs, such research should be considered.

Cohesive Consistency

A person's personality is established by his actions, speech, and mannerisms as repeated over time. There is a reasonable cohesiveness to these actions which stems from the inner personality of the individual. The formation of a company personality requires a similar cohesive consistency in the company's actions. These include everything from visual corporate identity systems (signs and logos) to the tone of voice used in news releases and sales correspondence. Establishing this consistency will involve the spirit of your employees in dealing with their customers, the community, and their families as they discuss the company. Even how your accountants handle delinquent accounts reflects the company persona. All of these public contacts ideally must seem to be coming from the same company. There must be a cohesiveness, a point of view on how the company does things. This has been called the corporate culture.

The CEO as Spokesman

A few years ago, a small ad agency sent out a new business letter to the CEOs of corporations that were using corporate advertising. The letter started, "If you appear in your company's corporate advertising it could be much more effective." I am not sure this new business effort turned up any new accounts. It may even have annoyed a few executives, who felt they were having their egos played upon. Nevertheless, there are many situations that can be handled best by a CEO who is willing to perform. For instance, it would be hard to imagine a more adept handling of the Tylenol crisis than the fast on-air discussions of the problem by James E. Burke, chairman of the board and chief executive officer of Johnson & Johnson. Clearly no one is in a better position to speak with authority in a crisis for the company than its CEO. No one else will carry quite the same credibility, providing you are good at it and have undergone some specialized training in survival techniques for press interviews.

A more usual situation also best handled by the CEO is the investor relations presentations to portfolio managers and analysts. Again and again research reveals the importance of confidence in management in evaluating a stock. Despite this, one of the most frequent complaints of analysts and portfolio managers is the lack of contact with CEOs. It is almost a given that that complaint will turn up whenever that audience is surveyed.

Presumably by now you should have come to a realistic understanding of your showmanship potential. If you have not, you may be lucky enough to have a longtime friend with no career stake in the outcome who's just blunt enough to level with you. Or a videotape of one of your efforts viewed alone may tell you a great deal. You *might* also want to try it on your spouse. Spouses have a habit of being candid.

It is in your appearances before stockholders and employee groups that your contribution to the company's personality will be greatest. Whether you hold these meetings with your jacket on or with sleeves rolled, whether you're folksy or brash, will mean a lot. It is here that a warm, friendly atmosphere can be developed or one that is crisp and businesslike. The degree to which you are candid, honest, and straightforward in your manner can set the ethical standard almost as well as the actual words you use.

There is a quantum difference between your role as spokesman in presentations and meetings with the press and Wall Street, and that of being spokesman in the company's advertising. There is also a great deal of difference between a CEO pitching his product and one talking about his company in corporate advertising. Most of the memorable advertising successes involve founders, people who became synonymous with the product—Tom Carvel, Frank Perdue, Earl Scheib, and Col. Harlan Sanders, to name a few. In effect, these people became living trademarks. Clearly, it is easier for a founder to assume this role. When a CEO such as David Mahoney, who was thought of as almost the quintessential conglomerate chief, spoke out for the Avis product, the result was generally judged less than successful.

CEOs as spokesmen in corporate advertising send out entirely different signals, principally that the company is in big trouble. In fact that is how most of them start. The ad agency vice president described Chrysler as in such bad shape that no one could speak for it but Lee Iaccoca. Eastern was in trouble when Frank Borman first started, and Charles Debutz was fighting to maintain AT&T as a single unit when he made his appearance in corporate advertising. As corporate advertising spokesman, you are a powerful weapon. Your speaking in this context is appropriate for very serious problems where great credibility is needed, perhaps to discuss the need for a rate hike, if you're a utility, or to lobby on legislative matters, as Peter Grace did. But for the usual corporate ad objectives, the big gun might just wipe out too much landscape even if he does hit the target.

If you do take this route, keep your expectations realistic. There is probably a vast difference in ad budget size between Lee Iaccoca's and your own campaign. No matter how good the commercials are, don't expect overnight fame. A number of CEOs, such as Richard L. Gelb of Bristol-Meyers and C. L. Brown of AT&T, are quoted in occasional corporate ads. Their signature is more in the nature of an endorsement of a point of view or a financial statement. This is hardly comparable to the show biz aspects of TV spokesmen. Nor is it as risky. However, either print or TV advertising will be more difficult for your agency to prepare if you are in it.

The advertising will have to fit you and be tailored to your own character, and if there are technical aspects to the copy, you had better start the campaign early because your middle management, those who must sign off on the accuracy of the copy, generally develop very cold feet when they realize these are words the boss will be speaking. Just a detail, but it could add a month to a production schedule.

The final consideration and a growing concern among executives in a society with increasing terrorism is kidnapping. It is still extremely rare and should probably not be a deterrent, although you might avoid excessive shows of opulence. In fact, when being interviewed for news stories, you may wish to leave your attractive family and million-dollar estate and prized antiques out of the setting. Including these elements may add to the rags-to-riches story, but it just might make you nervous.

Be Yourself

Don't lose sight of the old admonitions "Know thyself" and "To thine own self be true." Fortunately there are enough successful ways to run a company to allow for great variety in CEO personalities. Any attempt to be someone else will be short lived and can only result in inconsistency and crossed signals. The secret is to let that real personality come through loud and clear in somewhat larger-than-life dimensions so that it is consistent and understood throughout the organization and in your business contacts.

Finally

No company can realize its full potential without an adequate communication program. What the company is and does, however, will set the limits on that reputation. To have a meaningful role in society a company must be focused on the marketplace, its needs and wants, and provide products and services to meet them.

Unfortunately some CEOs have been distracted from the marketplace by the demands of Wall Street. If you feel yourself yielding to this powerful temptation you might remember this: *Directing the course of a company by watching Wall Street is like driving a car by looking in the rear view mirror. It's all there but it tells you more about where you've been, than where you are going.*

Index

About the Author

Thomas Garbett became something of a guru of corporate advertising following the success of his first book, *Corporate Advertising, the What, the Why, and the How,* published in 1981. It was virtually the first detailed study of the subject, and its success resulted in his forming his own corporate communications consulting business. This followed a successful thirty-year advertising career, the last twenty-three years with Doyle Dane Bernbach as Management Supervisor and Senior Vice President.

He has lectured on corporate communications both in the United States and abroad, and has written widely on the subject for many business publications, including the *Journal of Advertising Research* and *Harvard Business Review*.

His practice today, which he operates from his Waterford, Connecticut, home, includes many of the Fortune 500 corporations, as well as a number of major ad agencies and public relations firms. His current work ranges from the preparation of complete corporate ad programs to special projects, such as assistance in the selection of ad agencies, counsel during merger and business crisis periods, and analysis of and recommendations on specific communications problems.